COMPILING WITH CONTINUATIONS

COMPILING WITH CONTINUATIONS

ANDREW W. APPEL
Department of Computer Science, Princeton University

CAMBRIDGE UNIVERSITY PRESS

Cambridge

New York   Port Chester   Melbourne   Sydney

CAMBRIDGE UNIVERSITY PRESS
Cambridge, New York, Melbourne, Madrid, Cape Town, Singapore, São Paulo

Cambridge University Press
The Edinburgh Building, Cambridge CB2 2RU, UK

Published in the United States of America by Cambridge University Press, New York

www.cambridge.org
Information on this title: www.cambridge.org/9780521416955

First published 1992
This digitally printed first paperback version (with corrections) 2006

A catalogue record for this publication is available from the British Library

Library of Congress Cataloguing in Publication data

Appel, Andrew W., 1960-
    Compiling with continuations / Andrew W. Appel.
        p.   cm.
    Includes bibliographical references.
    ISBN 0-521-41695-7
    1. Compilers (Computer programs)   2. Standard ML of New Jersey.
    I. Title.
    QA76.76.C65A67 1992
    005.4´53–dc20   91-26651
                                                          CIP

ISBN-13 978-0-521-41695-5 hardback
ISBN-10 0-521-41695-7 hardback

ISBN-13 978-0-521-03311-4 paperback
ISBN-10 0-521-03311-X paperback

CONTENTS

ACKNOWLEDGMENTS

The compiler described in this book—**Standard ML of New Jersey**—is the work of many people. **David B. MacQueen** and I began the work in 1986; we intended to spend about one year making a Standard ML front end as a tool for further research. David did most of the work on the type checker and module system; we worked together on the parser, abstract syntax, static environment mechanism, and semantic analysis. My interest has been in dynamic semantics, intermediate representations, optimization, code generation, and runtime system.

Of course, we've ended up spending more than five years on the implementation, as the scope of project has become much more ambitious: a complete, robust, efficient, portable programming environment for Standard ML. We could not have done it without the help we've received from many talented people. In alphabetical order:

Bruce F. Duba helped improve the pattern-match compiler, the CPS constant-folding phase, the in-line expansion phase, the spill phase, and numerous other parts of the compiler. He also helped to design the *call with current continuation* mechanism.

Adam T. Dingle implemented the Emacs mode for the debugger.

Lal George taught the code generator about floating-point registers and made floating-point performance respectable. He also fixed several difficult bugs introduced by me and others.

Trevor Jim helped design the CPS representation, and implemented the match compiler and the closure-conversion phase, the original library of floating-point functions, and the original assembly-language implementation of external primitive functions.

James S. Mattson implemented the first version of the lexical-analyzer generator used in constructing the compiler.

James W. O'Toole implemented the NS32032 code generator.

Norman Ramsey implemented the MIPS code generator.

John H. Reppy contributed many improvements and rewrites of the runtime system. He implemented the signal-handling mechanism, improved the *call with current continuation* mechanism, designed the current mechanism for calls to C functions, implemented the sophisticated new garbage collector, and generally made the runtime system more robust. He also implemented the SPARC code generator.

Nick Rothwell helped implement the separate compilation mechanism.

Zhong Shao implemented common-subexpression elimination, as well as the callee-save convention that uses multiple-register continuations for faster procedure calls.

David R. Tarditi improved the lexical-analyzer generator and implemented the parser generator used to build parts of the front end; he helped in implementing the type-reconstruction algorithm used by the debugger; and he implemented the ML-to-C translator with **Anurag Acharya** and **Peter Lee**.

Mads Tofte helped implement the separate compilation mechanism.

Andrew P. Tolmach implemented the SML/NJ debugger. He also rewrote static environments (symbol tables) in a more functional style.

Peter Weinberger implemented the first version of the copying garbage collector.

Finally, I would like to thank those who gave me helpful comments on early drafts of this book: Ron Cytron, Mary Fernandez, Lal George, Peter Lee, Greg Morrisett, Zhong Shao, David Tarditi, and Andrew Tolmach.

CHAPTER ONE

OVERVIEW

ML is a strict higher-order functional programming language with statically checked polymorphic types, garbage collection, and a complete formally defined semantics. *Standard ML of New Jersey* is an optimizing compiler and runtime system for ML. The intermediate representation that SML/NJ uses for optimization and code generation—*continuation-passing style*—is applicable to the compilation of many modern programming languages, not just ML. This book is about compiling with continuation-passing style.

Prior knowledge of ML is helpful, but not necessary, to read this book. Since the Standard ML of New Jersey compiler is itself written in ML, we use ML notation for many of the examples. But will we use only a simple subset of the language for illustrations, and we will explain the notation as we go along. Readers completely unfamiliar with ML should refer to the introduction in Appendix A.

1.1 Continuation-passing style

The beauty of FORTRAN—and the reason it was an improvement over assembly language—is that it relieves the programmer of the obligation to make up names for intermediate results. For example, we write $x = (a+b)*(c+d)$ instead of the assembly language:

$$r_1 \leftarrow a + b$$
$$r_2 \leftarrow c + d$$
$$x \leftarrow r_1 \times r_2$$

The simple, one-line expression is easier to read and understand than the three-line assembly program; the names r_1 and r_2 don't really aid our understanding. Furthermore, the assembly program spells out explicitly the order of evaluation: $a+b$ is computed before $c+d$; this is something we did not really need to know.

The λ-calculus gives us these same advantages for functional values as well. We can write $f(\lambda x.x + 1)$ instead of (as in Pascal):

```
function g(x: integer): integer;
  begin g := x+1 end;
. . . f(g) . . .
```

Here, Pascal forces us to give a name (g) to this function; the name (and the consequent verbosity of the definition) may not help us understand what's going on. The λ-calculus also frees us from needing to know too much about order of evaluation, even across function-call boundaries.

These conveniences are quite appropriate for humans writing programs. But in fact, they may be just the wrong thing for compilers manipulating programs. A compiler might like to give a distinct name to *every* intermediate value of the program, so it can use these names for table lookups, manipulating sets of values, register allocation, scheduling, and so on.

Continuation-passing style (CPS) is a program notation that makes every aspect of control flow and data flow explicit. It also has the advantage that it's closely related to Church's λ-calculus, which has a well-defined and well-understood meaning.

We can illustrate CPS informally with an example. Start with a source program

```
fun prodprimes(n) =
  if n=1
  then 1
  else if isprime(n) then n*prodprimes(n-1)
                     else prodprimes(n-1)
```

This is an ML program that computes the product of all primes less than or equal to a positive integer n. The keyword **fun** introduces a function definition; the expression on the right-hand side of the equal sign is the body of the function. The **if-then-else** and arithmetic expression notation should be familiar to most readers.

Now, there are several points in the control flow of this program that deserve names. For example, when the function **isprime** is called, it will be passed a *return address*. It is helpful to name this return address—let's call it k. And **isprime** will return a Boolean value—call it b. The first call to **prodprimes** (in the **then** clause of the second **if**) will return to a point j with an integer p, but the second call to **prodprimes** (in the **else** clause) will return to a point h with an integer q. The first computation of $n - 1$ will be put in a temporary variable m, and the second one in a variable i, and so on.

We should also mention that the function **prodprimes**, when it is called, is handed a return address; we can call that c and treat it as one of the arguments (formal parameters) of the function. Then we can use c when it is time to leave the function.

We can express all of this using *continuations*. A continuation is a function that expresses "what to do next;" for example, we can say that **prodprimes** is given a continuation c as one of its arguments, and when **prodprimes** has computed its result a it will continue by applying c to a. Thus, returning from a function looks just like a function call!

The following program is a continuation-passing-style version of the program, written in ML. For those unfamiliar with ML, it will help to explain that **let** *declaration* **in** *expression* **end** declares some local value (a function, an integer, etc.) whose scope includes the *expression*; the result of the `let` is just that of the *expression*. A `fun` declaration declares a function (with formal parameters) and a `val` declaration (in this simple example) binds a variable to a value.

```
fun prodprimes(n,c) =
   if n=1
   then c(1)
   else let fun k(b) =
              if b=true
              then let fun j(p)=
                           let val a=n*p
                           in c(a)
                           end
                       val m=n-1
                   in prodprimes(m,j)
                   end
              else let fun h(q)=c(q)
                       val i=n-1
                       in prodprimes(i,h)
                       end
        in isprime(n,k)
        end
```

Observe that all the control points c, k, j, h discussed above are just continuation functions, and all the data labels b, p, a, m, q, i are just variables. In order to use continuation-passing style, we didn't have to change our notation very much; we just used a restricted form of the existing language. A full explanation of CPS will be given in Chapters 2 and 3.

The CPS representation is easy for optimizing compilers to manipulate and transform. For example, we would like to perform *tail-recursion elimination*: If a function f calls a function g as the very last thing it does, then instead of passing g a return address within f, it could pass to g the return address that f was given by f's caller. Then, when g returned, it would return directly to the caller of f.

If we look at the original version of `prodprimes`, we find that one of the calls is tail recursive (the last recursive call to `prodprimes`). In the CPS version of the program, this is manifested in the fact that the continuation function h is trivial: $h(q) = c(q)$. Now, whenever we have a function h that just calls another function c with the same argument, we can say that h is equivalent to c; and we might as well use c wherever h is referred to. So we can perform this simple transformation

```
let fun h(q)=c(q)
    val i=n-1
in prodprimes(i,h)
end
```
$\longrightarrow$
```
let val i=n-1
in prodprimes(i,c)
end
```

and now we have accomplished *tail-recursion elimination* in a clean way.

1.2   Advantages of CPS

There are many reasons to use continuation-passing style as a framework for compiling and optimization. In this discussion we will compare it to several alternatives:[1]

λ   The lambda calculus (without explicit continuations); this might seem like an appropriate language for reasoning about languages (such as ML and Scheme) that are "based on λ-calculus."

QUAD Register transfers, or "quadruples," that correspond (approximately) to the instructions of a very simple von Neumann machine.

PDG Program-dependence graphs, that can represent both control flow and data-flow without intertwining them more than necessary.

SSA Static single-assignment form [34], which is particularly designed for the efficient implementation of certain dataflow algorithms. In SSA, each variable is assigned exactly once; when control paths merge, explicit transfer functions are used to maintain the illusion of single assignment. SSA and CPS are similar in important ways, since CPS also has a kind of single-assignment property.

   These intermediate representations are designed to facilitate different transformations. Let us consider several different kinds of optimizations, and see how easy they are to perform with each of these representations.

In-line expansion   CPS   λ   QUAD   PDG   SSA

The λ-calculus has variable-binding and scope rules particularly designed for β-reduction, or in-line expansion of functions: The body of a function is substituted for the function call, and the actual parameters of the function are substituted for the formal parameters.

   But there is a problem with using λ-calculus to express the behavior of *strict* call-by-value languages (such as ML, Pascal, Lisp, Scheme, Smalltalk, etc.). In the programming language, the parameters of a function are supposed to be evaluated before the evaluation of the body begins; but in λ-calculus this is not necessary. The usual method of β-reduction for λ-calculus will just put a copy of the actual parameter at each location where the formal parameter had appeared in the body. This means:

- A program that was supposed to infinite loop (when interpreted *strictly*) may now terminate.

---

[1] Readers unfamiliar with the literature on compiler optimization might want to skip this section.

- An actual parameter that was evaluated once in the original program may now be evaluated several times (if the formal parameter is used several times in the original program).

- In a language with side effects (ML, Pascal, Lisp, etc.), the side effects of the actual parameter may now occur after *some* of the side effects in the body of the function, or may not occur at all, or may occur more than once.

It is just as easy in CPS to express substitution, but CPS has none of the problems listed in the previous paragraph. *All actual parameters to functions are variables or constants, never nontrivial subexpressions.* Thus the substitution of actuals for formals (and the consequent "moving" of the actual parameters into the body of the function) can't cause a problem.

As for the other representations—QUAD, PDG, SSA—they are primarily concerned with the representation of individual function bodies, not with optimizations across function boundaries. It is still possible to do in-line expansion with these frameworks, if additional mechanisms are added to represent function parameters and calling sequences; but the problems of termination, and out-of-order evaluation of side-effects, must still be solved.

Closure representations ~~CPS~~ λ⌣ ⌢QUAD ⌢PDG ⌢SSA

In languages with "block structure" or "nested functions"—such as Pascal, Scheme, ML—a function f may be nested inside a function g, which itself may be nested inside another function h. Then f may access its own formal parameters and local variables, but it may also access the formals and locals of g and h. One of the tasks of the compiler is to implement this access efficiently. Since the λ-calculus and CPS also have functions with nested scope, it is easier for the compiler to manipulate these functions and their representations in computing efficient access methods for nonlocal variables. The other three representations, since they are primarily concerned with control and dataflow within individual functions, cannot address this problem very easily.

Dataflow analysis CPS− λ⌢ QUAD− PDG− SSA⌣

Dataflow analysis involves the static propagation of values (more precisely, of compile-time tokens standing for runtime values) around a flow graph. It answers questions such as "does this definition of a variable reach that use of the variable?" which is useful when doing certain optimizations. Since the continuation-passing-style representation of a program contains a fairly faithful representation of the control-flow graph, dataflow analysis is as easy in cps as it is in more traditional representations such as QUADruples.

Static single-assignment form is designed to make forward dataflow analysis particularly efficient, since it is easy to identify the definition that reaches any use of a variable—each variable is defined (assigned) exactly once. Continuation-passing style has a property very much like single assignment, as we will discuss later. On the other hand, λ-calculus does not appear to be well suited for dataflow analysis.

Register allocation $\underset{\smile}{\text{CPS}}$ $\underset{\frown}{\lambda}$ $\underset{\smile}{\text{QUAD}}$ $\underset{-}{\text{PDG}}$ $\underset{\frown}{\text{SSA}}$

In allocating variables of the program to registers on a machine, it is useful to have a notation that can conveniently represent the lifetime—the creation and destruction—of values. This *liveness analysis* is really a kind of dataflow analysis, and so the observations of the previous paragraph apply equally well here. We note in particular that in certain phases of our CPS-based compiler, the *variables* of a CPS-expression correspond very closely to the *registers* of the target machine.

Vectorizing $\underset{-}{\text{CPS}}$ $\underset{\frown}{\lambda}$ $\underset{-}{\text{QUAD}}$ $\underset{\smile}{\text{PDG}}$ $\underset{-}{\text{SSA}}$

Program-dependence graphs are particularly designed for such optimizations as the synthesis of vector instructions out of ordinary loops. Such optimizations are still possible in other representations, but may in the end require auxiliary data structures that accomplish much of what is done by PDGs.

Instruction scheduling $\underset{-}{\text{CPS}}$ $\underset{\frown}{\lambda}$ $\underset{-}{\text{QUAD}}$ $\underset{-}{\text{PDG}}$ $\underset{-}{\text{SSA}}$

Modern, highly pipelined computers require *instruction scheduling* at the very back end of the compiler to avoid pipeline interlocks at runtime. Instruction scheduling requires the manipulation of individual instructions with detailed knowledge of their sizes, timings, and resource requirements. The representations described in this chapter are probably a bit too abstract for use in the scheduling phase of a compiler.

Conclusion

The intermediate representations described here have many similarities. Static single-assignment form is just a restricted form of quadruples. Continuation-passing style is a restricted form of λ-calculus. And in fact, there are many similarities between SSA and CPS, since CPS variables have a single-binding property. With continuations, we get both the clean substitution operations of λ-calculus and the dataflow and register analyses appropriate for von Neumann machines.

1.3   What is ML?

This book will demonstrate the use of continuations for compilation and optimization in a real compiler. Our compiler—*Standard ML of New Jersey*—compiles *ML*; but continuation-passing style is not tied in any way to ML, and has been used in compilers for several languages [52].

The programming language ML was originally developed in the late 1970s as the Meta-Language of the Edinburgh *Logic for Computable Functions* (LCF) theorem-proving system [42]. In the early 1980s it was recognized as a useful language in its own right (even for people who don't want to prove theorems) and a stand-alone ML system was implemented [26]. Since then, the *Standard ML* language has been defined [64], a formal semantics has been written [65], several compilers have become available [13, 63], and several hundred programmers at scores of locations are actively using the language.

ML has several advantages as a practical programming language:

- ML is *strict*—arguments to a function are evaluated before the function call, as in Pascal, C, Lisp, and Scheme but not as in Miranda or Haskell, which are *lazy*.

- It has *higher-order functions*, meaning that a function can be passed as an argument and returned as the result of another function—as in Scheme, C, and Haskell, but not Pascal and Lisp. But unlike C, ML has *nested functions* (so do Scheme and Haskell), which make the higher-order functions much more useful.

- It has *parametric polymorphic types*, meaning that a function can be applied to arguments of several different types as long as it does exactly the same thing to the argument regardless of the type. Lisp, Scheme, and Haskell also have parametic polymorphism, but Pascal and C do not. Parametric polymorphism is different from *overloading*, with which a function can be applied to arguments of different types only if a different implementation of the function is written for each type.

- Types are *statically checked* at compile time, so there is no need for runtime type checking (and many bugs may be found before running the program). Other statically checked languages are Pascal, C, Ada, and Haskell; dynamically type-checked (at runtime) languages include Lisp, Scheme, and Smalltalk. But ML (like Haskell) has *type inference*, which relieves the programmer of writing down most type declarations; in Pascal, C, Ada, and other languages descended from Algol the programmer must declare explicitly the type of each variable.

- ML has *garbage collection*, which automatically reclaims unreachable pieces of storage; this is typical of functional languages such as Scheme and Haskell, but Lisp and Smalltalk also have garbage collection; Pascal, C, and Ada usually do not.

- Variable bindings are *statically determined*; as in Pascal, C, and Scheme the variable declaration corresponding to any particular use can be determined by lexical scope in the program text. This is in contrast to Smalltalk, which has dynamic binding for functions ("dynamic method lookup").

- ML has *side effects*: input/output, and reference variables with assignment and update. In this respect it is like most languages (such as Pascal, C, Smalltalk, Lisp, and Scheme), but differs from *purely functional* languages like Haskell. In ML, however, the updateable variables and data structures are constrained and statically identifiable by the compile-time type system. In a typical program, the vast majority of variables and data structures are not updateable.

- ML has a *formally defined semantics* [65] that is *complete* in the sense that each legal program has a deterministic result, and all illegal programs are recognizable as such by a compiler. This is in contrast to Ada, for which formal semantics have been written but are not complete, in the sense that some "erroneous" programs must be accepted by compilers; Pascal, which is recognized to have certain "ambiguities and insecurities" [95]; and C, in which it is very easy for programmers to trash arbitrary parts of the runtime environment by careless use of pointers. Lisp and Scheme are not too bad in this respect; in principle, "erroneous" programs are detected either at compile time or at runtime, though certain things (such as order of evaluation of arguments) are left unspecified [69].

From this summary we see that the problems and language features that our compiler must address have much in common with those addressed by other compilers. But there are several ways in which compilers for "modern" languages like ML must differ from compilers for "traditional" languages like C.

The higher-order functions of ML (Scheme, Smalltalk, etc.) require the compiler to introduce runtime data structures to represent the free variables of these functions. And because the lifetimes of these "closures" are not always determinable at compile time, some form of garbage collection is required.

The presence of garbage collection requires that all runtime data structures be in a format that the collector can understand; the machine registers and other temporaries used by the compiled code must also be accessible and understandable to the collector.

Since a "functional" programming style is encouraged—in which old data is rarely updated, but instead new data is produced—the garbage collector must be particularly efficient. In some older Lisp systems, and in some Algol descendents with garbage collection, much less load is placed on the collector because new objects are less frequently allocated.

Most control flow is indicated by source-language function calls (instead of built-in constructs like **while** and **repeat**). So function calls—especially tail-recursive ones—must have very low overhead.

There is no "macro" facility. Macros in C and Lisp are often used for in-line expansion of frequently executed code fragments. A good compiler for a macro-free language should do some in-line expansion of functions—a much safer way to provide this kind of efficiency.

A unique feature of ML, shared by no other commonly used language, is that most data structures are *immutable* once created. That is, once a variable—or a list cell, or a record on the heap—is created and initialized, it cannot be modified. Of course, a local variable of a function will be *instantiated* each time the function is invoked, with a different value each time; list cells on the heap eventually become garbage (because no local variable points to them anymore) as new cells are created. But the fact that list cells can't be modified means that the *aliasing problem* becomes trivial. In compiling a conventional language, the statements

$$a \leftarrow \#1(p); \quad \#1(q) \leftarrow b$$

(where $\#1(x)$ means the first field of the record that x points to) can't be exchanged, because p and q might be *aliased*—might point to the same object. Similarly,

$$a \leftarrow \#1(p); \quad b \leftarrow f(x)$$

can't be exchanged unless a great deal is known about the behavior of f.

In ML, mutable variables and data structures—those that can be modified (stored into) *after* their creation—have a different static type than immutable ones. That is, they are distinguished by the type-checking phase of the compiler. In a typical program, the vast majority of variables and data structures are immutable. Thus, the aliasing problem mostly disappears: If p is an immutable variable (as is usually the case), the fetch from p commutes with just about anything. Our compiler exploits this property in several ways.

Lazy languages such as Haskell have immutable variables in principle, but in fact the update of a variable to replace a thunk by an evaluated result looks very much like a mutation to some parts of the compiler and runtime system.

Finally, the fact that ML has a rather abstract formal semantics is quite useful in some ways. Any optimization or change in the representation that leads to the same computable function is legal. In C, on the other hand, there is no formal semantics. Even allowing that there is a reasonably good informal understanding of what a C program is supposed to do, this "semantics" is tied to low-level machine representations. And there are many C programs that "break the rules" and are still expected to work in any "reasonable" compiler. In this situation, the compiler has limited freedom to transform the program.

1.4 Compiler organization

Standard ML of New Jersey [13] is a compiler for ML written in ML. It is a multipass compiler which transforms a source program into a machine-language program in a series of phases:

1. Lexical analysis, parsing, type checking, and producing an annotated abstract syntax tree.

2. Translation into a simple, λ-calculus-like representation (described in Chapter 4).

3. Conversion into continuation-passing style (CPS, described in Chapter 5).

4. Optimization of the CPS expression, producing a "better" CPS expression (Chapters 6–9).

5. Closure conversion, producing a CPS expression in which each function is closed, i.e., has no free variables (Chapter 10).

6. Elimination of nested scopes, producing a CPS expression with one global set of mutually recursive, nonnested function definitions (Chapter 10).

7. "Register spilling," producing a CPS expression in which no subexpression has more than n free variables, where n is related to the number of registers on the target machine (Chapter 11).

8. Generation of target-machine "assembly-language" instructions—in abstract, not textual form (Chapter 13).

9. Instruction scheduling, jump-size optimization, backpatching, and the generation of target-machine instructions (Chapter 14).

The rest of this book is organized very much like the compiler, except that the first phase—which is specific to the ML language—is not described. In fact, this "front-end" part of the compiler is much larger than the back-end phases covered in the book. But our focus here is the use of continuations for optimization and code generation, not how to compile ML.

CHAPTER TWO

CONTINUATION-PASSING STYLE

The first compilers that used continuation-passing style (CPS) as an intermediate language [83, 54] represented the CPS using Scheme [69] notation—in those compilers, a CPS expression was just a Scheme program satisfying certain syntactic properties. In the Standard ML of New Jersey compiler (and in this book) we use a more specialized representation. An ML datatype represents CPS expression trees; the syntax of the datatype itself automatically assures most of the syntactic properties that were just conventions in the Scheme approach. Also, we ensure that every function has a name; we have a syntactic operator for defining mutually recursive functions, instead of just an "external" fixed point function; and we have n-tuple operators that make modeling record and closures more convenient.

This chapter introduces the concrete CPS data structure used as the intermediate representation for programs, and informally sketches how continuation-passing style works.

An important property of well-formed CPS expressions is that the arguments to a function (or a primitive operator such as $+$) are always atomic (variables or constants); a function application can never be an argument of another application. This is because the CPS language is meant to model the program executed by a von Neumann machine, which likes to do just one thing at a time, with all the arguments to an operation ready-at-hand in registers.

2.1 The CPS datatype

We express such restrictions directly in an ML datatype cexp (*continuation expression*), as shown in figure 2.1. For those unfamiliar with ML, we explain that the datatype keyword defines a "disjoint-union" or "variant-record" type (see also Appendix A). In this case, each value of type cexp is "tagged" as a RECORD, SELECT, OFFSET, and so on. If the tag (called a *constructor*) is SELECT, then there are also four fields of type *integer*, *value*, *var*, and *cexp*; and so on.

Each continuation expression takes zero or more atomic arguments, binds zero or more results, and continues via zero or more continuation expressions. For example integer addition of variables a and b yielding c, continuing with the evaluation of expression e, is written as

11

```
signature CPS = sig

eqtype var

datatype value = VAR of var
               | LABEL of var
               | INT of int
               | REAL of string
               | STRING of string

datatype accesspath = OFFp of int
                    | SELp of int * accesspath

datatype primop =
      * | + | - | div | ~
    | ieql | ineq | < | <= | > | >= | rangechk
    | ! | subscript | ordof
    | := | unboxedassign | update | unboxedupdate | store
    | makeref | makerefunboxed | alength | slength
    | gethdlr | sethdlr
    | boxed
    | fadd | fsub | fdiv | fmul
    | feql | fneq | fge | fgt | fle | flt
    | rshift | lshift | orb | andb | xorb | notb

datatype cexp =
        RECORD of (value * accesspath) list * var * cexp
      | SELECT of int * value * var * cexp
      | OFFSET of int * value * var * cexp
      | APP of value * value list
      | FIX of (var * var list * cexp) list * cexp
      | SWITCH of value * cexp list
      | PRIMOP of primop * value list * var list * cexp list

end
```

Figure 2.1. The CPS data type.

```
PRIMOP(+, [VAR a, VAR b], [c], [e])
```

(For ML novices: The square brackets denote a list, and `VAR` is just a constructor of the user-defined `value` datatype. So the second argument to `PRIMOP` is just a list of two values, the third argument is a list of one `var`, etc. Also, + is an identifier just like `a` or `PRIMOP`; usually it is bound to a function that adds its arguments but here we have rebound it as a datatype constructor that takes no arguments. The entire *ML* expression `PRIMOP(...)` simply builds a data structure that *represents* a *continuation expression* that a compiler might want to manipulate.)

The arguments to CPS operations are *atomic* in the sense that they may be variables or constants, but not subexpressions. This is the essence of continuation-passing style; instead of writing $e = (a + 1) * (3 + c)$ one must make up names for all the subexpressions, yielding

$$u = a + 1, v = 3 + c, e = u * v$$

Using the CPS datatype one would write

$$\text{PRIMOP}(+, [\text{VAR a, INT 1}], [\text{u}],$$
$$[\text{PRIMOP}(+, [\text{INT 3, VAR c}], [\text{v}],$$
$$[\text{PRIMOP}(*, [\text{VAR u, VAR v}], [\text{e}], [M])])])$$

where we assume that the continuation expression M makes some use of the variable e.

The datatype *value* is the union of all the different kinds of atomic arguments that can be provided to the CPS operators. Each argument can be a variable (`VAR`), an integer constant (`INT`), a string constant (`STRING`), or a floating-point constant (`REAL`). The use of `LABEL` will be explained in Section 2.4.

Although the mathematical expression $(a + 1) * (3 + c)$ makes no assumption about whether $a + 1$ or $3 + c$ is to be evaluated first, any translation into continuation-passing style must choose one or the other. In the example above, $a + 1$ is to be evaluated first. This is another essential feature of CPS: many decisions about control flow are made during the conversion from the source language into CPS. These decisions are not irreversible, however—an optimizer could, after some analysis, determine that the continuation expression could be rearranged to evaluate $3 + c$ first.

Continuations express control flow very naturally. The "integer greater than" comparison operator takes two integer arguments (constants or variables), produces no result, and continues using one of two continuation expressions. For example, "if $a > b$ then F else G" can be expressed as

$$\text{PRIMOP}(>, [\text{VAR } a, \text{ VAR } b], [\,], [F, G])$$

where F and G are continuation expressions.

Multiway branches (i.e., indexed jumps) are expressed using the `SWITCH` operator: the expression

$$\text{SWITCH}(\text{VAR } i, [E_0, E_1, E_3, E_4])$$

continues as $E_0, E_1, \ldots$ depending on whether i has the value $0, 1, \ldots$; there may be an arbitrary number of continuation expressions in the list. If the runtime value of i is negative, or greater than or equal to the number of elements in the list, the evaluation is erroneous.

Continuation expressions may build records (n-tuples) on the heap, and may select fields of records. The expression

RECORD([(VAR a, OFFp 0), (INT 2, OFFp 0), (VAR c, OFFp 0)], w, E)

makes a three-word record initialized to $(a, 2, c)$ and binds its address to w, continuing with E. The meaning of the access paths (OFFp 0) will be explained later. Note that any object on the heap created with RECORD is immutable and may not later be assigned into or modified in any way.

The expression SELECT(i, v, w, E) fetches the ith field of record v and binds the result to w, continuing with E. If the ith field doesn't exist, the expression is meaningless. Fields are numbered starting from 0.

A variable in the CPS language may point at a record value; but it may also point into the middle of the record. The OFFSET primitive allows a pointer to be adjusted; if variable v points at the jth field of a record (where possibly $j = 0$), then OFFSET(i, v, w, E) makes w point to the $(j + i)$th field and continues with E. The constant i may be negative, but $j + i$ must be nonnegative.

Mutually recursive functions are defined using the FIX operator. The expression

$$\text{FIX}([\quad (f_1, [v_{11}, v_{12}, \ldots, v_{1m_1}], B_1),$$
$$(f_2, [v_{21}, v_{22}, \ldots, v_{2m_2}], B_2),$$
$$\ldots$$
$$(f_n, [v_{n1}, v_{n2}, \ldots, v_{nm_n}], B_n)],$$
$$E)$$

defines zero or more functions f_i that can be called from the expression E or from each other's bodies B_j. The formal parameters of each function f_i are the variables v_{ik}. The effect of evaluating FIX($\vec{f}, E$) is just to define the functions in the list $\vec{f}$ and then to evaluate E, which (usually) calls one or more of the f_i by means of the APP operator, or passes one of the f_i as an argument to another function, or stores some of the f_i in a data structure.

All function calls in continuation-passing style are "tail" calls; that is, they do not return to the calling function. This can be seen from the form of the APP continuation expression, which does not have any continuation expression as a subexpression. Unlike SELECT($3, v, w, $ SELECT($2, w, z, E$)), which fetches the third field of v, continues by fetching the second field of the result, and then continues by evaluating E, the expression APP($f, [a_1, a_2, \ldots, a_k]$) calls the function f and then does nothing at all. That is, the body of f is evaluated with the actual parameters a_i substituted for the formal parameters of f.

The function f will have formal parameters and a body bound to it by a FIX declaration. Of course, since functions may be passed as parameters and stored into data structures (they are "first-class"), the variable f may in fact be bound as a formal parameter of a statically enclosing function, or as the result of a SELECT operation, and so on. However, the value to which f refers must have originally been created by a FIX operator.

Of course, in most programming languages, a function is allowed to return to its caller! But recall the example of Section 1.1, in which one of the calls to prodprimes could return directly to its *caller's caller*. This was because whatever value the call to prodprimes(n-1) returned, it was returned directly as the result of prodprimes(n). If all function calls were like this, then no function would return until the very end of the program execution, when all functions would return; there wouldn't need to be a runtime stack of return addresses (and local variables, etc.) indicating "where to return to."

In a continuation-passing-style compiler, all function calls must be translated into such "tail" calls. This is accomplished by introducing *continuation functions*: A continuation expresses the "rest" of the computation after the called function was to have returned. Continuation functions are bound by ordinary FIX operators and passed as arguments to functions; the algorithm for introducing them will be explained in Chapter 5.

A simple example will serve to illustrate. Suppose we have a source-language program

```
let fun f(x) = 2*x+1
 in f(a+b)*f(c+d)
end
```

This might be (mostly) converted into continuation-passing style as follows:

```
let fun f(x,k) = k(2*x+1)
    fun k1(i) = let fun k2(j) = r(i*j)
                 in f(c+d, k2)
                end
 in f(a+b, k1)
end
```

where r is the "rest" of the computation, to which the original program fragment was to have returned its answer. Now, since every function call in this (converted) program is the last thing that the enclosing function does, it may readily be translated into the CPS language:

```
FIX([(f, [x,k], PRIMOP(*, [INT 2, VAR x], [u], [
                PRIMOP(+, [VAR u, INT 1], [v], [
                  APP(VAR k, [VAR v])])])),
       (k1, [i], FIX([(k2, [j],
                  PRIMOP(*, [VAR i, VAR j], [w], [
                    APP(VAR r, [VAR w])]))],
                PRIMOP(+, [VAR c, VAR d], [m], [
                  APP(VAR f, [VAR m, VAR k2])])))],
     PRIMOP(+, [VAR a, VAR b], [n], [
       APP(VAR f, [VAR n, VAR k1])]))
```

The functions k_1 and k_2 are called *continuations*. They express the "rest of the computation" after the two function calls to f (respectively). The function f is written so that instead of returning in the ordinary way, it calls its continuation argument k. This has the effect of evaluating the "rest of the computation," just as a function in an ordinary programming language would *return* in order to evaluate the rest of the computation.

When an "ordinary" function returns, it often produces a "return value" as well. The return value in continuation-passing style is simply an argument to the continuation function, captured—in the example above—by the variables i and j in the continuations k_1 and k_2.

2.2   Functions that escape

Consider the following two programs:

```
let fun f(a,b,c) = a+c              let fun g(a,b,c) = a+c
  in f(1,2,3)                         in (g, g(1,2,3))
end                                 end
```

The function f is used only locally, but the function g is both used locally and exported to the outside; we say that g *escapes* but f does not.

Now, we can do a simple program transformation to remove the unused argument b from f, as long as we also modify all the places where f is called:

```
let fun f(a,c) = a+c
  in f(1,3)
end
```

But it's not easy to do so for g, since we don't know all the places g is called. Since g might be held in a data structure and extracted at arbitrary points in the program; or worse, might be exported and used in some other "compilation unit" about which we know nothing at all, its representation (as a function that takes a triple, not a pair) must not be changed.

When using CPS to compile a particular programming language, we may want to make some restrictions on the behavior of escaping functions. We will take ML as an example here; other programming languages might have quite different restrictions. Functions that do not escape (such as f above) need no restrictions, since at any call site where it might be useful to analyze their behavior, the function body can be easily found syntactically.

In ML, all functions take exactly one argument. The effect of multiple arguments can be achieved by passing an n-tuple as the argument; the pattern matching of n-tuples makes this syntactically convenient. In the example above, the functions f and g are actually one-argument functions that take 3-tuples as arguments.

Now, when ML is converted into continuation-passing style, each one-argument user-defined function now becomes a two-argument function: The additional argument is a continuation function. The continuation functions themselves are just one-argument functions.

So, in the translation of ML, we have the following rules about escaping functions:

- Every escaping function has either one argument or two arguments.

- The second argument of a two-argument escaping function (a *user function*) is always a one-argument escaping function (a *continuation*).

- The current exception handler[1] (set using the `sethdlr` primop) is always a one-argument escaping function—a *continuation*.

Since the straightforward conversion of ML into CPS establishes these invariants, we might want the optimizer to make use of them in reasoning about the behavior of escaping functions. Since the escaping functions might be from some other compilation unit, we cannot derive this information by examining their function bodies. However, we can arrange for the optimizer to preserve the invariants in all compilation units.

For functions that can take several arguments (as most languages allow), we could make similar conventions; it is still true of those languages that there are *user functions* and *continuations*. On the other hand, for Prolog—where each predicate might take *two* continuations—we would make quite a different convention.

2.3 Scope rules

The results produced by CPS operators are *bound* to variables with lexical scope. No variable can be bound in more than one place within a continuation expression, and no variable can be mentioned outside its syntactic scope. The scope rules for CPS are simple and straightforward:

- In the expression `PRIMOP(p, vl, [w], [e1, e2, ...])` the scope of w is the expressions $e_1, e_2, \ldots$.

- In the expression `RECORD(vl, w, e)` the scope of w is just the expression e.

- In `SELECT(i,v,w,e)` or `OFFSET(i,v,w,e)`, the scope of w is just e.

- In `FIX([(v,[w1, w2, ...], b)], e)` the scope of w_i is just b, and the scope of v includes exactly b and e. This generalizes for a mutually recursive

---

[1] The *exception* mechanism of the ML language will be mentioned from time to time, and its translation and optimization described. Readers unfamiliar with ML exceptions may safely ignore these mentions, as they are not central to the subject of this book.

function definition: In the expression

$$\text{FIX}([\quad (f_1, [v_{11}, v_{12}, ..., v_{1m_1}], B_1),$$
$$(f_2, [v_{21}, v_{22}, ..., v_{2m_2}], B_2),$$
$$...$$
$$(f_n, [v_{n1}, v_{n2}, ..., v_{nm_n}], B_n)],$$
$$E)$$

the scope of each f_i includes all of the B_j and E; the scope of v_{ij} is just B_i.

- The operators APP, SWITCH, and some instances of PRIMOP (in the case where the third argument is empty) do not bind variables, and thus need no scope rule.

Each use of a variable (in a *value*) must be within the scope of its binding. Once a variable is bound, it retains the same value within its entire scope and cannot be reassigned. Of course, a piece of CPS code may be executed many times (for example, if it is the body of a function called more than once); a variable binding executed many times may bind a different value each time.

2.4   Closure conversion

The reason to use CPS as a compiler intermediate representation is that it is quite close to the instruction set of a von Neumann computer. Most CPS operators (such as PRIMOP(+,...)) correspond closely to machine instructions. However, the notion of function definition is more primitive on a von Neumann machine than in the CPS. CPS functions (like those in λ-calculus or, for that matter, Pascal) can have "free variables": expressions can refer to variables defined outside the innermost-enclosing function. For example, the function k_2 on page 15 refers to the variable j defined as an argument of k_2, but also to the variable i which is defined outside of k_2. We say that j is a *bound* variable of k_2 and i is a *free* variable of k_2. Of course, every variable is bound somewhere; i is a bound variable of k_1.

Now, a "von Neumann" machine represents a function just by an address in the machine-code. Such an address cannot describe the current values of the free variables of the function. (It's not necessary to describe values of bound variables of the function, since those won't even acquire values until the function is called.) The usual way to represent functions with free variables is by a *closure* [57]: a pair of *machine-code pointer* and *free-variable information*. For example, in a situation where k_1 has been called with argument $i = 7$, we might represent k_2 by the record $(L_2, 7)$, where L_2 is the address of the machine code for k_2, and 7 is the value of i in this instantiation of k_2.

We represent closure records explicitly in the CPS language. The translation of a program in CPS, into another CPS program in which none of the functions have free variables, is called "closure conversion." Every function will be given an extra argument, which will be a closure record. The first field of the closure record will be a pointer to the function itself; the other fields will be the values of free variables of the function. When the "function" is passed as an argument to another function, or stored into data structure, it is actually the closure that will be passed or stored. Then, when another function needs to call the closure, it performs the following steps:

1. To call a closure f, first extract the function pointer f' from the first field of f.

2. Then APPly the function f', passing the closure f as the first argument (and the other arguments afterwards).

It is important that the caller of f need not know the format of the closure record, or even how large it is. The only thing the caller needs to know is how to extract the function (machine-code) pointer. The function f' itself will know where to find the free variables in the closure record.

We will use the example from page 15 (with functions f, k_1, and k_2) to illustrate, using ML notation instead of CPS (for brevity):

```
let fun f'(f'', x, k) = let val k' = #1(k)
                          in k'(k,2*x+1)
                        end
    val f = (f')
    fun k1'(k1'', i) = let fun k2'(k2'', j) =
                            let val r' = #1(r)
                            in r'(r,#2(k2'')+j)
                          end
                        val k2 = (k2', i)
                      in f'(f, #2(k1'') + #3(k1''), k2)
                    end
    val k1 = (k1',c,d,f)
  in f'(f, a+b, k1)
end
```

(This fragment doesn't quite type check in ML, but it's not intended to.) The function f doesn't have any free variables, so its closure is trivial: a one-element record containing the function "code." But the function k_1 had three free variables c, d, and f; its closure is a four-element record containing those free variables as well as k_1', which is a new version of k_1 that expects a closure as the first argument. The important thing is that, in each closure, the "closed" function is the first field, so another function in a different context does not need to know about the format of the closure in order to call it. This is evident in the call to r; the closure r may have several fields, but to call it all that is necessary is to extract the first field and pass the closure itself as one of the arguments. (The notation #1 in ML selects the first field of an n-tuple.) Thus, f' receives its closure in argument f'', k_1' receives its closure in k_1'', and k_2' in k_2''.

We have taken the shortcut of referring directly to f' in the two calls to that function, rather than extracting it from f.

The input to the closure-conversion phase of the compiler is a CPS expression that obeys the scope rules described in the previous section. The output is also a CPS expression, but one that obeys an additional rule: none of the functions have free variables.

More precisely, the only free variables in the body of a function g are:

- Formal parameters of the function g;

- Names of functions—those appearing as the first element of a (function, formals,body) triple in a FIX.

In the implementation on a von Neumann machine, the function names (i.e., machine-code addresses of functions) are really constants. They may appear free in other functions without requiring a closure to locate them. In the output of the closure-conversion phase, we will use LABEL instead of VAR to refer to such variables in the CPS notation, to indicate that they are essentially constants; and we will not consider them to be "free variables."

So we can say that the CPS after closure conversion obeys the following *free-variable rule*:

In a mutually recursive function definition, the expression

$$
\begin{aligned}
\text{FIX}([\quad &(f_1, [v_{11}, v_{12}, ..., v_{1m_1}], B_1), \\
&(f_2, [v_{21}, v_{22}, ..., v_{2m_2}], B_2), \\
&\cdots \\
&(f_n, [v_{n1}, v_{n2}, ..., v_{nm_n}], B_n)], \\
&E)
\end{aligned}
$$

the free variables of B_i can include *only* v_{ik} **and all of the** f_j. Furthermore, all references to the f_j (and *only* references to variables defined as functions by FIX operators) will use the LABEL constructor instead of VAR.

The primary reason for using LABEL is to make the computation of free-variable sets for register allocation easier; from the code generator's point of view, a VAR occupies a register and a LABEL does not.

Now that no function has any nontrivial free variable, there is no need for functions to be nested; we can define all the functions in one top-level FIX. The entire compilation unit now has the form:

$$
\begin{aligned}
\text{FIX}([\quad &(f_1, [v_{11}, v_{12}, ..., v_{1m_1}], B_1), \\
&(f_2, [v_{21}, v_{22}, ..., v_{2m_2}], B_2), \\
&\cdots \\
&(f_n, [v_{n1}, v_{n2}, ..., v_{nm_n}], B_n)], \\
&E)
\end{aligned}
$$

where none of the B_i or E contain a FIX operator. To simplify even further, we can take the free variables of E and make them into formal parameters, yielding

$$
\begin{aligned}
\text{FIX}([\quad & (f_0, [v_{01}, v_{02}, ..., v_{0m_0}], E), \\
& (f_1, [v_{11}, v_{12}, ..., v_{1m_1}], B_1), \\
& (f_2, [v_{21}, v_{22}, ..., v_{2m_2}], B_2), \\
& \cdots \\
& (f_n, [v_{n1}, v_{n2}, ..., v_{nm_n}], B_n)], \\
& \text{APP}(\text{VAR } f_0, [\text{VAR } v_{01}, \text{ VAR } v_{02}, ..., \text{ VAR } v_{0m_0}])])
\end{aligned}
$$

Later phases of the compiler can be concerned only with a set of triples of the form $(f_i, \vec{v}_i, B_i)$, and need not process the final APP expression because it's trivial and contains nothing of interest.

A full description of our closure-conversion algorithm is in Chapter 10. However, it is worthwhile to give a formal definition of the free variables of an expression. We use the auxiliary function **fvl** which yields the set of variables used in a list of values:

$$
\begin{aligned}
\text{fvl}(\text{nil}) &= \phi \\
\text{fvl}((\text{VAR } v)::l) &= \{v\} \cup \text{fvl}(l) \\
\text{fvl}((\text{LABEL } v)::l) &= \text{fvl}(l) \\
\text{fvl}((\text{INT } i)::l) &= \text{fvl}(l) \\
\text{fvl}((\text{REAL } r)::l) &= \text{fvl}(l) \\
\text{fvl}((\text{STRING } s)::l) &= \text{fvl}(l)
\end{aligned}
$$

Now, the computation of free variables is quite straightforward:

$$
\begin{aligned}
\text{fv}(\text{APP}(v, l_a)) &= \text{fvl}(v::l_a) \\
\text{fv}(\text{SWITCH}(v, [C_1, C_2, \ldots])) &= \text{fvl}[v] \cup \bigcup_i \text{fv}(C_i) \\
\text{fv}(\text{RECORD}([(v_1, p_1), (v_2, p_2), \ldots], w, E)) &= \text{fvl}[v_1, v_2, \ldots] \cup \text{fv}(E) - \{w\} \\
\text{fv}(\text{SELECT}(i, v, w, E)) &= \text{fvl}[v] \cup \text{fv}(E) - \{w\} \\
\text{fv}(\text{OFFSET}(i, v, w, E)) &= \text{fvl}[v] \cup \text{fv}(E) - \{w\}
\end{aligned}
$$

$$
\text{fv}(\text{PRIMOP}(p, l_a, [w_1, \ldots], [C_1, \ldots])) = \text{fvl}(l_a) \cup \bigcup_i \text{fv}(C_i) - \bigcup_j \{w_j\}
$$

$$
\begin{aligned}
\text{fv}(\text{FIX}([(f_1, [w_{11}, \ldots, w_{1m_1}], B_1), \\
\cdots \\
(f_n, [w_{n1}, \ldots, w_{nm_n}], B_n)], E)) = \\
(\text{fv}(E) \cup \bigcup_i (\text{fv}(B_i) - \bigcup_{j=1}^{m_i} \{w_{ij}\})) - \bigcup_i \{f_i\}
\end{aligned}
$$

2.5 Spilling

The use of variables in the CPS language resembles in many ways the use of registers on a von Neumann machine. Arithmetic operators take their operands in variables (registers), and produce their results in variables (registers); the SELECT (memory fetch) takes a variable (register) and a constant offset, and fetches into a variable (register), and so on.

However, von Neumann machines have only a fixed number of registers, and CPS expressions can have an arbitrary number of variables. To correct this mismatch, we will map many CPS variables onto the the same register. But two CPS variables can be implemented by the same register only if they are not both simultaneously "live," that is, if only one of them is required by the rest of the computation. A (statically) live variable in traditional dataflow analysis [1] is exactly the same as a free variable in the CPS: a variable used in a continuation expression but not bound in it. This analogy is easy to prove: Simply note that the free-variable function defined above is the same as the dataflow algorithm for computing liveness of variables in a directed acyclic graph.

The *finite-register rule* for the CPS is this:

For compilation to a machine with k registers, no subexpression of the CPS may have more than k free variables.

After the closure phase, the *spill* phase rewrites the CPS to satisfy this rule. Certain other phases are also limited by variants of the finite-register rule: Even prior to the spill phase,

For compilation to a machine with k registers, no function of the CPS may have more than k formal parameters.

A full description of the spill phase is in Chapter 11.

CHAPTER THREE

SEMANTICS OF THE CPS

The meaning of CPS expressions can be given via a simple denotational semantics. The complete semantics is given in Appendix B; here we follow the structure of the semantic definition for a more informal discussion. Those readers uncomfortable with denotational semantics would do well to read the text of this chapter and skip the "semantics", in this font. All variants of the CPS—no matter which subset of the scope rules, free-variable rules, and language-dependent rules has been applied—follow this semantics.

What follows is a straightforward continuation semantics written in Standard ML. It will be helpful if the reader is familiar with continuation semantics (see, e.g., Stoy [84], Gordon [43], or Schmidt [77]), and with ML (see, e.g., Milner [65], Reade [68], or Paulson [67]).

By presenting a formal semantics for our CPS representation, we hope to make the transformations presented in later chapters independently verifiable by the reader, though we will rarely present formal proofs.

```
functor CPSsemantics(
        structure CPS: CPS
```

The semantics is written as a functor in Standard ML.[1] It takes (pro forma) a CPS structure (see figure 2.1) as an argument, along with:

```
        val minint: int    val maxint: int
        val minreal: real  val maxreal: real
```

We don't expect the low-level machine architecture—for which the CPS is a model—to have infinite-precision arithmetic. There must be some maximum and minimum representable integer and real.

```
        val string2real: string -> real
```

The CPS language represents real (floating-point) numbers as string literals, just as they might have been written in the source program (e.g., "0.0"). We assume that there is some way of translating them into machine representation. The

---

[1] Readers unfamiliar with the ML module system (structures and functors) may simply ignore this line of the semantics; or refer to Section 4.8 where a summary of ML modules is given.

practical reason for expressing reals as strings (at this phase of the compilation) is
to make the CPS language independent of any particular machine representation—
accurate cross compilation is much easier this way. A disadvantage of this representation is that constant folding of real-valued expressions becomes very difficult.

```
eqtype loc
val nextloc: loc -> loc
```

As is typical in a denotational semantics, operations that have side effects on
memory are represented by means of a "store." Each store value can be thought
as a mapping from locations (addresses) to denotable values. The type *loc* of
locations, and a function to generate new locations, is a parameter to the semantics.
It must be a type on which the equality of values is testable (an *eqtype*).

```
val arbitrarily: 'a * 'a -> 'a
```

Some things cannot be predicted by the semantics. To model this unpredictabil-
ity, the expression arbitrarily(*a, b*) evaluates either to *a* or to *b*. It is used only in
conjunction with pointer comparison; see Section 3 on equality testing.

```
type answer
```

As is traditional in a continuation semantics, we have a type "answer" standing
for the result of the entire execution of the program. We don't really need to know
anything about the structure of this type.

```
datatype dvalue = RECORD of dvalue list * int
               | INT of int
               | REAL of real
               | FUNC of dvalue list ->
                   (loc*(loc->dvalue)*(loc->int))->
                   answer
               | STRING of string
               | BYTEARRAY of loc list
               | ARRAY of loc list
               | UARRAY of loc list
```

These are the denotable values of the semantics. These values may be bound
to variables, passed as parameters, and stored in data structures. In an implementation, the denotable values are just those that can be held in one machine word
(as pointers into the heap or as single-precision integers).

A denotable value can be a RECORD containing a list of denotable values. It
is possible to point into the middle of a record, not just at the beginning, so the
denotable value for records also has an integer indicating the offset into the record.

A denotable value can be an integer (INT) or a REAL. One might expect the
implementation to represent integers "unboxed" (not on the heap, but in a single

machine word in place of a pointer); the same might even be true of reals, if pointers are large enough or floating-point values are small enough.

ARRAY values are represented using the store, so their contents can be modified after they are created. An array of length n is represented in the semantics as an arbitrary list of locations, though presumably in an implementation the locations will be consecutive. Note that records are not kept in the store, and thus record values are "pure" and cannot be modified once created. There are two kinds of arrays: ARRAYs can contain arbitrary denotable values, and UARRAYs can contain only integers.

A denotable value can be a STRING of characters or a BYTEARRAY. The same operations apply to strings and byte arrays, except that byte arrays can be stored into (modified) and strings cannot. The elements of strings and byte arrays must be small (byte-sized) integers, in contrast to the elements of UARRAYs, which can be larger (word-sized) integers, and elements of ARRAYs, which can be of any type (including integer).

Finally, a function value (FUNC) takes a list of actual parameters and a store, and continues the computation to yield an answer. The store (whose type is (loc*(loc->dvalue)*(loc->int))) has three components: the next unused location, a mapping from locations to denotable values, and a mapping from locations to integers. Why are there two mappings? We have broken the store into two parts: one part that can hold arbitrary values, and another part that can hold only integers. This turns out to make the task of a generational garbage collector much easier, as we will explain in Section 16.3.

```
val handler_ref : loc
val overflow_exn : dvalue
val div_exn : dvalue
```

The store has a special location in which the "current exception handler" is kept. This is a continuation function which is called in order to "raise" an exception. Also, there are two "special" exceptions, for arithmetic overflow and dividing by zero. These are special in that the "machine" can raise them directly: In an implementation, that means that the runtime system must know where these exception values are, so on an overflow interrupt the runtime system can raise the exception.

```
                   ) :
     sig val eval: CPS.var list * CPS.cexp ->
                   dvalue list ->
                   (loc*(loc->dvalue)*(loc->int)) ->
                   answer
         end
struct
```

Forgive the typography here! The closing parenthesis indicates that we have come to the end of the functor arguments, the sig...end describes the signature

of the result structure produced by this functor (a single function `eval`), and the
word `struct` indicates the beginning of the functor body.

The `eval` function takes a list of CPS variables, a continuation expression, a
list of denotable values, and a store. It yields the "answer" obtained by evaluating
the *cexp* in an environment where the variables are bound to the values, respectively. This allows a form of "linkage" from one "compilation unit" to another;
the "externals" of a continuation expression are represented by a specified set of
variables, with corresponding values.

Here begins the body of the semantics:

```
type store = loc * (loc -> dvalue) * (loc -> int)
fun fetch ((_,f,_): store) (l: loc) = f l
fun upd ((n,f,g):store, l: loc, v: dvalue) =
                (n, fn i => if i=l then v else f i, g)
fun fetchi ((_,_,g): store) (l: loc) = g l
fun updi ((n,f,g):store, l: loc, v: int) =
                (n, f, fn i => if i=l then v else g i)
```

It's convenient to have functions for elementary manipulation of stores: one
for fetching a value from a location in the value store; one for updating a location
with a new value (producing, of course, an entirely new store); one for fetching an
integer from a location in the integer store; and one for updating the integer store.

```
exception Undefined
```

In the CPS language it is possible to write syntactically correct but meaningless
programs. The semantics will fail to yield a denotation for such programs.

We might also want to treat this semantics as an ML program that could serve
as an interpreter for the CPS language. For erroneous programs, the interpreter
will raise an ML exception: either `Undefined` (declared here) or one of the predefined exceptions `Bind`, `Match`, or `Nth`. This is not to be confused with a CPS
program invoking a CPS exception handler.

```
fun eq(RECORD(a,i),RECORD(b,j)) =
                arbitrarily(i=j andalso eqlist(a,b), false)
  | eq(INT i, INT j) = i=j
  | eq(REAL a, REAL b) = arbitrarily(a=b, false)
  | eq(STRING a, STRING b) = arbitrarily(a=b, false)
  | eq(BYTEARRAY nil, BYTEARRAY nil) = true
  | eq(BYTEARRAY(a::_), BYTEARRAY(b::_)) = a=b
  | eq(ARRAY nil, ARRAY nil) = true
  | eq(ARRAY(a::_), ARRAY(b::_)) = a=b
  | eq(UARRAY nil, UARRAY nil) = true
  | eq(UARRAY(a::_), UARRAY(b::_)) = a=b
  | eq(FUNC a, FUNC b) = raise Undefined
  | eq(_,_) = false
```

```
and eqlist(a::al, b::bl) = eq(a,b) andalso eqlist(al,bl)
  | eqlist(nil, nil) = true
```

This function is explained in detail in Appendix A.4.

Records and strings in the CPS language are "pure values," and cannot reliably be compared using "pointer equality." For example, the record (4,5) is meant to be indistinguishable from the record (4,5) even if the latter was created at a different time than the former. This means that the implementation is permitted to use "hash-consing" to put both records at the same address; or, on the other hand, a garbage collector might take a record to which there are several pointers, and make each pointer point to its own copy.

The "eq" test here—intended to represent pointer-equality comparison—denotes the places where pointers arbitrarily may or may not be equal. For example, testing the equality of two arrays must accurately determine whether they start at the same location; testing the equality of two integers must also be accurate. But, in order to accommodate implementations as described in the previous paragraph, testing the equality of two records is permitted to be "conservative": If the two records are unequal, eq will return *false*, but if they are equal, eq might return *true* or *false*. The three kinds of comparisons for which different pointers can point to equivalent values are records, reals (which might be represented by pointers to double-precision values), and strings.

This version of the "eq" test distinguishes all pointers from all integers. Thus, in an implementation it is necessary that pointers have a different bit representation from integers. To avoid this requirement, we might want to say that only "small" integers can be distinguished from pointers (see Section 4.1). In this case, we would insert the following clauses just before the last clause for eq:

```
  | eq(INT i, _) = arbitrarily(false, i<0 orelse i>255)
  | eq(_, INT i) = arbitrarily(false, i<0 orelse i>255)
```

The number 255 is arbitrary, and indicates (in an implementation) that we won't put heap objects in the first 255 bytes of the machine's memory.

```
fun do_raise exn s =
    let val FUNC f = fetch s handler_ref in f [exn] s end

fun overflow(n: unit->int, c: dvalue list -> store -> answer) =
    if (n() >= minint andalso n() <= maxint)
          handle Overflow=> false
       then c [INT(n())]
       else do_raise overflow_exn

fun overflowr(n,c) =
    if (n() >= minreal andalso n() <= maxreal)
          handle Overflow => false
       then c [REAL(n())]
       else do_raise overflow_exn
```

Some of the integer and floating-point arithmetic operators can produce an "overflow," that is, a result not representable because it's out of range. The `overflow` function evaluates a number n, turns it into a *dvalue* list, and hands it to its continuation argument c; but if it overflows, then it raises an exception instead.

The line "`handle Overflow => false`" is there just in case it is desired to execute this semantics in an ML system with finite-precision integers. The word `Overflow` refers to the overflow exception *of the meta-language*, and should not be confused with `overflow_exn`, which is the overflow exception of the CPS.

To raise an exception *exn*, `do_raise` first extracts the current exception handler from the store (at location `handler_ref`), and then applies it to *exn* and the current store.

The function `evalprim`, below, evaluates a `PRIMOP` applied to arguments. The function takes three arguments: a primitive operator, a list of *dvalue* arguments, and a list of possible continuations. Then it produces a list of result values (possibly empty, depending on the operator), and selects one of the continuations to apply to the result list; this yields a `store->answer` function. Of course, the list of continuations will have more than one element only in the case that the primop is a "conditional branch" of some sort.

```
fun evalprim (CPS.+ : CPS.primop,
              [INT i, INT j]: dvalue list,
              [c]: (dvalue list -> store -> answer) list) =
                          overflow(fn()=>i+j, c)
```

So, to add two integers, one simply calculates $i + j$, and if it does not overflow, applies c to the result. Since the `evalprim` function does not have a clause that matches the application of `CPS.+` to noninteger values, such an application would be undefined and would result in the semantics failing to produce a denotation.

```
| evalprim (CPS.-,[INT i, INT j],[c]) =
                          overflow(fn()=>i-j, c)
| evalprim (CPS. *,[INT i, INT j],[c]) =
                          overflow(fn()=>i*j, c)
| evalprim (CPS.div,[INT i, INT 0],[c]) =
                          do_raise div_exn
| evalprim (CPS.div,[INT i, INT j],[c]) =
                          overflow(fn()=>i div j, c)
```

Integer subtraction, multiplication, and division are similar; for division by zero it is necessary to raise the divide exception.

```
| evalprim (CPS.~,[INT i],[c]) = overflow(fn()=>0-i, c)
```

Integer negation is like subtraction from zero; note that there is only one `dvalue` argument. It is possible for integer negation to overflow, for example, on a two's complement machine where the most negative integer has a larger absolute value than any positive integer.

```
| evalprim (CPS.<,[INT i,INT j],[t,f]) =
                            if i<j then t[] else f[]
| evalprim (CPS.<=,[INT i,INT j],[t,f]) =
                            if j<i then f[] else t[]
| evalprim (CPS.>,[INT i,INT j],[t,f]) =
                            if j<i then t[] else f[]
| evalprim (CPS.>=,[INT i,INT j],[t,f]) =
                            if i<j then f[] else t[]
```

The inequality operators <, <=, >, and >= apply only to integers. Depending on the result of the test, one of the two continuations t or f is applied to the (empty) result list.

```
| evalprim (CPS.ieql,[a,b],[t,f]) =
                        if eq(a,b) then t[] else f[]
| evalprim (CPS.ineq,[a,b],[t,f]) =
                        if eq(a,b) then f[] else t[]
```

The primop ieql stands for "integer equality", but this is clearly a misnomer since the eq function tests many types. It is intended that the implementation just compare the two machine words a and b for integer equality; if a and b are pointers this turns out to be pointer equality.

```
| evalprim (CPS.rangechk, [INT i, INT j],[t,f]) =
                    if j<0
                    then if i<0
                        then if i<j then t[] else f[]
                        else t[]
                    else if i<0
                        then f[] else if i<j then t[]
                        else f[]
```

This complicated-looking operator is simply "unsigned comparison." When two's complement is used to represent negative numbers, and j is nonnegative, the test $0 \leq i < j$ can be most efficiently accomplished using an unsigned comparison operator. The rangechk is just "unsigned less than;" the nested if statements here just express unsigned comparison using signed operators. When $j < 0$, the unsigned comparison is not useful for anything reasonable, but its semantics can be expressed nonetheless.

```
| evalprim (CPS.boxed, [INT _],[t,f]) = f[]
| evalprim (CPS.boxed, [RECORD _],[t,f]) = t[]
| evalprim (CPS.boxed, [STRING _],[t,f]) = t[]
| evalprim (CPS.boxed, [ARRAY _],[t,f]) = t[]
| evalprim (CPS.boxed, [UARRAY _],[t,f]) = t[]
| evalprim (CPS.boxed, [BYTEARRAY _],[t,f]) =t[]
| evalprim (CPS.boxed, [FUNC _],[t,f]) = t[]
```

The `boxed` predicate returns true if a value is "boxed" (represented as a pointer), and false if unboxed. An implementation might ensure that pointers have a bit-pattern unlike nonpointers, so this operator is a simple bit-test or comparison. The use of `boxed` in implementing ML is mainly for determining which data constructor has been applied to a value; see Section 4.1.

If we want to say that only *small* integers can be distinguished from pointers, we would replace the first clause for `boxed` by:

```
| evalprim (CPS.boxed, [INT i],[t,f]) =
                if i<0 orelse i>255
                        then arbitrarily(t[],f[]) else f[]
```

The reasons for wanting to do this are explained in Section 4.1.

```
| evalprim (CPS.!, [a],[c]) =
                evalprim(CPS.subscript, [a, INT 0],[c])
| evalprim (CPS.subscript, [ARRAY a, INT n],[c]) =
                (fn s => c [fetch s (nth(a,n))] s)
| evalprim (CPS.subscript, [UARRAY a, INT n],[c]) =
                (fn s => c [INT(fetchi s (nth(a,n)))] s)
| evalprim (CPS.subscript, [RECORD(a,i), INT j],[c]) =
                        c [nth(a,i+j)]
```

The subscript operator can be used to fetch elements of either arrays or records, though record fields are usually fetched using SELECT. It would be cleaner, in fact, to use different operators for indexing mutable and immutable objects. In any case, subscript on arrays selects the nth location of the array, and then fetches at that location in the store. The result is used as an argument to the continuation c. The operator ! is equivalent to subscript at index 0. On records, subscript does not need to refer to the store; but it does need to take care to adjust the index j by the offset i. In an implementation, a nonzero i just indicates that the record pointer is pointing into the middle of the record, so subscript is just an add followed by a fetch (with a left shift necessary on byte-addressible machines).

There is no bounds checking on the subscript operator; a fetch out of bounds is erroneous and fails to yield a denotation. However, it is expected that a compiler (for a safe language such as ML) will put in explicit bounds checks using integer comparison and the array length operator (`alength`) described below.

The function `nth` just returns the nth element of a list, counting from zero. If $n < 0$ or $n \geq \text{length}(l)$, then $\text{nth}(l, n)$ raises the `Nth` exception, indicating a semantically undefined CPS expression.

```
| evalprim (CPS.ordof, [STRING a, INT i],[c]) =
                        c [INT(String.ordof(a,i))]
| evalprim (CPS.ordof, [BYTEARRAY a, INT i],[c]) =
                (fn s => c [INT(fetchi s(nth(a,i)))] s)
```

The operator `ordof` subscripts strings and byte arrays just as `subscript` operates on arrays and records. The implementation will probably represent strings as contiguous sequences of characters, and in fact byte arrays have the same representation. However, strings are treated as constants, since (for example) they might be literals in the machine-language program.

```
| evalprim (CPS.:=, [a, v],[c]) =
                 evalprim(CPS.update, [a, INT 0, v], [c])
| evalprim (CPS.update, [ARRAY a, INT n, v],[c]) =
                 (fn s => c [] (upd(s,nth(a,n),v)))
| evalprim (CPS.update, [UARRAY a, INT n, INT v],[c]) =
                 (fn s => c [] (updi(s,nth(a,n),v)))
```

The assignment operator `:=` is equivalent to `update` at index zero. To perform an update, the nth location in the array is updated in the store, producing a new store that is passed (along with a pro forma empty list of arguments) to the continuation c. As with `subscript`, no bounds checking is done. Updating of a `UARRAY` with an integer value is similar; it is erroneous to update a `UARRAY` with a noninteger value.

```
| evalprim (CPS.unboxedassign, [a, v], [c]) =
                 evalprim(CPS.unboxedupdate, [a, INT 0, v], [c])
| evalprim (CPS.unboxedupdate,
             [ARRAY a, INT n, INT v],[c]) =
                 (fn s => c [] (upd(s,nth(a,n), INT v)))
| evalprim (CPS.unboxedupdate,
             [UARRAY a, INT n, INT v],[c]) =
                 (fn s => c [] (updi(s,nth(a,n),v)))
```

In some implementations, a generational garbage collector will want to know about all stores of pointers into older generation arrays (this will be explained fully in Section 16.3). Because of this bookkeeping, such store operations may be more expensive to implement. However, in many cases the compiler knows that the value being stored is *not* a pointer; for example, the value may be of an always-unboxed type such as `int`, or it might be an unboxed constant of a sometimes-unboxed type. In such cases, the compiler can use the cheaper `unboxedassign` or `unboxedupdate` operators, which are semantically identical to `:=` and `update`, respectively, except that they apply only to integer values.

```
| evalprim (CPS.store,
         [BYTEARRAY a, INT i, INT v],[c]) =
     if v < 0 orelse v >= 256
         then raise Undefined
         else (fn s => c [] (updi(s,nth(a,i),v)))
```

The `store` operator is the equivalent for byte arrays of the `update` operator for arrays. Strings cannot be stored into. Strings and byte arrays can hold only "one-byte" values (integers between 0 and 255).

```
| evalprim (CPS.makeref, [v],[c]) = (fn (l,f,g) =>
               c [ARRAY[l]] (upd((nextloc l, f,g),l,v)))
| evalprim (CPS.makerefunboxed, [INT v],[c]) = (fn (l,f,g) =>
               c [UARRAY[l]] (updi((nextloc l, f,g),l,v)))
```

An array of length one (called a "ref" in ML) can be allocated using the makeref operator. Larger arrays cannot be allocated in the CPS language; it is expected that the implementation will provide an external function (part of the runtime system, for example) to do this. Such functions can be made accessible to CPS programs by means of the *dvalue* arguments to the eval function.

The makerefunboxed operator makes a reference that will contain only integer values; this is useful when a generational garbage collector is used. Note that either := or *unboxedassign* can be used with either kind of reference, as long as *unboxedassign* is used only to store integer values (of possibly not-always-boxed types), and "unboxed" references contain only integer values.

```
| evalprim (CPS.alength, [ARRAY a], [c]) =
                           c [INT(List.length a)]
| evalprim (CPS.alength, [UARRAY a], [c]) =
                           c [INT(List.length a)]
| evalprim (CPS.slength, [BYTEARRAY a], [c]) =
                           c [INT(List.length a)]
| evalprim (CPS.slength, [STRING a], [c]) =
                           c [INT(String.size a)]
```

The alength function can extract the length (number of elements) of an array; slength does the same for strings and byte arrays. Note that the length of an array is fixed, even though the values of its elements are mutable in the store.

```
| evalprim (CPS.gethdlr, [], [c]) =
                     (fn s => c [fetch s handler_ref] s)
| evalprim (CPS.sethdlr, [h], [c]) =
                     (fn s => c [] (upd(s,handler_ref,h)))
```

The operator gethdlr returns the current exception handler (extracting it from the store), and sethdlr updates the store with a new exception handler. The implementation can choose to implement the exception handler in a register instead of memory, since the location handler_ref is not used in a very general way in this semantics.

```
| evalprim (CPS.fadd, [REAL a, REAL b],[c]) =
                           overflowr(fn()=>a+b, c)
| evalprim (CPS.fsub, [REAL a, REAL b],[c]) =
                           overflowr(fn()=>a-b, c)
| evalprim (CPS.fmul, [REAL a, REAL b],[c]) =
                           overflowr(fn()=>a*b, c)
```

```
| evalprim (CPS.fdiv, [REAL a, REAL 0.0],[c]) =
                        do_raise div_exn
| evalprim (CPS.fdiv, [REAL a, REAL b],[c]) =
                        overflowr(fn()=>a/b, c)
| evalprim (CPS.feql, [REAL a, REAL b],[t,f]) =
                        if a=b then t[] else f[]
| evalprim (CPS.fneq, [REAL a, REAL b],[t,f]) =
                        if a=b then f[] else t[]
| evalprim (CPS.flt,[REAL i,REAL j],[t,f]) =
                        if i<j then t[] else f[]
| evalprim (CPS.fle,[REAL i,REAL j],[t,f]) =
                        if j<i then f[] else t[]
| evalprim (CPS.fgt,[REAL i,REAL j],[t,f]) =
                        if j<i then t[] else f[]
| evalprim (CPS.fge,[REAL i,REAL j],[t,f]) =
                        if i<j then f[] else t[]
```

The floating-point arithmetic and comparison operators are similar to those for integers.

```
type env = CPS.var -> dvalue
```

The rest of the semantics uses the notion of an "environment": a mapping from CPS variables to denotable values. CPS operators that bind a result to a variable will do so by augmenting an environment. CPS operators that take variables as arguments will extract values for those variables from the environment.

```
fun V env (CPS.INT i) = INT i
  | V env (CPS.REAL r) = REAL(string2real r)
  | V env (CPS.STRING s) = STRING s
  | V env (CPS.VAR v) = env v
  | V env (CPS.LABEL v) = env v
```

The function V is used to turn a CPS value into a denotable value. For constants, it's quite straightforward; variables (and labels, which are equivalent in this semantics) must be looked up in the environment.

```
fun bind(env:env, v:CPS.var, d) =
                fn w => if v=w then d else env w

fun bindn(env, v::vl, d::dl) = bindn(bind(env,v,d),vl,dl)
  | bindn(env, nil, nil) = env
```

The bind function just performs an update on an environment, producing a new environment. To bind several values to several variables, bindn is used.

```
fun F (x, CPS.OFFp 0) = x
  | F (RECORD(l,i), CPS.OFFp j) = RECORD(l,i+j)
  | F (RECORD(l,i), CPS.SELp(j,p)) = F(nth(l,i+j), p)
```

A record field in the CPS language is written as a value and an "access path." The access path is just a chain of selections terminated by an offset. For example, the record field expression (v,SELp(3,SELp(1, OFFp 2))) indicates that the third field of v is to be fetched, then the first field of the result is to be fetched, the result of that is to be offset by two words without a fetch, and the result of *that* is what goes into the new record. The need for this is explained in Chapter 11.

The access path OFFp 0 has no effect on the field value; it is the only path that can be applied to non-record values (such as integers, reals, an so on).

The function E is used to take the denotation of a CPS expression. Such a denotation has the type env->store->answer, and there are just seven cases:

```
fun E (CPS.SELECT(i,v,w,e)) env =
                    let val RECORD(l,j) = V env v
                      in E e (bind(env,w,nth(l,i+j)))
                    end
  | E (CPS.OFFSET(i,v,w,e)) env =
                    let val RECORD(l,j) = V env v
                      in E e (bind(env,w,RECORD(l,i+j)))
                    end
```

To evaluate a SELECT, the value v is first extracted from the environment; it must be a record, or the expression is undefined. Then, the index i is added to the offset j and the corresponding element of the record is bound to the variable w in a new environment. This new environment is then used as the argument in the evaluation of the subexpression e. The evaluation of OFFSET is similar, except that after the index and the offset are added, no field is selected; instead, the record with a new offset is bound to w.

```
  | E (CPS.APP(f,vl)) env =
                    let val FUNC g = V env f
                      in g (map (V env) vl)
                    end
```

Function application is quite simple: The variable f must stand for some function g. The arguments vl are all extracted from the environment, and g is applied to the list of resulting values. Note that no environment is passed to g; this is an indication that the CPS language has lexical (static), not dynamic scope.

For ML novices, we note here that the map function takes a function (in this case, V env and a list (in this case, vl), and returns a new list whose elements are obtained by applying the function to each of the elements of the list (in this case, the result of looking up each of the values of vl in the environment).

```
| E (CPS.RECORD(vl,w,e)) env =
            E e (bind(env,w,
                RECORD(map (fn (x,p) =>
                                F(V env x, p)) vl, 0)))
```

To make a record, it is first necessary to extract all the fields from the environment (`V env x`); then, the selects and offset (`SELp` and `OFFp`) implicit in the access path p for each field are evaluated by the function F. Then, a `RECORD` is made with offset 0 and bound to w.

```
| E (CPS.SWITCH(v,el)) env =
            let val INT i = V env v
             in E (nth(el,i)) env
            end
```

Switch expressions are quite simple: v is evaluated to get an integer i, and then the ith continuation is evaluated. It should be noticed that every continuation expression continues with the evaluation of exactly one continuation. For `RECORD`, `SELECT`, and `OFFSET` this is obvious syntactically; for a `SWITCH` or `PRIMOP` that may have several syntactic continuation expressions as arguments, it is enforced by the semantics; for `APP` the continuation expression may be found "hidden" in the body of the applied function f.

```
| E (CPS.PRIMOP(p,vl,wl,el)) env =
                evalprim(p,
                        map (V env) vl,
                        map (fn e => fn al =>
                            E e (bindn(env,wl,al)))
                        el)
```

To evaluate a primitive operator, it is first necessary to extract all the atomic arguments from the environment (`map (V env) vl`). Then the *cexp* arguments are all converted to functions of type `dvalue list -> store -> answer`. The list of atomic arguments and the list of continuations are handed (along with the operator p) to the `evalprim` function, which performs the appropriate operation and then selects one of the continuations to hand the result to.

```
| E (CPS.FIX(fl,e)) env =
            let fun h r1 (f,vl,b) =
                    FUNC(fn al => E b (bindn(g r1,vl,al)))
                and g r = bindn(r, map #1 fl, map (h r) fl)
             in E e (g env)
            end
```

The definition of mutually recursive functions is a bit complicated. In essence, we just evaluate the expression e in the augmented environment $g(env)$. The function g takes an environment r as an argument and returns r augmented by binding all the function names (`map #1 fl`) to the function bodies (`map (h r) fl`).

The function h defines an individual function; it takes an environment r_1 and a function definition `(f,vl,b)`, where f is the function name, vl is the list of formal parameters, and b is the function body. The result is a function (`fn al => ...`) that takes a list of actual parameters al, and augments r_1 in two ways: First it applies g to redefine all the (mutually recursive) functions in fl, and then it binds the actual parameters to the formal parameters. The resulting environment is then used to evaluate the body b.

The functions g and h are mutually recursive; we use a recursion in the semantics to implement the mutual recursion of the CPS functions.

Note that the number of actual parameters must be the same as the number of formal parameters, or else `bindn` will not be defined. There are no functions in our CPS with a variable number of arguments.

```
val env0 = fn x => raise Undefined

fun eval (vl,e) dl = E e (bindn(env0,vl,dl))

end
```

Finally, the function `eval` takes a variable list, a value list, and an continuation expression; binds the values to the variables in the empty environment; and then returns the denotation of the expression in the resulting environment.

CHAPTER FOUR

ML-SPECIFIC OPTIMIZATIONS

In a compiler using continuation-passing style, most optimizations (partial evaluation, dataflow, register allocation, etc.) should be done in the CPS representation. However, some representation decisions are best done at a level closer to the source language. Here we describe several optimizations, specific to ML, that are done before conversion into continuation-passing style. Most of them are related to static types, which is why they are most naturally done before the types are stripped off during the conversion into CPS.

4.1   Data representation

Standard ML has *record* types that are essentially Cartesian products of other types (like records in Pascal or structs in C, except that their fields may not be modified after the record is created), and *datatypes* that are disjoint sums (like variant records in Pascal or unions in C).

A record type is a set of named fields, each of a given (possibly polymorphic) type. For example, the type

```
type t = {name: string, number: int}
```

contains values such as {name="Sam",number=5}; the order in which the fields are written down is immaterial (this value is the same as {number=5,name="Sam"}).

Since types in ML can be polymorphic, type *t* is also an instantiation of the type constructor

```
type 'a r = {name: string, number: 'a}
```

so $t = int\ r$. Similarly, `type s = real r` is a record type of which each element contains a string a real number. (ML novices should note that the parameter of a type constructor is put *before* the constructor, not after!)

Since an ML program can only access a record field in a context where the names of all the fields are known, the implementation can represent records as simple *n*-tuples. We choose in our implementation to number the fields in alphabetical order starting at zero, so (in this case) name is field 0, and number is field 1. The alphabetization is necessary because the field names might occur in any order in expressions where the record type is used. Presumably, the fields will all be contiguous in storage.

However, because ML is a polymorphic language, the (ground) types of all the fields are not necessarily known. For example, the function `printname`

```
fun printname {name=s, number=n} = output(std_out, s)
```

has type $\alpha\ r\ \rightarrow\ unit$, that is, a function from $\alpha\ r$ (for any α) to *unit*, which is just a placeholder for functions that don't return any interesting result (like `void` in the C language). But this means that the type of n is not known at compile time! The solution to this problem is to make all record fields the same size—for example, one word each. Every ML object will be represented in exactly one word; of course, that word may be a pointer to some data structure in memory.

Polymorphism is not unique to ML. Lisp, Scheme, Prolog, and other languages also have variables whose complete types are not known until runtime. When it is necessary to manipulate these values (e.g. to make lists of them), they must all have the same size—in most implementations, one word.

So, a record of n fields will be represented using n contiguous words in memory. ML also has a *tuple* type, which is like a record type with unlabeled fields; the type `int*bool*int` contains values such as `(4,true,7)`, and is represented in an implementation just like a three-element record.

A disjoint union type, called a "datatype" in ML, is represented in the source language by a set of constructors that may be applied to values, for example,

```
type posint = int (* positive integers *)
datatype money = COIN of posint | BILL of posint
                | CHECK of {amount:real, from: string}
datatype color = RED | BLUE | GREEN | YELLOW
datatype 'a list = nil | :: of 'a * 'a list
datatype register = REG of int
datatype tree = LEAF of int | TREE of tree * tree
datatype xxx = M | N | P of int list
datatype yyy = W of int * int | X of real * real * real
datatype gen = A | B | C | D of int | E of real
              | F of gen * gen | G of int * int * gen
```

A value of type `money` is either a "coin" with an integer value, a "bill" with an integer value, or a "check" with a value that consists of a real number and a string. A program can examine a piece of `money` to see which constructor has been applied, and can extract the associated value carried by the constructor. This is done using a "pattern match" in ML:

```
val evaluate = (* calculate value of a piece of money *)
    fn COIN c => c
     | BILL b => b * 100
     | CHECK{amount=r, from="Joe Deadbeat"} = floor(r*50)
     | CHECK{amount=r, from=f} = floor(r*100)
```

Some constructors (such as RED, BLUE, nil, A, etc.) do not carry values. Thus, the datatype color is like an enumeration type in Pascal.

How are constructors to be represented in memory? The most straightforward way is to say that each value of a datatype is represented as a two-word value, with the constructor (represented as a small integer) in one word, and the carried value (if any) in the other word. However, there are several improvements that can be made. First, datatypes with only one constructor (such as the register type above) can be represented completely transparently; the representation can be exactly the same as the representation of the carried value. Such datatypes are used in ML mainly to assist in catching type errors (in this case, for example, the mistake of using an integer as a register number).

It is possible to make more specialized representations for datatypes [26]. We might make the assumption:

Assumption 1: At runtime, pointers can be distinguished from small integers. This might be true if, for example, no pointer pointed into the first 256 bytes of memory, or if the low-order bit of each word is used as a tag to distinguish pointers from integers.

Using this assumption, we can say that all "constant" constructors (those that don't carry values) are represented as small integers, whereas value-carrying constructors are still represented as two-word records with the (small-integer) tag in one of the words and the value in the other. This makes the representation of constant constructors much more efficient, as they won't require allocation of memory on the heap.

Also, datatypes with only one value-carrying constructor don't need the tag in their record. For example, the datatype xxx has three constructors, but only one is not a constant. Therefore, if a value of type xxx is a pointer, it must be an application of the P constructor. The pointer will point to a single-word record containing the value of type int list. Note that the value of type P needs the extra indirection; it can't be an int list directly, since lists are not always pointers—sometimes they are nil. And the value nil has the same representation as the constructor M of the xxx datatype. Thus, we need the indirection so values with the P constructor will always be boxed, and distinguishable from M and N.

Datatypes with only one value-carrying constructor applied to an *always-boxed* value don't even need the extra indirection. A *boxed* value is simply one represented as a pointer; an *unboxed* value is represented as an integer (or other nonpointer). Consider the type 'a list: Since the :: (pronounced *cons*) constructor is always applied to a record, the value it carries is always a pointer. Since the nil value is represented as a small integer, we know that :: values can always be distinguished from nil values. Thus, we can represent 5::nil as a record containing 5 and nil, without any extra indirection.

More specialization is possible. Consider:

Assumption 2: All pointers can be distinguished from all integers. This might be true if one bit of each word is used as a tag to distinguish pointers from integers. The boxed predicate of the CPS language performs exactly this test. Of course, this assumption might be unpalatable for several reasons. It makes the represen-

tation of "big" (arbitrary precision) integers more difficult, since those are usually
represented by pointers to some complicated representation. Also, it uses up one
bit of precision in the representation of integers, which can be a great inconve-
nience. Usually, Assumption 2 is required by the garbage collector anyway. But it
is possible to make a collector for ML that does not need any runtime tags on data,
even to distinguish pointers from integers [5]. Therefore, we might prefer to have
full 32-bit integers, and no overhead to tag and untag integers when performing
arithmetic; in this case, Assumption 2 would not be valid.

Using Assumption 2, we can specialize the representation of datatypes such as
tree above. Any LEAF value can be represented by the integer that the constructor
is "carrying," and any TREE value can be represented by the two-word record. Then
no "extra" indirections are required in either case.

If we are willing to presume the existence of lots of runtime tags, we can make
more assumptions:

*Assumption 3: Two-element records can be distinguished from three-element
records, and so forth.* This is easy enough with a record descriptor at the beginning
of each record (or built into the record pointer itself). But the use of Assumption
3 may unduly constrain the implementation of the runtime system. In particular,
it makes the use of a BIBOP ("BIg Bag Of Pages") scheme more difficult. With
such an arrangement, objects of the same type are grouped together on a page,
and there is just one descriptor for each page—this saves the space required by
descriptors on each object. But then, if the compiler generates pattern-matching
code that must distinguish between different types of records, the compiled code
must use the BIBOP descriptor table. This is inefficient and clumsy.

Using this assumption, we can specialize the implementation of type yyy; since
the value carried by constructor X can be distinguished from the value carried by
Y, we don't need any extra bits or words for the constructors themselves.

There are many variants on Assumption 3, for example,

*Assumption 4: Secords of different sizes, strings, integers, reals, and arrays are all
distinguishable at runtime.* This has the same sorts of disadvantages as assumption 3.

Then the type gen can have the following representation:

- Constructors A, B, and C will be represented as the integers 0, 1, and 2.

- The value D(i) will be represented as a one-word record containing *i* (to
  distinguish it from the constant constructors).

- The constructors E, F, and G will be represented transparently, since the
  values they carry can all be distinguished.

For languages like Lisp that have *runtime type checking*, Assumption 4 (or something even stronger) is required. Because ML has compile-time type checking, it is
not necessary to distinguish all the different types at runtime—these assumptions
merely allow more efficient data constructor representations.

*Assumption 5: The type posint will be enforced by the compiler to contain
only positive integers.*

Then the datatype `money` can be represented without any extra indirection: Coins will be represented as negative integers, bills as positive integers, and checks as records.

Clearly, we are proceeding *ad absurdem* with these assumptions. We can use arbitrarily complicated encodings of constructors, with diminishing returns in the representations of datatypes. But there is a problem with many of these representations in Standard ML: Types can be abstract, so the details of their representation are not known at compile time. Consider:

```
datatype ('a,'b) t = A of 'a | B of 'b
type u = (int, real*real) t
```

In this case, the type constructor t can be applied to any pair of types, so the representation of A and B cannot be specialized. On the other hand, the representation of u might be specialized, since its values are all of known type. However, any function applicable to values of type t can also be applied to values of type u, so the representation must be the same, or conversion must take place.

Things get worse. Consider the functor:

```
functor F(S: sig  type 'a t
                  datatype 'a list = nil | :: of 'a t
            end
         ) = struct . . . end
```

applied to the structure

```
structure A =
struct  datatype 'a list = nil | :: of 'a * 'a list
        type 'a t = 'a * 'a list
end
```

Now, the functor F must assume nothing about the structure of t, and must therefore use an extra indirection in the representation of `::` to ensure that it is boxed. On the other hand, structure A makes use of Assumption 1 to avoid the extra indirection. Since the modules F and A can be compiled separately, there is no perfect solution to this problem.

If functors in ML behaved like the "generic" modules of Ada, this problem would not exist: It is expected of an Ada implementation that each application of a "generic" will generate new code specialized to the particular argument. But in ML the intent of the designers was that machine-code generation (and type checking, etc.) needs to be done only once for each functor, and is independent of the actual parameter to the functor.

In the implementation of Standard ML of New Jersey, we wished to avoid the functor problem, and we wanted to avoid too many constraints on the runtime system. On the other hand, we felt it was unacceptable to have extra indirections in the `list` datatype. Therefore, we rely only on Assumption 1 in the representation of datatype constructors (though we use Assumption 2 elsewhere in the compiler),

and we assume types are boxed *only* when they are records explicitly written down
in the `datatype` declaration, for example,

```
datatype a = A | B of int * int
type pair = int * int
datatype c = D | E of pair
```

The datatype *a* will be represented without extra indirections, but *c* will use extra indirections. This makes functor mismatches very rare, though it does not
completely eliminate them; we detect this problem at functor application time,
however, and print an error message for the user.

There is one last twist to constructor representation. Standard ML has an *exn*
datatype to represent exceptions that can be raised (by the `raise` operator) and
handled (by `handle`). This datatype has an unbounded number of "exception constructors," some of which carry values and some of which are "constant." Clearly,
we cannot associate *small* integer tags with each one, since there are so many of
them. We have chosen to represent the *exn* type as a pair of words, where one word
is the carried value (if any) and the other word is the tag—just as for ordinary
value-carrying constructors. This will be true even for "constant" constructors;
for them the "value word" will just be zero.

To represent the tag, any type with an unbounded number of values and that
admits equality (to test the identity of a constructor) will do. We have chosen to
use "string ref" instead of integer type for this purpose, since the string is useful
to hold the name of the exception for error reporting by the runtime system (as
in "Uncaught exception Match," when the `Match` exception is propagated to top
level).

In summary, we have discussed several different kinds of constructor representation:

Tagged: A two-word record; one word is the value and one word is a small-integer
tag. The value-carrying constructors in any one datatype are numbered
contiguously starting at zero.

Constant: An unboxed integer representing a constant data constructor. The
constant constructors for any one datatype are numbered contiguously starting at zero.

Transparent: A value-carrying constructor in a datatype with only one constructor need not be represented at all; $c(v)$ will have the same representation as
v.

TransB: Transparent boxed: A value-carrying constructor which is known to be
applied to an always-boxed type, in a datatype with no other value-carrying
constructors, can be transparent (if Assumption 1 is used).

TransU: Transparent unboxed: A value-carrying constructor which is known to
be applied to an always-unboxed type, if there are no constant constructors
in the datatype and all other constructors are boxed, can be transparent (if

Assumption 2 is used). We have chosen not to use this representation at present in Standard ML of New Jersey.

Variable: A value-carrying exception constructor, as described above.

VariableC: An exception constructor without an argument, as described above.

As each datatype is defined, the compiler analyzes the constructors and types to choose a representation for each constructor.

4.2 Pattern matching

One important and nontrivial job of the ML-specific part of the compiler is to select optimal comparison sequences for the compilation of pattern-matching. A *match* in ML is a sequence of pattern–expression pairs, called *rules*. When a match is applied to an argument, the argument is matched against the patterns, and the first rule with a matching pattern is selected and its expression is evaluated. A pattern is either a constant, which must match the argument exactly; a variable, which matches any argument (and is bound to it for the purposes of evaluating the expression); a tuple of patterns, which matches a corresponding tuple argument whose components match the components of the pattern tuple; or a constructor applied to a pattern, which matches an argument built using that constructor if the rest of the pattern matches.

As an example, consider the case statement:

```
case a
 of (false, nil)   => nil
  | (true, w)      =>  w
  | (false, x::nil) =>  x::x::nil
  | (false, y::z)   =>  z
```

The argument (`false, 4::nil`) matches the third pattern, whereas the argument (`true, 4::nil`) matches the second pattern.

One could imagine a naive compilation of matches just by testing the rules in turn as called for by the semantics. Our approach is to transform a sequence of patterns into a decision tree [19]. Each internal node of the decision tree corresponds to a test, and each branch is labeled with one of the possible results of the test and with a list of the patterns that remain potential candidates in that case. It is then straightforward to translate the decision tree into code for pattern matching. During the construction of the decision tree it is also easy to determine whether the pattern set is "exhaustive," meaning that every possible argument value matches at least one pattern, and whether there are any "redundant" patterns that only match arguments covered by previous rules. Nonexhaustive and redundant patterns result in warning messages by the compiler.

Our goal in constructing the decision tree is simply to minimize the total number of test nodes. This minimizes the size of the generated code and also generally reduces the number of tests performed on value terms. However, finding the decision tree with the minimum number of nodes is an NP-complete problem [19]; so a set of efficient heuristics is used that in practice produces an optimal decision tree in almost all cases.

In the example above, testing the first component of the pair for truth or falsity suffices to distinguish the second rule from the others; then testing the second component to see whether it is :: or `nil` distinguishes the first rule from the last two; one more test suffices to separate the last two rules. Thus, in just two or three tests, the appropriate rule can be selected; instead of two or three tests *per rule* that the naive algorithm would use.

The result of the decision-tree algorithm for pattern matches is a sequence of multiway branches, each testing which constructor is attached to a given value. For example, the *case* expression

```
case mygen
 of (true, A) => a
  | (false, B) => b
  | (true, E x) => e(x)
  | (false, F(x,y)) => f(x)
  | (true, G(1,_,x)) => f(x)
  | (false, _) => c
  | (_, G(2,_,_)) => c
  | _ => d
```

might be compiled by the "match compiler" in one of several different ways. For example, the Boolean could be tested first, followed by tests of the *gen* constructor (defined on page 38) lower in the tree; or the *gen* constructor could be tested first as follows (written in ML, though the compiler actually uses a much simpler intermediate representation):

```
let val (i,j) = mygen
 in case j
     of A => (case i of true => a | false => c)
      | B => (case i of true => d | false => b)
      | E x => (case i of true => e(x) | false => c)
      | F(x,y) => (case i of true => d | false => f(x))
      | G(z,y,x) => (case i of true => (case z of 1 => f(x)
                                              | 2 => c
                                              | _ => d)
                              | false => c)
      | _ => (case i of true => d | false => c)
end
```

Now, each *case* expression tests only one datatype to see which constructor has been applied (Boolean and integer values are like "constant" constructors).

4.3 Equality

In Standard ML a programmer may compare two values for equality if they are of
the same type, and the type is not a function type or a data type that contains
function types. The equality is *structural:* two lists containing equal values are
considered equal. However, two references (mutable cells) are considered equal
only if they are the same cell (i.e., at the same address). This simplifies the testing
of structural equality, as cycles need not be considered—every cycle in an ML data
structure goes through a `ref`.

Equality may be tested even if the types are not fully known, for example,

```
fun member(x, a::rest) = x=a orelse member(x,rest)
  | member(x, nil) = false
```

This is a polymorphic function (type $\alpha \times \alpha$ list $\to$ bool), and the type of x
cannot be known at compile time. The type checking rules will enforce, however,
that α cannot be a function type or a data structure containing function types.

In some cases, however, the type is known:

```
fun f(x:tree, y:tree, z:tree) = x=y orelse y=z
fun g(i) = if i=0 then j else i
```

(using the tree datatype shown on page 38).

When the type of the equality test is known (i.e., is a ground type, not containing any type variables), then the compiler can generate special-purpose functions
to implement each instance of equality. For example, we automatically generate a
function such as the following to implement the equal sign in `x=y` above:

```
fun eqtree(LEAF i, LEAF j) = Integer.=(i,j)
  | eqtree(TREE(a,b), TREE(c,d)) =
             eqtree(a,c) andalso eqtree(b,d)
  | eqtree _ = false
```

and for the test `i=0` in `g(i)` we just use the integer equality primitive. In general, the automatically generated functions are mutually recursive, to follow the
structure of mutually recursive datatypes.

When the type of the equality test is not known, we must rely on runtime tags.
In particular, it is necessary to make use of Assumption 4 (page 40), that the size
of each object can be determined at runtime. This is the only place in the implementation of ML where this assumption is necessary; even the garbage collector
could in principle learn the sizes and types of objects from a static description of
the compile-time type system [5]. It is conceivable that the representation of each
and every "equality type" could contain within it an equality predicate, but this
would be quite expensive [92].

How is the size of an object to be determined at runtime? There is no `PRIMOP`
in the CPS language, for example, that tells the size of a record; this is to allow
an implementation's runtime system some freedom in representation decisions. A
simple runtime system might put a descriptor word before every record; a fancier

system might use a "big bag of pages" (BIBOP) scheme to use just one descriptor for a large collection of similar records.

To implement "polymorphic equality," we assume that the runtime system provides an *externally defined* function that tells the number of fields of a record; this is accessed using the linkage convention described in Chapter 3. Then we can write an ML function that recursively compares the structure of two values, returning false if there is any difference. The pointer-equality test (*ieql*) is used as a shortcut *at each level of recursion*; when pointer equality fails on any object, structural equality is tried. In fact, this shortcut is also used in the case of known types—we generate a test for object identity in the special-case code for each datatype—but for clarity this was not shown in the *eqtree* function above.

Interpreting tags of polymorphic objects is significantly less efficient than using the specially compiled functions that are used for known types.

In summary: Polymorphic equality is no fun at all.

4.4   Unboxed updates

As mentioned in Chapter 3 and explained more fully in Section 16.3, it is helpful for the compiler to identify those `ref` cells and arrays that can hold only unboxed (nonpointer) objects, and to identify those assignment (`:=`) and `update` operations that are guaranteed to store unboxed objects (even if into a `ref` cell that might also hold boxed values). The ML type system helps to identify such `ref` creations and `update`s, and thus it is helpful to mark them prior to CPS conversion, which will strip off the type annotations. Because of type abstractions in ML, there will be some `ref` cells that the compiler can't determine the "boxity" of, and in this case we settle for a conservative approximation, using the general-purpose `ref`-creation or update operators that can handle either boxed or unboxed values. The result of this analysis will be to replace some of the `:=` operators in the program by `unboxedassign`, some of the `makeref` operators (that create `ref` cells) by `makerefunboxed`, and some of the `update` operators by `unboxedupdate`.

4.5   The mini-ML sublanguage

We now describe a "mini-ML" language, into which Standard ML programs can be translated. The translation will simplify the program significantly, and will incorporate all of the optimizations described earlier in this chapter.

Mini-ML is an untyped language; however, any mini-ML program could in principle be embedded in a parametric-polymorphic (second-order) lambda calculus [75]. Mini-ML programs can't be type checked as ML programs for two reasons: Mini-ML has no `let` expressions, and the parametric modules of ML (functors) are encoded as ordinary functions of mini-ML.

The datatypes of mini-ML are a subset of Standard ML's:

- integers, reals, and strings;

- datatypes with constructors, as in Standard ML;

- n-tuples, for $n \geq 0$;

- mutable arrays;

- single-argument, single-result functions.

The other ML datatypes can be translated into these. Records with named fields can be translated into n-tuples, with the loss of the distinction between different record types of arity n. But this translation is done *after* ML type checking, so the loss of some type information is not harmful.

The expressions of mini-ML are a subset of Standard ML's:

- variables;

- integer, real, and string literals;

- application of data constructors;

- removal of data constructors (see below);

- very simple case expressions (see below);

- n-tuple creation;

- selection of fields from n-tuples;

- function application, which is *strict* (as in ML)—the argument of a function is evaluated before substitution for the bound variable;

- function definition using λ (or **fn** in ML syntax), where each function binds a single variable (not a pattern as in ML);

- mutually recursive function definition using **let val rec**;

- primitive arithmetic and comparison operators;

- operators for manipulating references and arrays;

- simple exception handling (see below).

Significant components of Standard ML that are lacking in mini-ML are pattern matching, abstract types, and the module system (structures and functors). All of these are expressed using the simpler primitives of mini-ML.

The mini-ML **case** expression takes one argument—an element of a datatype— and determines which constructor has been applied. Each case rule must be an expression of the form c or c _, where c is a constant or value carrying constructor, respectively; the final rule can be a wildcard (_). Case expressions can range over integer, real, and string types as well, just as in Standard ML.

Note that case expressions do not bind variables in mini-ML, as they do in ML. Once it has been determined (using a case expression) that a datatype value has been made using a certain constructor, the carried value (for a nonconstant constructor) may be accessed by stripping off the constructor (by *deconstructing*, or *projecting*). For each value-carrying constructor c there will be a deconstructor $decon_c$ with the semantics

```
decon_c(e) = case e of c x => x | _ => error
```

for any expression e. Clearly, $decon_c$ must only be used in a context where it is guaranteed to work, for example, in the right-hand side of a case rule that has tested for the constructor c.

Section 4.2 shows how ML case expressions can be simplified to test only one datatype value at a time; now, using deconstructors, we show (for the example of Section 4.2) how variable-binding is handled:

```
let val (i,j) = mygen
  in case j
     of A => (case i of true => a | false => c)
      | B => (case i of true => d | false => b)
      | E _ => (fn x => (case i of true => e(x) | false => c))
               (decon_E j)
      | F _ => (fn (x,y) =>
                       (case i of true => d | false => f(x)))
               (decon_F j)
      | G _ => (fn (z,y,x) =>
                    (case i of true => (case z of 1 => f(x)
                                             | 2 => c
                                             | _ => d)
                             | false => c))
               (decon_G j)
      | _ => (case i of true => d | false => c)
  end
```

In each case rule that matches a value-carrying constructor c, the carried value is extracted from the constructed object j by a projection operator $decon_c$. Since mini-ML does not have *let* expressions, we use a λ (fn) applied to an argument. Strictly speaking, mini-ML does not have multiargument λs either, so we must use the selection operator to implement them:

```
fn (x,y,z) => M
```

for variables x, y, z and expression M becomes

```
fn xyz => (fn x => (fn y => (fn z => M)
                            (#3 xyz))
                   (#2 xyz))
          (#1 xyz)
```

where #i is the operator to select the ith field of an n-tuple.

In Standard ML, the `ref` operator that creates a mutable reference to the store is treated as a constructor; a use of `ref` in an expression creates a ref cell, and a use of `ref` in a pattern extracts the contents. Mutation of the contents is done by the assignment operator (`:=`). In mini-ML we abandon the fiction that `ref` is a constructor, and two new primitive functions are introduced: `makeref`(x) to create a ref and initialize it to x, and the fetch operator (written with an exclamation point `!`) to extract the contents. The assignment operator is unchanged.

Exception handling is simpler in mini-ML than in Standard ML. An exception handler in ML is a pattern match on the *exn* (exception) type; in mini-ML a handler is just a function taking an *exn* as an argument. Decision trees are used to simplify exception pattern matches just as for `fn` and `case` expressions.

4.6 Exception declarations

Mini-ML contains no special syntax for declaring exceptions. Each `exception` declaration of Standard ML is turned into a `val` declaration of `mini-ML`. The declarations

```
exception E of int
exception C
exception D = J
```

are translated into

```
val E = ref "E"
val C = ((), ref "C")
val D = J
```

We choose a **string ref** for the representation of exception constructors for three reasons:

- We need some type which can cheaply be compared for equality; `ref` cells can be compared "by reference," which is as cheaply as any type can be tested.

- We need to be able to make new values conveniently; if we used integers there would have to be some central counter to specify which numbers have been used.

- It is convenient to extract the name of an exception, as a diagnostic, when it is raised all the way to the top level.

In each case, the *string ref* behaves like the integer tag of an ordinary value-carrying constructor. But unlike those constructors, the boxity test cannot distinguish constant from value-carrying constructors, since a *string ref* is boxed. So the value-carrying constructors are represented as string refs that will be used as

tags (in two-element records) when applied to values; and the constant constructors are two-element records with the string-ref tag in the second element, and a
placeholder in the first element.

4.7   The lambda language

In the Standard ML of New Jersey compiler, mini-ML is encoded into a concrete
data structure called the *lambda language* (figure 4.1). The datatype `conrep` is
used to specify constructor representations, and is explained in Section 4.1. All of
the previous discussion of mini-ML applies to the lambda language. A "lambda
expression" *lexp* can be:

- a variable (`VAR`);

- a lambda function (`FN`);

- a "val rec" declaration (`FIX`) that recursively binds several function names
  (`var list`) to several lambda functions (`lexp list`) in the scope of an expression;

- a `SELECT(i,e)` expression of the lambda language that selects the ith field
  of an evaluated expression e (fields in the lambda language are numbered
  starting at zero, instead of starting at one as in ML);

- a `SWITCH` expression that detects which constant or constructor (from the
  (`con*lexp`) `list`) was used to build a datatype value, and then evaluates
  the resulting expression. The `lexp option` is the default case, to be used
  if none of the constructors on the list matches. For matches where all the
  constructors of the datatype are used, the `lexp option` may be `NONE`. The
  `conrep list` field of the `SWITCH` specifies all the legal constructors of the
  datatype; this is useful in optimizing the code generated for the `SWITCH`.
  For switches over integer, real, string, and exception types (i.e., all but the
  "ordinary" datatypes), this list is `nil`;

- a data constructor—constant or value-carrying—applied to an argument
  (`CON`). In the constant case, the argument is merely pro forma;

- a data value-carrying constructor removed from an argument (`DECON`);

- the `RAISE`-ing of an exception;

- the evaluation of an expression in the scope of an exception `HANDLE`r;

- a primitive operator (`PRIM`).

The lambda language is not really a lambda calculus: It is a call-by-value
langauge with an implied state. The side effects are hidden in the `primops`, which
are roughly the same as those of the CPS language and include such things as
assignment (`:=`) to the store.

```
datatype 'a option = NONE | SOME of 'a

eqtype var   (* = int *)

datatype accesspath = OFFp of int | SELp of int * accesspath

datatype conrep = UNDECIDED
                | TAGGED of int
                | CONSTANT of int
                | TRANSPARENT
                | TRANSU
                | TRANSB
                | REF
                | VARIABLE of var * accesspath
                | VARIABLEc of var * accesspath

datatype con = DATAcon of conrep
             | INTcon of int
             | REALcon of string
             | STRINGcon of string

datatype lexp
  = VAR of var
  | FN of var * lexp
  | FIX of var list * lexp list * lexp
  | APP of lexp * lexp
  | INT of int
  | REAL of string
  | STRING of string
  | SWITCH of lexp * conrep list * (con * lexp) list * lexp option
  | CON of conrep * lexp
  | DECON of conrep * lexp
  | RECORD of lexp list
  | SELECT of int * lexp
  | RAISE of lexp
  | HANDLE of lexp * lexp
  | PRIM of primop
```

Figure 4.1. The lambda language.

The primops of the lambda language include some that are not in the CPS primop set, including `callcc` (*call with current continuation*) and `throw` (*throw to a continuation*) [37]. When these are converted into CPS (see Chapter 5), they are expressed using the FIX and APP operators of the CPS language.

4.8   The module system

Standard ML has a *module* system to facilitate the structuring of large ML programs and to support separate compilation and generic library units. Figure 4.2 shows the syntax of the module system. An ordinary (unparametrized) module is

$$
\begin{array}{rcl}
decl & \rightarrow & \text{ordinary ML } \texttt{val} \text{ or } \texttt{type} \text{ declaration, etc.} \\
decl & \rightarrow & \texttt{structure } name \;=\; strexp \\
decl & \rightarrow & \texttt{structure } name : signature \;=\; strexp \\
decl & \rightarrow & \texttt{functor } name(name : signature) \;=\; strexp \\
decl & \rightarrow & \texttt{functor } name(name : signature) : signature \;=\; strexp \\
decl & \rightarrow & \texttt{signature } name \;=\; signature \\
\\
strexp & \rightarrow & \texttt{struct } decl \texttt{ end} \\
strexp & \rightarrow & name \\
strexp & \rightarrow & name(strexp) \\
\\
signature & \rightarrow & \texttt{sig } specifications \texttt{ end} \\
signature & \rightarrow & name
\end{array}
$$

Figure 4.2. Syntax of the ML module system (simplified).

called a *structure*. Any set of core ML declarations (such as `val`, `fun`, `type`, or `datatype` declarations) can be bracketed by `struct...end` and made into a structure S. Thereafter, in the scope of the declaration of S, names i, j, k from those declarations can be accessed using *qualified identifiers* $S.i, S.j, S.k$.

If it is desired to export only some of the names from a module, a *signature* can be used in the structure declaration to restrict visibility of names and to constrain the types of exported values.

A parametrized module is called a `functor`, and takes a structure as an argument. The "type" of the formal parameter structure must be specified using a signature, and the "type" of the result structure can optionally be specified using a signature. Functors and signatures cannot be nested inside structures or functors.

Figure 4.3 shows an example of the use of structures and signatures. The signature `STACK` is implemented in two different ways, by structures `Stack1` and `Stack2`. The structure `User` uses some of the primitives of structure `Stack1`. The functor `F` uses stacks, but doesn't care which implementation is used; it can be applied to any structure that matches the STACK signature. The structure T is an application of F to the Stack2 structure.

The definition of Stack1 doesn't specify—as Stack2 does—that it must match the STACK signature, but it does have all the right fields and can be used anywhere a STACK is required (e.g., as an argument to F). Similarly, the definition of Stack2 would have been just as adequate without the signature constraint.

To translate structures and functors into mini-ML, we will use RECORDs. The representation of Stack1 will be a five-element record containing the values Empty, push, top, pop, and empty in that order. We don't need to represent types (such as stack), because they are compile-time entities that don't have runtime manifestations.

When elements of structures are accessed from outside (e.g., Stack1.push in the User structure), this is translated as a selection from the structure record (e.g., SELECT(1,VAR Stack1)).

Now, if the structures Stack1 and User are compiled one at a time, the interface between them is quite simple. The Stack1 module is a single value (which happens to be a record), the names of interface files have been compiled into record offsets, and the link-loader need not be concerned with the internals of modules.

On the other hand, if the two modules are compiled together, the CPS optimizer (as will be described) can quite easily evaluate the SELECT at compile time, so the User function can apply push just as efficiently as it could have had structures not been used.

When a signature constrains a structure definition, this can have some effect on the representation of the structure. For example, the representation of any structure matching the STACK signature must be a five-element record empty, Empty, push, top, pop, in that order. Therefore, if this signature is applied to the Stack1 structure, the fields must be reordered. Furthermore, when STACK constrains Stack2, the value extra will not be represented in the interface record. It will still be evaluated, but its result will be discarded.

Furthermore, the name push inside Stack2 refers to a data constructor, but in the signature it is an ordinary function. Thus, the record built for Stack2 must have a function push that simply applies the data constructor. In general, the application of a signature to a structure may result in "thinning," meaning that some fields may be discarded, some constructors will turn into ordinary values, and the fields may be rearranged.

Functors in the module system are translated into ordinary functions in mini-ML. Thus F will just be a function that takes a structure (record) as an argument, and returns another structure (record) as a result.

This translation means that the mini-ML language given to the back end of the compiler contains no special notation for the ML module system. All of the complexities of the module system are handled statically or translated into the RECORD, SELECT, and FN operators of mini-ML. This is a great convenience, not only for the optimizer but also for the Standard ML of New Jersey link-loader and runtime system.

```
signature STACK =
   sig   type 'a stack
         exception Empty
         val empty : 'a stack
         val push: 'a * 'a stack -> 'a stack
         val top : 'a stack -> 'a
         val pop : 'a stack -> 'a stack
   end

structure Stack1 =
struct type 'a stack = 'a list
       exception Empty
       fun push(a,s) = a::s
       fun top(a::rest) = a | top(nil) = raise Empty
       fun pop(a::rest) = rest | pop(nil) = raise Empty
       val empty = nil
end

structure Stack2 : STACK =
struct datatype 'a stack = empty | push of 'a * 'a stack
       val extra = print "hello"
       exception Empty = Match
       fun top(push(a,rest)) = a
       fun pop(push(a,rest)) = rest
end

structure User =
struct val j = Stack1.push(7,Stack1.empty)
end

functor F(S : STACK) = struct  . . . S.empty . . . end

structure T = F(Stack2)
```

Figure 4.3. An example of ML modules.

CHAPTER FIVE

CONVERSION INTO CPS

After the language-specific optimizations and representation decisions have been made, the program being compiled is converted into continuation-passing style. This is done by a recursive traversal over the source-language abstract syntax tree; in Standard ML of New Jersey, we traverse the *lambda-language* expression that's a simplified version of the abstract syntax tree.

The conversion function $\mathcal{F}$ takes two arguments: a lambda-language expression E and a "continuation" function c of type $value \rightarrow cexp$. The result is a continuation expression: the original lambda expresson, converted to CPS and *nested inside* the continuation expression (*cexp*) produced by c.

The function c is not a continuation expression of the target language (CPS); nor is it a continuation of the metalanguage in the sense of *call with current continuation*. Rather, it is a continuation in a more informal sense: It is simply a function passed as an argument to $\mathcal{F}$ that is applied by $\mathcal{F}$ to the translation of the argument E.

5.1 Variables and constants

To CPS convert a variable v, one just hands it off to the contination:

$$\mathcal{F}(\text{L.VAR } v, \ c) \ = \ c(\text{VAR } v)$$

Note that we use the same representation—named **var** in figures 2.1 and 4.1—for variables of the lambda language and variables of the CPS language. This is not necessary, but it reduces the amount of verbiage required in the implementation of $\mathcal{F}$. Also note that the operators of the lambda language are prefixed by "L." in this chapter to distinguish them from CPS operators.

Conversion of a numeric constant is just like conversion of a variable:

$$\mathcal{F}(\text{L.REAL } r, \ c) \ = \ c(\text{REAL } r)$$

$$\mathcal{F}(\text{L.INT } i, \ c) \ = \ c(\text{INT } i)$$

We have chosen to represent each single-character string as an unboxed integer (the ASCII character code), and empty or multiple-character strings using

55

a pointer (i.e., a CPS STRING object). The utility of this dual representation is debatable; it saves space and time for single-character strings at the expense of continual checks to see which representation has been used on operands. This dual representation is in no way imposed by the CPS language or runtime system; it is simply a choice we made in representing ML programs. In any case, the conversion into CPS is not too difficult:

$$\mathcal{F}(\text{L.STRING } s, \ c) \ = \ c(\text{if size}(s) = 1 \text{ then } \text{INT}(\text{ord}(s)) \text{ else } \text{STRING } s)$$

5.2   Records and selection

Building records, and selecting from them, is reasonably straightforward. We take care not to produce empty (zero-length) records, as the runtime system does not like them; instead we represent an empty record as an integer zero:

$$\mathcal{F}(\text{L.RECORD nil}, \ c) \ = \ c(\text{INT } 0)$$

$$\mathcal{F}(\text{L.RECORD } \vec{A}, \ c) \ = \ \mathcal{F}_l(\vec{A}, \ \lambda\vec{a}.\text{RECORD}(\text{map}(\lambda v.(v, \text{OFFp } 0)) \ \vec{a}, \ \mathbf{x}, \ c(\text{VAR } \mathbf{x})))$$

In the nontrivial case, $\vec{A}$ is a list of lambda-expressions. The auxiliary function $\mathcal{F}_l$ converts this list, binding their results to a list $\vec{a}$ of CPS variables. The function $\lambda\vec{a}...$ produces a RECORD $cexp$ that $\mathcal{F}_l$ puts inside the $cexp$ produced by $\mathcal{F}_l(\vec{A}, ...)$ that binds the variables $\vec{a}$; therefore, the RECORD in the equation above will be in the scope of all of its arguments. A new variable $\mathbf{x}$ is created here; it is formally bound by the RECORD operator to hold the newly created record, and then is passed to c. We use boldface to indicate CPS variables newly introduced into expressions. Note that the variables $\vec{a}$ are not newly introduced at this time; instead, they are created in the recursive call to $\mathcal{F}$ and passed as arguments into the *meta-variable* $\vec{a}$—a subtle point that may or may not be helpful to the reader. By *meta-variable* we mean a variable of the compiler, and not of the compiled code.

The definition of $\mathcal{F}_l$ is

$$\mathcal{F}_l(\vec{A}, c) = \quad \begin{aligned} &\text{let} \quad g(E::\vec{R}, \ \vec{w}) \ = \ \mathcal{F}(E, \lambda v.g(\vec{R}, v::\vec{w})) \\ &\qquad\quad g(\text{nil}, \ \vec{w}) \ = \ c(\text{reverse } \vec{w}) \\ &\text{in} \quad g(\vec{A}, \text{nil}) \end{aligned}$$

Each expression in the list $\vec{A}$ is converted in turn by a call to $\mathcal{F}$; then the continuation ($\lambda v...$) converts the remainder of the expressions. When all the expressions have been converted, the list $\vec{w}$ of variables holds all the results (note that $\vec{w}$ has been accumulated backwards and needs to be reversed). Now the original list continuation c can be applied to this list of variables.

To select from a record is quite easy:

$$\mathcal{F}(\text{L.SELECT}(i, E), \ c) \ = \ \mathcal{F}(E, \lambda v.\text{SELECT}(i, v, \mathbf{w}, c(\text{VAR } \mathbf{w})))$$

To evaluate a selection from an expression E, first the expression must be evaluated (by a call to $\mathcal{F}$) and then the CPS SELECT operator can be applied. One can use the word "evaluate" anywhere in place of "convert;" this often helps in the visualization of what will happen when the program is run.

As above, w is a newly invented variable not appearing elsewhere; it holds the newly fetched value.

At this point an example may be helpful. We show the translation of an ML expression (4,#1(m)). This translates into lambda language as

L.RECORD[L.INT 4, L.SELECT(0, L.VAR m)]

(recall that record fields are numbered starting at #1 in ML but starting at 0 in the lambda language and CPS). Then, we apply $\mathcal{F}$ to this, in a context c_0:

$$\mathcal{F}(\text{L.RECORD}[\text{L.INT } 4, \text{ L.SELECT}(0, \text{ L.VAR } m)], c_0) =$$
$$\mathcal{F}_l([\text{L.INT } 4, \text{ L.SELECT}(0, \text{ L.VAR } m)],$$
$$\lambda \vec{a}.\text{RECORD}(\text{map}(\lambda v.(v, \text{OFFp } 0)) \ \vec{a}, \ \text{x}, \ c_0(\text{VAR x})))$$

Now, let $c_1 = \lambda \vec{a} \ldots (\ldots \text{x}))$ in the expression above, and we have:

$$\mathcal{F}_l([\text{L.INT } 4, \text{ L.SELECT}(0, \text{ L.VAR } m)], \ c_1) =$$
$$g_{c_1}([\text{L.INT } 4, \text{ L.SELECT}(0, \text{ L.VAR } m)], \text{nil}) =$$
$$\mathcal{F}(\text{L.INT } 4, \ \lambda v.g_{c_1}([\text{L.SELECT}(0, \text{L.VAR } m)], [v])) =$$
$$(\lambda v.g_{c_1}([\text{L.SELECT}(0, \text{L.VAR } m)], [v])) \ (\text{INT } 4) =$$
$$g_{c_1}([\text{L.SELECT}(0, \text{ L.VAR } m)], [\text{INT } 4]) =$$
$$\mathcal{F}(\text{L.SELECT}(0, \text{ L.VAR } m), \lambda v.g_{c_1}(\text{nil}, \ v :: [\text{INT } 4])) =$$
$$\mathcal{F}(\text{L.VAR } m, \lambda u.\text{SELECT}(0, u, w, g_{c_1}(\text{nil}, [\text{VAR } w, \text{ INT } 4]))) =$$
$$\text{SELECT}(i, \text{VAR } m, \ w, g_{c_1}(\text{nil}, [\text{VAR } w, \text{ INT } 4])) =$$
$$\text{SELECT}(i, \text{VAR } m, \ w, c_1([\text{INT } 4, \text{ VAR } w])) =$$
$$\text{SELECT}(i, \text{VAR } m, \ w,$$
$$\text{RECORD}([(\text{INT } 4, \text{ OFFp } 0), (\text{VAR } w, \text{ OFFp } 0)], \ \text{x}, \ c_0(\text{VAR x})))$$

Notice that u and v are not variables of the CPS like m and w. The meta-variable v is bound to the CPS constant INT 4, and u is bound to the CPS variable VAR m.

5.3 Primitive arithmetic operators

The primitive operators (*primops*) can be classified into categories based on the number of results they return, and whether they branch. There are approximately four such categories:

1. Operators that take n arguments, return one result, and continue in only one way. These include all the arithmetic operators such integer add, integer negate, floating multiply, as well as operators like fetch from ref cell.

2. Operators that take n arguments, return no result, and continue in only one way. These operators—ref assignment, array update, set current exception handler—are executed only for their side effect on the store.

3. Operators that take n arguments, return no result, and continue in one of two ways. These are the conditional branches: integer greater than, floating less than, is boxed?, and so on.

4. Unusual operators that require special translation, such as *call with current continuation*.

Each category is converted into continuation-passing style in one of two ways, depending on whether the operator takes one argument or more than one. This is because Standard ML (and mini-ML) represent multiple-argument functions by passing (pro forma) a single argument that's an n-tuple of the actual arguments. When there is just one actual argument, however, the n-tuple is omitted. Here's the case for a one-argument arithmetic primop:

$$\mathcal{F}(\texttt{L.APP}(\texttt{L.PRIM}\ i,\ E),\ c)\ =\ \mathcal{F}(E, \lambda v.\texttt{PRIMOP}(i, [v], [\mathbf{w}], [c(\texttt{VAR}\ \mathbf{w})]))$$

where, as usual, the bold-faced variable $\mathbf{w}$ is a new, distinct variable.

When a lambda-language primop is found in some other context (i.e., not directly applied to an argument), an inverse η-reduction can be performed in the lambda language to make it match the pattern above:

$$\texttt{L.PRIM}\ i\quad \rightarrow \quad \texttt{L.FN}(\mathbf{x}, \texttt{L.APP}(\texttt{L.PRIM}\ i, \texttt{L.VAR}\ \mathbf{x}))$$

When an n-argument primop $(n > 1)$ is found applied to a record, the conversion is simple:

$$\mathcal{F}(\texttt{L.APP}(\texttt{L.PRIM}\ i,\ \texttt{L.RECORD}\ \vec{A}),\ c)\ =\ \mathcal{F}_l(\vec{A}, \lambda\vec{a}.\texttt{PRIMOP}(i, \vec{a}, [\mathbf{w}], [c(\texttt{VAR}\ \mathbf{w})]))$$

Here $\vec{A}$ is the list of n argument expressions and $\vec{a}$ is the list of variables holding the results of evaluating those expressions.

If an n-argument primop is found applied to something other than a record, then a simple transformation is useful in the lambda language; for readability, we will express the transformation in the source language instead:

$$\texttt{p}(E) \rightarrow \texttt{let val}\ (v_1, v_2, ..., v_n) = E\ \texttt{in}\ \texttt{p}(v_1, v_2, ..., v_n)\ \texttt{end}$$

Of course, in lambda language the `let` and the pattern match are expressed via `FN`, `APP`, and `SELECT` operators.

For primops that return no result, the conversion algorithm $\mathcal{F}$ just passes a placeholder (0) to the continuation c:

$$\mathcal{F}(\texttt{L.APP}(\texttt{L.PRIM}\ i,\ E),\ c)\ =\ \mathcal{F}(E, \lambda v.\texttt{PRIMOP}(i, [v], [], [c(\texttt{INT}\ 0)]))$$

The `INT` 0 placeholder is likely to be eliminated in the optimization of the CPS expression after the conversion is completed, in most contexts.

For no-result primops that take several arguments, or that are in need of an inverse η-reduction, the same transformations apply as for arithmetic primops that return a result. The assignment (:=) and **update** primops are examples of this kind.

We now consider the branching primops. In ML (and in mini-ML), the comparison operators such as > and = return a Boolean result; the Boolean type is simply a datatype with two constant constructors, **false** and **true**. The representations of these constructors are the integers 0 and 1. In the CPS language, however, the comparison primops return no result; instead, they take one of two different continuations. We address this slight semantic gap by making the two different continuations pass 1 and 0, respectively, to the original continuation.

We start with the one-argument case (e.g., $\text{boxed}(x)$) that tests whether x is represented as a pointer. A naive approach is:

$$\mathcal{F}(\texttt{L.APP}(\texttt{L.PRIM } i, \ E), \ c) \ = \ \mathcal{F}(E, \lambda v.\texttt{PRIMOP}(i, [v], [\,], [c(\texttt{INT 1}), c(\texttt{INT 0})]))$$

This is not quite right, since the application of c (a metalanguage function that constructs a CPS expression) to two different arguments will lead to two different copies of the same CPS code. This leads to a possibly exponential blowup of the code size. What we must do is call c only once: We define a CPS function whose body contains the expression c, and then write two applications of that function

$$\mathcal{F}(\texttt{L.APP}(\texttt{L.PRIM } i, \ E), \ c) \ =$$
$$\mathcal{F}(E, \lambda v.\texttt{FIX}([(\mathbf{k}, [\mathbf{x}], c(\texttt{VAR x}))], \texttt{PRIMOP}(i, [v], [\,], [\texttt{APP}(\texttt{VAR k}, \texttt{INT 1}),$$
$$\texttt{APP}(\texttt{VAR k}, \texttt{INT 0})])))$$

For multiple-argument comparison operators, and for operators needing inverse η-reduction, the transformations are similar to those for the arithmetic operators.

The conversion of the primops **callcc** (call with current continuation) and **throw** (invoke a continuation) is discussed in Section 5.9.

5.4 Function calls

A single function definition in the lambda language translates into a single function definition in the CPS language. However, the CPS function takes one additional argument: the continuation **k** to invoke upon function exit. The application of this continuation function to the result of the lambda function is made explicit:

$$\mathcal{F}(\texttt{L.FN}(v, E), \ c) \ = \ \texttt{FIX}([(\mathbf{f}, [v, \mathbf{k}], \mathcal{F}(E, \ \lambda z.\texttt{APP}(\texttt{VAR k}, [z])))], \ c(\texttt{VAR f}))$$

The function is given a name **f**, and takes the (original) argument v along with a continuation argument **k**. The body of **f** is given by converting E so when E is finished, it will bind its result to some variable x (or will produce some constant z) and then apply **k** to that. Finally, we apply c to **f** to hand the function off to the context that expects it.

To translate a lambda language function call, a continuation function **r** (for the "return address") must be defined. The lambda function F and the lambda argument E must both be evaluated (f and e will refer to these values). Then a CPS-language APP applies the function f to the argument e and continuation r.

$$\mathcal{F}(\texttt{L.APP}(F, E),\ c) =$$
$$\texttt{FIX}([[(\mathbf{r}, [\mathbf{x}], c(\texttt{VAR x}))], \mathcal{F}(F, \lambda f.\mathcal{F}(E, \lambda e.\texttt{APP}(f, [e, \texttt{VAR r}]))))$$

5.5   Mutually recursive functions

Both the lambda language and the CPS language have constructs for defining a set of mutually recursive functions visible in some limited scope, so the conversion is not difficult:

$$\mathcal{F}(\texttt{L.FIX}(\vec{h}, \vec{b}, E),\ c)\ =\ \texttt{FIX}(g(\vec{h}, \vec{b}),\ \mathcal{F}(E, c))$$

where the function g is applied to the list of function names and the list of function bodies:

$$g(h_1 :: \vec{h},\ \texttt{L.FN}(v, B) :: \vec{b})\ =\ (h_1, [v, \mathbf{w}], \mathcal{F}(B, \lambda z.\texttt{APP}(\texttt{VAR w}, [z]))) :: g(\vec{h}, \vec{b})$$
$$g(\texttt{nil},\ \texttt{nil})\ =\ \texttt{nil}$$

5.6   Data constructors

The lambda language has an operator for the application of a data constructor; the CPS language has no such operator. In the translation, we rewrite constructor applications using the RECORDs (etc.) of the lambda language, and then translate those into CPS. Since the representation of each constructor has already been decided, this is quite simple:

$$\begin{aligned}
\mathcal{F}(\texttt{L.CON}(\texttt{CONSTANT } i,\ E),\ c)\ &=\ \mathcal{F}(\texttt{L.INT } i,\ c) \\
\mathcal{F}(\texttt{L.CON}(\texttt{TAGGED } i,\ E),\ c)\ &=\ \mathcal{F}(\texttt{L.RECORD}[E,\ \texttt{L.INT } i],\ c) \\
\mathcal{F}(\texttt{L.CON}(\texttt{TRANSPARENT},\ E),\ c)\ &=\ \mathcal{F}(E,\ c) \\
\mathcal{F}(\texttt{L.CON}(\texttt{TRANSB},\ E),\ c)\ &=\ \mathcal{F}(E,\ c) \\
\mathcal{F}(\texttt{L.CON}(\texttt{TRANSU},\ E),\ c)\ &=\ \mathcal{F}(E,\ c)
\end{aligned}$$

A constant constructor is represented just as an integer. A tagged constructor is a two-element record; arbitrarily, the tag comes second and the value comes first. Transparent constructors (of three flavors) have no effect on the expression they are applied to.

The variable-tagged constructors, used for the exception type, have a slightly more complicated representation. Instead of a constant integer tag, the tag is found by traversing a path of SELECTs rooted at a variable. This is to model the situation in which an exception defined in some other ML module is applied to an argument; to extract the exception constructor from another module may require a chain of selections. The chain (v, p) is expressed using the CPS path notation (SELp and OFFp), which can be used directly in the CPS-converted expression:

$$\mathcal{F}(\text{L.CON}(\text{VARIABLE}(v,p),\ E),\ c)\ =$$
$$\mathcal{F}(E,\ \lambda w.\text{RECORD}([(w,\ \text{OFFp}\ 0),\ (v,p)],\ \text{x},\ c(\text{VAR}\ \text{x})))$$

Finally, the "constant" exception constructors—those that in ML are not applied to an argument—must have a very similar representation to the tagged exception constructors. They must, in fact, be applied to a pro forma argument using a two-element record. This is unlike the constant constructors of ordinary datatypes; the source of the difference is that the ordinary constant constructors are small integers, distinguishable from the boxed records used for the application of tagged constructors. However, for exception constructors, the constant constructors themselves are already pointers (they're *string refs*), and could not be easily distinguished from the two-element records.

Even so, there is a choice about when to create the two-element record; is it done when the exception constructor is declared, or when it is applied? Since every application of the constructor would lead to an operationally equivalent record, it is more efficient to create the record at declaration time. Thus, to "apply" a constant exception constructor (to an irrelevant placeholder argument), one simply grabs the already-existing two-element record:

$$\mathcal{F}(\text{L.CON}(\text{VARIABLEc}(v,p),\ E),\ c)\ =$$
$$\text{RECORD}([(v,p)],\mathbf{w},\text{SELECT}(0,\mathbf{w},\mathbf{x},c(\text{VAR}\ \mathbf{x})))$$

The reason for building a RECORD and then immediately selecting from it is merely pro forma; the path notation (v, p) is easy to translate into CPS as a record field, and the RECORD and SELECT will be quickly optimized away by the CPS optimization phase.

It is also necessary to explain how the lambda-language deconstruction operators (DECON) are converted into CPS. This is quite simple; for ordinary tagged constructors we just fetch the first element (recall that the tag is the second element), and for transparent constructors we do nothing at all:

$$\mathcal{F}(\text{L.DECON}(\text{TAGGED}(i),\ E),\ c)\ =\ \mathcal{F}(\text{L.SELECT}(0,\ E),\ c)$$
$$\mathcal{F}(\text{L.DECON}(\text{TRANSPARENT},\ E),\ c)\ =\ \mathcal{F}(E,\ c)$$
$$\mathcal{F}(\text{L.DECON}(\text{TRANSB},\ E),\ c)\ =\ \mathcal{F}(E,\ c)$$
$$\mathcal{F}(\text{L.DECON}(\text{TRANSU},\ E),\ c)\ =\ \mathcal{F}(E,\ c)$$
$$\mathcal{F}(\text{L.DECON}(\text{VARIABLE},\ E),\ c)\ =\ \mathcal{F}(\text{L.SELECT}(0,\ E),\ c)$$

Of course, L.DECON cannot be applied to values constructed with the "constant" constructors CONSTANT and VARIABLEc.

5.7 Case statements

Generating code for case statements is made easier by the fact that much of the heavy lifting has already been done by the "match compiler," as described in sections 4.2 and 4.5. What's left is the simple SWITCH operator of the lambda language, which takes an expression to be evaluated and a list of constructor–expression pairs, with the expression to be evaluated if the corresponding constructor matches.

There is also an optional default case, for use if none of the constructors matches. If the default is not present, then it is erroneous for none of the explicit cases to match. This is unlike Standard ML, in which a system-defined "Match" exception is raised if none of the cases is matched; in the lambda language, a default case that explicitly raises this exception must be written into the SWITCH expression on any nonexhaustive match.

Finally, for datatypes with a finite number of constructors, the SWITCH operator has an argument that lists all the possible constructor representations in the type; this facilitates the generation of good code by eliminating useless tests (i.e., range-checks that can't possibly be violated).

The translation of lambda-language SWITCHes to CPS is not completely trivial. First, it is necessary (for datatypes that have both boxed and unboxed constructors) to test the argument for "boxity." Then, for the unboxed case we must test an integer value against several integer constants; for the boxed case (if there is more than one boxed constructor) we have the same situation after fetching the tag word from the two-element record.

There are several ways that a value may be compared with several integers to see which one it is (and which continuation to execute). A chain of compare-and-branches may be used; this is equivalent to *linear search*. A *binary search* may be used by comparing against the median integer in the range, recursively. Finally, a *jump table* can be used to find the right continuation in constant time.

If there are just a few cases, then a linear search works fine; if there are many cases and they are sparsely distributed among the range of possible values that an integer can take on, then a binary search works best; and if there are many values densely distributed, then a jump table works best.

These three methods may be combined judiciously [20]: Each "clump" of densely distributed cases will have its own jump table; then a binary search will be used to decide which clump the test value is in. Tiny clumps (e.g., fewer than five cases) will use linear search.

We have implemented this technique. Perhaps it is overkill, since most datatypes do not have too many constructors; but we did not want programs with large datatypes (or large case statements on integer values) to suffer. Such programs are often generated, for example, by parser generators and other programs that produce source code as output.

There are four "special" datatypes with infinite numbers of constructors: the integer, real, string, and exception types. Each merits some discussion.

Switch expressions on integers can be handled using the same tree of indexed jumps as is used for ordinary data constructors.

Switch expressions on real numbers cannot make use of indexed jumps, but a binary decision tree is certainly possible to ensure a logarithmic-time (in the number of cases) resolution. At present, though, Standard ML of New Jersey eschews any interpretation of floating-point literals until final machine-code generation, so cross compilation can be completely accurate. Therefore we use a simple (and potentially slow) linear search for pattern matches on reals.

Since we represent single-character strings unboxed and all other strings boxed, the first thing that a switch on strings has to do is test the argument for boxity. The unboxed cases are handled (efficiently) as if they were integers; the boxed cases are then handled (expensively) by a linear search with calls to an ML-coded string equality function. In principle, the boxed cases could use a decision tree based on individual characters, or on string length, but we have not bothered. Finally, exception constructors have tag values that are not known at compile time, so no precomputation of a decision tree is possible. A linear search of ref-cell pointer comparisons is used.

5.8   Exception handling

The lambda-language primitives for exception handling are RAISE, which evaluates an expression of type *exn* and then raises that exception; and HANDLE which evaluates its first argument, and if an exception occurs it applies the second argument to that exception. The second argument is an expression of type $exn \rightarrow A$, where A is the type of the first argument.

There are at least two ways that exception handlers of this kind could be implemented. We have chosen to have a distinguished location in the store, containing the current exception handler; each exception handler is just a continuation taking an *exn* argument. A HANDLE just installs a new exception handler upon entry, and re-installs the previous handler upon exit. A RAISE just passes its argument to the current handler. The primitive operators necessary for this method are *get-handler* and *set-handler*. A minor variant of this scheme would be to use the fetch and assignment operators on this location, but we have chosen special operators to give the implementation more freedom to make the implementation of exception handlers different from that of ordinary refs. In particular, a machine register can be used to hold the current exception-handler continuation.

The other method of doing exception handling is to give every function in the CPS an extra argument: the current exception handler. A function could leave the current handler untouched, and pass it to every function that it calls, or it could "install" a new one by passing a different handler to functions that it calls. This method is at least as efficient as the store-based method, since arguments left untouched typically require (in the implementation) no instructions to pass to another function; and the implementation might be able to optimize more easily the manipulation of handlers.

However, there is a serious problem with the "extra argument" approach. The arithmetic operators on a typical machine automatically raise a signal on overflow (or division by zero). The runtime system would like to be able to handle this signal by raising an ML exception. To do so, the runtime system must be able to find the exception handler. By having a known location for the handler, we enable the runtime system to find it. If the handler were just a function argument, then transformations on the program might hide the handler in a place the runtime system couldn't understand, or alter its representation, or in-line expand it entirely.

So the translation of HANDLE must first save the old handler **h**. Then it makes a continuation **k** corresponding to the context of the entire handle expression. Then it makes and installs a new exception handler **n**. Finally, the first operand A of the handle expression is executed, with a continuation that re-installs **h** and then invokes **k**.

The new handler **n**, if invoked, first re-installs **h** and then evaluates the second operand B of the HANDLE expression, continuing with **k**.

$$\mathcal{F}(\text{L.HANDLE}(A, B),\ c) =$$
$$\text{PRIMOP}(\text{gethdlr}, [\,], [\mathbf{h}],$$
$$\text{FIX}([[(\mathbf{k}, [\mathbf{x}],\ c(\text{VAR } \mathbf{x})),$$
$$(\mathbf{n}, [\mathbf{e}],\ \text{PRIMOP}(\text{sethdlr}, [\text{VAR } \mathbf{h}], [\,], [$$
$$\mathcal{F}(B,\ \lambda f.\text{APP}(f, [\text{VAR } \mathbf{e},\ \text{VAR } \mathbf{k}]))])))],$$
$$\text{PRIMOP}(\text{sethdlr}, [\text{VAR } \mathbf{n}], [\,],$$
$$[\mathcal{F}(A,\ \lambda v.\text{PRIMOP}(\text{sethdlr}, [\text{VAR } \mathbf{h}], [\,], [\text{APP}(\text{VAR } \mathbf{k}, [v])]))])))))$$

Raising an exception is much simpler:

$$\mathcal{F}(\text{L.RAISE } E,\ c) = \mathcal{F}(E,\ \lambda w.\text{PRIMOP}(\text{gethdlr}, [\,], [\mathbf{h}], [\text{APP}(\text{VAR } \mathbf{h},\ [w])]))$$

We first evaluate the exception value E, yielding a value referred to by meta-variable w. Then the current handler **h** is extracted and applied to w.

5.9   Call with current continuation

Standard ML of New Jersey has a set of primitives [37] to allow programs to manipulate their continuations directly:

```
type 'a cont
val callcc : ('a cont -> 'a) -> 'a
val throw : 'a cont -> 'a -> 'b
```

The continuation of an expression is an abstraction of what the system will do with the value of the expression. For example, in the expression

```
            if a orelse b then foo() else goo()
```

the continuation of the expression `a orelse b` can be described in words as "if the value is true then compute foo() otherwise compute goo() and then continue in the context of the **if** expression." Usually the continuation of an expression is implicit; however, the primitive `callcc` allows the programmer to capture and use these continuations.

The `callcc` (call-with-current-continuation) operator takes a function as an argument and applies it to the current continuation. The continuation of an expression of type α has type α *cont* and is a first-class object. To capture the continuation of `a orelse b` described above, one would write:

```
if callcc(fn k => a orelse b) then foo() else goo
```

Here the continuation of the `callcc` application is captured by being bound to k, but it is not used. Because the continuation is not used the predicate tested by `if` is the result of the expression `a orelse b`. To use the continuation k it must be invoked with some argument; then the computation would continue as if that value were the result of the `callcc` application. This is called *throwing* the continuation a value; it is performed by applying `throw` to the continuation and the value.

```
if callcc(fn k => (throw k false) orelse b) then foo() else goo()
```

Here, when the continuation k is thrown the value *false*, `orelse b` is simply ignored, the `callcc` application returns *false*, and `goo()` is then evaluated.

The type returned by a `throw` expression is unconstrained like that of a `raise` expression and for the same reason: Neither of these expressions ever return.

One of the less interesting uses of `callcc` is as an alternative to exception handlers. For example,

```
exception Prod

fun prod l = let fun loop [] = 1
                   | loop(0::r) = raise Prod
                   | loop(a::r) = a * loop r
             in loop l handle Prod => 0
             end
```

can be written with `callcc` as follows:

```
fun prod l = callcc(fn exit =>
                  let fun loop [] = 1
                        | loop(0::r) = throw exit 0
                        | loop(a::r) = a * loop r
                  in loop l
                  end)
```

But continuations are more general than exception handlers and can be used to implement sophisticated control structures. Chapter 17 discusses this further.

A naive (but explicatory) approach to the implementation of `callcc` just grabs the continuation in the obvious way:

$$\mathcal{F}_{\text{naive}}(\text{L.APP}(\text{L.PRIM L.callcc}, F), c) =$$
$$\text{FIX}([(\mathbf{k}, [\mathbf{x}], c(\text{VAR } \mathbf{x}))], \mathcal{F}(F, \lambda v.\text{APP}(v, [\text{VAR } \mathbf{k}, \text{VAR } \mathbf{k}])))$$

$$\mathcal{F}_{\text{naive}}(\text{L.APP}(\text{L.PRIM L.throw}, E), c) =$$
$$\mathcal{F}(E, \lambda k.\text{FIX}([(\mathbf{f}, [\mathbf{x}, \mathbf{j}], \text{APP}(k, [\text{VAR } \mathbf{x}]))], c(\text{VAR } \mathbf{f})))$$

The context c of a `callcc` expression is abstracted as a function $\mathbf{k}(\hat{x})$ that just evaluates the continuation expression $c(x)$. Then the argument F of the `callcc` is applied to $(\mathbf{k}, \mathbf{k})$. The first $\mathbf{k}$ is the "argument" of F and the second is the "continuation" of F; thus, if F simply returns then $\mathbf{k}$ will be the continuation, and if F throws to its argument then $\mathbf{k}$ will also be the continuation. The interesting uses of `callcc` involve F saving $\mathbf{k}$ in a data structure, or passing it to another function.

Then `throw` E A just evaluates E into a continuation-variable k, and applies k to the evaluated A. The `FIX` in this definition is merely to express the curried `throw` operator of ML.

The naive approach is not quite right, because we want each continuation to inherit the exception handler of its creator, not the handler of its invoker. With proper manipulation of handlers, `callcc` is translated thus:

$$\mathcal{F}(\texttt{L.APP(L.PRIM L.callcc}, \ F), \ c) \ =$$
$$\quad \texttt{PRIMOP(gethdlr}, [\,], [\mathbf{h}], [$$
$$\quad\quad \texttt{FIX}([(\mathbf{k}, [\mathbf{x}], \ c(\texttt{VAR } \mathbf{x})),$$
$$\quad\quad\quad\quad (\mathbf{k}', [\mathbf{x}'], \texttt{PRIMOP(sethdlr}, [\texttt{VAR } \mathbf{h}], [\,], [\ \texttt{APP(VAR } \mathbf{k}, [\texttt{VAR } \mathbf{x}])]))],$$
$$\quad\quad\quad\quad \mathcal{F}(F, \ \lambda v.\texttt{APP}(v, [\texttt{VAR } \mathbf{k}', \ \texttt{VAR } \mathbf{k}]))))])$$

$$\mathcal{F}(\texttt{L.APP(L.PRIM L.throw}, \ E), \ c) \ = \ \mathcal{F}_{\text{naive}}(\texttt{L.APP(L.PRIM L.throw}, \ E), \ c)$$

Note that the `throw` operator doesn't have to know about the exception-handler manipulation, in this formulation. The reason for making two separate functions k and k' is that if f simply returns (calls its continuation) directly, there is no need to reset the exception handler after it returns—any function in the lambda language is guaranteed to leave the handler as it found it. By letting k be essentially the same as c, we enable `callcc` to be tail recursive in many cases where k' would not lead to tail calls.

Another way to save the exception handler would be to represent each reified continuation (that is, each continuation saved by `callcc`) as a pair of underlying continuations: one for normal invocation and one for the exception handler. Then `throw` would have to install the exception handler before invoking the normal continuation. This has the disadvantage that there would be an extra record creation on each `callcc`, but it has the putative advantage that one could make a function

```
handler_of : 'a cont -> exn cont
```

that extracts the exception handler of any reified continuation.

However, `handler_of` is not a good thing to have around. In the presence of signal handlers that can grab the current continuation at any time [72], that means that any exception could be raised in any program fragment. This impairs the ability of the optimizing compiler, or of the human reader of the program, to reason about control flow.

CHAPTER SIX

OPTIMIZATION OF THE CPS

After conversion from mini-ML (the lambda language) into continuation-passing style, the program being compiled is in need of three kinds of work:

1. The CPS program is very inefficient, and the application of many simple transformations (such as β-reduction, constant folding, argument expansion) will lead to a smaller, more efficient CPS program with the same semantics.

2. The representations of functions (FIXes) are not exactly as a von Neumann machine would like them, since functions are nested with lexical scope. A rewrite of the CPS can unnest all functions and simplify the environments of variable bindings.

3. The CPS must eventually be translated into machine code.

These three jobs will be split into separate phases, called *CPS optimization*, *closure introduction*, and *abstract machine-code generation*, respectively. There are also other phases between the ones mentioned here, as summarized in Section 1.4. This chapter covers the CPS optimization: rewriting a CPS expression to produce a more efficient representation of the same computable function.

Many different kinds of optimizations are performed, and each pass over the expression performs some subset of the optimizations. Each time an optimization is performed (e.g., the constant folding of the expression $5 + 7$ within the larger expression $3 + (5 + 7)$), some other optimization might be enabled on the next pass (e.g., constant folding of the resultant $3 + 12$).

Each pass performs many optimizations in parallel, so it is necessary that the different optimizations performed in each pass do not interfere with each other. We have grouped the different transformations into five separate groups, so each group contains noninterfering optimizations:

1. Constant folding, function-argument expansion, β-contraction of functions called only once, and other "contractions;"

2. β-expansion, that is, the β-reduction of functions called more than once;

3. η-reduction and uncurrying;

4. Hoisting, that is, the interchange of bindings to reduce or expand the scope of individual definitions;

5. Common subexpression elimination.

Each round of the optimizer might involve one pass of each of these five groups of optimizations. These optimization rounds are repeated until no more transformations (more strictly speaking, until few transformations) are accomplished in each round—a normal form is reached.

Unfortunately, optimization is a tricky business. We cannot hope to (automatically) achieve the optimal representation of a general computable function—the problem is Turing complete. Any optimizer of which we require termination on all inputs (that is, we don't want it to execute the user's infinite loops at compile time—just at runtime!) must of necessity be just a batch of heuristics; there can be no "algorithm." We can have "algorithms" only for small pieces of the problem; for example, once a (presumably suboptimal) representation of the program is found, we can "optimally" allocate registers for it, if we're lucky.

Thus, the emphasis here is on finding small, correct transformations of the program that will probably improve its efficiency (run time or program size, or both). We can then measure the improvement on "typical," "realistic" programs. And we can measure the cost— how much compile time does each optimization take? We will be less concerned with such things as (for example) the Church–Rosser property: Does the optimizer produce the same CPS output regardless of the order it performs its optimizations? Probably not. A more interesting question: Is the result of executing the CPS invariant under the optimization? We hope so.

We now describe the individual optimizations, and give a sketch of the algorithms and data structures used in performing them.

6.1   Constant folding and β-contraction

The "constant-folding" phase of the optimizer performs a large number of transformations that improve both the size and speed of the program. These include the elimination of arithmetic operators when both arguments are constants, but more important are the elimination of selections from "known" records, and the in-line expansion (β-reduction) of functions called only once. Also, parameter passing in calls to known functions is streamlined. Each of these optimizations merits separate discussion.

Beta contraction: When a variable f is statically bound as a function in a FIX declaration, and that variable is then applied to arguments, a β-reduction can take place: The body of the function can replace the APP expression, with the actual parameters substituted for the formals of the function. Since the (entire) continuation expression obeys the rule of unique bindings, that is, each variable is bound in only once place, there is no danger of "variable capture" that might occur in ordinary λ-calculus. Thus, if we have the expression

$$\texttt{FIX}([\ldots,(f,\vec{v},B),\ldots],\ldots \texttt{APP}(f,\vec{a})\ldots)$$

where $\vec{v}$ are the formal parameters of the function f, and $\vec{a}$ are the actual parameters of a call to f, we can replace the function call (APP) with the body B of f, in which we substitute $\vec{a}$, respectively, for $\vec{v}$:

$$\texttt{FIX}([\ldots,(f,\vec{v},B),\ldots],\ldots B\{\vec{v}\mapsto \vec{a}\}\ldots)$$

The notation $B\{\vec{v}\mapsto \vec{a}\}$ means the expression B with each occurrence of v_i replaced by the corresponding a_i.

However, if f contains internal variable bindings (as it is likely to do), this will violate the unique-binding rule. One solution is to α-convert B, that is, rename all the bound variables of B. This solution will be resorted to in the β-expansion phase (which does β-reduction of functions called more than once). But here we have a much simpler solution: If we do β-reduction only on functions called just once, then we can delete the function definition at the same time as we expand the body, thus preserving the unique-binding rule:

$$\texttt{FIX}([\ldots,\ldots],\ldots B\{\vec{v}\mapsto \vec{a}\}\ldots)$$

To clean up after this transformation, it is useful to remove any FIX that binds no functions:

$$\texttt{FIX}([\,],A) \;\rightarrow\; A$$

We will define β-contraction as β-reduction of functions called just once, and β-expansion as β-reduction of functions called more than once. (Functions called not at all can be "reduced" as a special case of dead-variable elimination.) It is not just for simplicity of implementation that we avoid β-expansion in this phase. To "reduce" a function called more than once means copying its body; if the body is large, then this a "reduction" only in name. Since we want the "constant-folding" phase to consist only of optimizations that improve the size and speed of the program, we will perform only β-contraction in this phase.

Selection from known records: When a variable r is statically bound by a RECORD operator, and r is the operand of a SELECT operator, then we can eliminate the selection entirely, and substitute the nth field of the record for r. Since the operands of the RECORD must all be atomic—variables or constants—the substitution of one of these operands for every occurrence of r cannot cause the duplication of any operation, so the program size is guaranteed to go down.

It must be noted, however, that this optimization may cause the number of free variables of an expression to go up, making register allocation more difficult or causing spills. Spills will be handled in a much later phase, and we will ignore the effect of register allocation in our claim that program size and speed are always improved by the **select** optimization.

Dead-variable elimination: If a variable is bound by an operator that cannot raise an exception or modify the store, and is never used, then its binding may be removed. For example:

$$\text{FIX}([\ldots,(f,\vec{v},B),\ldots],A) \ \rightarrow \ \text{FIX}([\ldots,\ldots],A) \quad f \text{ not free anywhere}$$

$$\text{RECORD}(\vec{a},v,A) \ \rightarrow \ A \quad v \notin \text{fv}(A)$$

This optimization can be applied to a variable that is the result of a RECORD, SELECT, FIX, or PRIMOP, except for arithmetic operators that can raise exceptions. These are ~, +, -, *, div, fadd, fsub, fmul, fdiv. In principle, operators that modify the store should not be eliminated, but it happens that none of them binds a variable, so this is a nonissue.

There may be cases where an arithmetic operator is known not to raise an exception (e.g., division by a constant other than -1), and in this case the dead variable may be eliminated.

We have chosen to be conservative in reducing the exception-raising operators just so the CPS optimization phase will be completely transparent to the programmer. One of the nice attributes of Standard ML is that it is completely defined, that is, any program accepted by the compiler has a deterministic semantics; we would like to preserve that attribute. (Of course, we may add less-deterministic functions for such things as input/output, but the programmer knows where to expect this nondeterminism.)

Argument flattening: In ML, every function has exactly one argument; where the effect of n arguments is desired, the programmer may pass an n-tuple. The pattern matching of arguments in ML makes it convenient to receive an n-tuple into formal parameters, as in

```
let fun f(a,b,c) = a+b+c
in . . . f(x,y,z) . . .
end
```

In the CPS language, the syntactic sugar of pattern matching is stripped away, and we have:

```
FIX([ (f, [t,k], SELECT(0,VAR t, a,
                SELECT(1,VAR t, b,
                 SELECT(2,VAR t, c,
                  PRIMOP(+,[VAR a, VAR b], [e],
                  PRIMOP(+,[VAR e, VAR c], [g],
                   APP(VAR k,[VAR g])))))))))],
   . . .
        RECORD([(VAR x,OFFp0),(VAR y,OFFp0),(VAR z,OFFp0)], r,
        APP(VAR f,[VAR r, VAR k1]))
   . . . )
```

Records (n-tuples) are constructed on the heap in the implementation, and it is clearly undesirable to heap allocate an argument record for each function call.

Furthermore, the CPS language allows for multiargument functions. Therefore, we would like to "flatten" the structured arguments of functions such as f (this also applies to nested tuples like h((a,b),(c,d)), etc.). In understanding the motivation for this optimization, it may be helpful to realize that all arguments to functions will be passed in machine registers, once the CPS is translated to machine instructions.

To flatten the arguments of a function, we must change the function definition and each of the applications of the function. Therefore, we can do this only for *known* functions; we can't flatten the arguments of escaping functions because we don't know all the call sites.

The "conservative" version of this optimization is as follows: When a known function f uses an argument t only as the operand of SELECT operations, and in all the calls the actual parameters corresponding to t are variables bound by RECORD operators, and the records all have the same number n of fields, then the parameter t can be replaced by n parameters t_i, the SELECTions in f's body can be replaced by the appropriate t_j, and the actual parameters can be replaced by the record fields.

Thus for the example of the known function f(a,b,c) we have:

```
FIX([ (f, [a,b,c,k], PRIMOP(+,[VAR a, VAR b], [e],
                PRIMOP(+,[VAR e, VAR c], [g],
                APP(VAR k,[VAR g]))))],
  . . .
        APP(VAR f,[VAR x, VAR y, VAR z, VAR k1])
  . . .)
```

This version of argument flattening applies only when all the calls to f pass an explicitly created n-tuple. But consider this case:

```
fun f(i,j) = if i=0 then j else f(i-1,j+j)
fun h(t) = f(t)+4
```

One of the calls to f (the recursive one) passes an explicit tuple, but the other does not. This case often comes up when an escaping function of a pair introduced by inverse η-reduction (see Section 6.2) calls the known function of the pair.

We might like to rewrite this program so the recursive call (which is probably executed more often than the nonrecursive call) has flattened arguments. To do this, we need to add explicit select operators on the nonrecursive call, to extract two arguments from the tuple t:

```
fun h(t) = f(#1 t, #2 t) + 4
```

That's not difficult to do, but consider the next example:

```
fun g(i,t) = if i=0 then #1(t) + #2(t) else 5

g(0,(2,8)) + g(1,7)
```

This doesn't type check in Standard ML: If the argument i of g is 0, then the argument t is a pair of integers, but if the i is nonzero, then t is an integer. But even though this is not a legal source program, it illustrates the state of affairs after a few rounds of optimization: The CPS is not a typed language, and the argument i is probably the type tag of a data constructor.

In this case, it is not at all a good idea to flatten the argument t and insert selection operators at the calls to g. In that case, we would get:

```
fun g(i,a,b) = if i=0 then a+b else #1(t) + #2(t) else 5

g(0,2,8) + g(1,#1(7)+#2(7))
```

The construct #1(7), representing the selection of the first field of the integer 7, is not only illegal, but is likely to crash the program at runtime.

So, to make a more "liberal" version of argument flattening, we must be careful. One way to be careful is to have some approximate type information in the CPS language; see Section 18.2. Another way is to avoid flattening arguments—such as t above—that we are not sure about. More precisely:

When a known function f uses an argument t only as the operand of SELECT operations, then let n be the highest field number that is selected from t. If field n is selected from t on *all* paths inside f (from the root to the leaves, which are APP nodes), then the parameter t can be replaced by n parameters t_i, the SELECTions in f's body can be replaced by the appropriate t_j, and in each call to f the corresponding actual parameter a can be replaced by n different SELECTions from a.

Recall that all arguments to functions are passed in machine registers. Since argument flattening increases the number of arguments to functions, we might end up with a function that has more arguments than our machine has registers, a contradiction. Therefore, we will make the number of registers a parameter of the CPS optimization functor; a candidate for argument-flattening will be rejected if it would have too many arguments after flattening. On an N register machine no function will have more than N arguments (but see Section 13.4 for a more precise bound).

Dropping unused arguments: If a known function f has an argument a that is not used in the body of f, then a can be removed, along with the corresponding actual parameters in all the calls to f. This is just a slightly more complicated case of dead-variable elimination.

A more sophisticated version of dead-argument elimination—which we have not implemented—also proves variables "useless" by inductions around loops[80]. For example, the variable i in the following program is "useless":

```
fun f(i,j,x) = if j=0 then x else f(i+1,j-1,x*x)
```

Unfortunately, this is a bad example, because $i + 1$ might overflow! Unless we can prove that $i <$ maxint, the computation of $i+1$ may have some noticeable effect on the program, and i is not truly useless. This limits the useless-variable elimination to those variables to which side-effecting operators (including exception-raising operators) are not applied.

Constant folding of SWITCH: If a SWITCH expression has a constant argument i, then it may be replaced by its ith continuation argument.

Record optimizations: The CPS language allows record fields to be not just variables or constants, but also variables with selection paths attached. This allows, for example, the expression

```
SELECT(7, VAR a, x,
 SELECT(3, VAR x, y,
  RECORD([...,(y, OFFp 0),...], ... )))
```

to be rewritten as

```
 RECORD([...,(a, SELp(7,SELp(3,OFFp 0))),...], ... )
```

Why is this desirable? It does not reduce the number of fetches that are done at runtime; the implementation of SELp is just the same as the implementation of SELECT. However, register usage improves significantly. It is not unusual to have a record with many fields, each of which is calculated by selecting from the same variable (or some small set of variables). If the selections are done before the record is created, every field must be held in registers simultaneously. By using the selection paths inside the records, the value of one field can be fetched and disposed of before the next field is started.

This is particularly important for large records. In fact, some records have more fields than the machine has registers! The translation of Standard ML structures and functors often leads to large records. After the CPS has been through its last transformation, it will be necessary that each CPS variable corresponds to one machine register. If a large RECORD expression needed all of its arguments in registers simultaneously, this would be impossible. Thus we see the need for the path notation in the fields of records. (See also Chapter 11, which describes the *spill* phase of the compiler.)

So, the record-path optimization is: If a variable w is bound by SELECTing field i from variable v, and (w,p) is used as the field of a RECORD (where p is a path), then the record field is rewritten as $(v, \text{SELp}(i, p))$. If there are no other uses of w, of course, the original SELECT will then be removed by dead-variable elimination.

Arithmetic constant folding: When an arithmetic operator is applied to constant arguments, the operation can be removed and the (constant) result of the operation can be substituted for the variable bound by the operation. If the particular constant arguments will lead to a runtime exception (e.g., an overflow), the operation should not be eliminated, of course. The following kinds of constant expressions are folded (we use **boldface** to denote compile-time constants):

- boxed(INT i, t, f) $\rightarrow$ f; the boxity test on an unboxed value yields false ("applies the false continuation").

- boxed(STRING s, t, f) $\rightarrow$ t; all strings are boxed.

- boxed(VAR v, t, f) $\rightarrow$ t, when v is bound by a RECORD operation.

- $1 \times x \rightarrow x$, and $x \times 1 \rightarrow x$.

- $0 \times x \rightarrow 0$, and $x \times 0 \rightarrow 0$.

- $\mathbf{i} \times \mathbf{j} \rightarrow \mathbf{ij}$, provided $\mathbf{ij}$ is representable.

- x div $1 \rightarrow x$.

- $\mathbf{x}$ div $\mathbf{y} \rightarrow (\mathbf{x}/\mathbf{y})$, provided $\mathbf{x}/\mathbf{y}$ is representable.

- $0 + x \rightarrow x$, and $x + 0 \rightarrow x$.

- $\mathbf{x} + \mathbf{y} \rightarrow (\mathbf{x} + \mathbf{y})$ (here the informal notation is a bit inadequate!), provided the result is representable.

- $x - 0 \rightarrow x$.

- $\mathbf{x} - \mathbf{y} \rightarrow (\dot{\mathbf{x}} - \mathbf{y})$ provided the result is representable.

- $\tilde{\mathbf{i}} \rightarrow -\mathbf{i}$.

- slength(STRING s) $\rightarrow |s|$.

- ordof(STRING s, INT i) $\rightarrow s_i$.

Folding of comparison operators: The numeric comparison operators can also be folded. There are two kinds of simplifications possible on an expression that compares a and b, branching to c or d depending on which is greater:

$$\text{PRIMOP}(>, [a, b], [], , [c, d])$$

If both a and b are integer constants, then expression c or d can be substituted for the PRIMOP depending on whether $a > b$. Similarly, if a is the minimum integer or b is the maximum integer, d can be chosen. There may be range information; if, for example, b is the result of taking the length of an array and a is the integer 0, then the comparison must yield false (d can be chosen). One can go to great lengths to maintain range information using dataflow analysis or subtyping, though we do not do much of this.

On the other hand, it could be that nothing useful is known about a and b, but c and d are the same (modulo α-conversion, that is, renaming of bound variables). In this case c (or d) can be substituted for the PRIMOP expression, and the comparsion is unnecessary.

Analysis of operations on the store: In principle, an assignment into the store followed by a fetch from the same location can be analyzed, eliminating the fetch. But it is not clear that this kind of optimization is worthwhile. After all, in a mostly functional programming style encouraged by ML, most of the variables on which such analysis would be fruitful—in a conventional compiler— are likely to be "functional," nonstore variables. Potentially more important, there may in the future be parallel implementations in which sequential store analysis is not guaranteed to be accurate. Thus, we eschew such optimizations.

Exception-handler shortcuts: If a gethdlr operation occurs in the "scope" of a sethdlr, that is,

$$\text{PRIMOP}(\texttt{sethdlr}, [v], [\,], [(\ldots \text{PRIMOP}(\texttt{gethdlr}, [\,], [w], [B])\ldots)])$$

with no intervening sethdlr, then $B\{w \mapsto v\}$ can be substituted for the gethdlr. In fact, this is just a specialization of the fetch-after-store optimization described in the previous paragraph. Why is it "permissible" to make this optimization when we are refraining from optimizing the more general case of fetch and store operations? The answer lies in the distinguished nature of the current-exception-handler location in the semantics of the CPS. We have more control over the exception-handler location than over most locations; in particular, we are willing to guarantee that *each thread* in a multithreaded system will have its own exception-handler location, and will not be able to alter the other threads' handlers.

Another optimization on exception handlers is that if there are two successive sethdlr operations (perhaps with other intervening instructions) that install the same handler, the later one can be eliminated. Also, if a sethdlr is "dead" (there is no gethdlr or exception-raising arithmetic operator before the next sethdlr), it can be removed; although we do not implement this optimization at present.

Boolean idiom simplification: In Standard ML, the result of a comparison (etc.) is a member of *bool*, an ordinary two-constructor datatype. Just as in any programming language where a "Boolean" value is just a piece of data, there is a slight mismatch between the conditional jump provided by the machine and the operator in the programming language. To implement $a > b$, we must (in the CPS language, or on a typical machine) do a conditional branch to store either a 0 or 1 into a register; to add insult to injury, the next thing that's typically done is a conditional branch on the resulting value. Thus, the expression if $a > b$ then E_1 else E_2 translates into:

$$\text{FIX}([[(\texttt{c}, [\texttt{z}], \text{PRIMOP}(\texttt{ineq}, [\texttt{VAR z, INT 0}], [\,], [E_1, E_2]))],$$
$$\text{PRIMOP}(>, [a, b], [\,], [\text{APP}(\texttt{c}, [\texttt{INT1}]), \text{APP}(\texttt{c}, [\texttt{INT0}])]))$$

We would like this to reduce to

$$\text{PRIMOP}(>, [a, b], [\,], [E_1, E_2])$$

This reduction can be done by in-line expansion (β-expansion) of the function c. However, the body of c (the expressions E_1 and E_2) might be quite large, and the "ordinary" β-expander is wary about expanding large functions; consider the result:

$$\text{PRIMOP}(>, [a, b], [\,], [$$
$$\text{PRIMOP}(\texttt{ineq}, [\texttt{INT 1, INT 0}], [\,], [E_1, E_2]),$$
$$\text{PRIMOP}(\texttt{ineq}, [\texttt{INT 0, INT 0}], [\,], [E_1', E_2'])])$$

Now there are two copies of E_1 and E_2. Of course, we know that by further constant folding of the ineq operators, half of these expressions will fall away. But

the β-expander doesn't know that, and we have chosen not to add this kind of
heuristic to the expansion phase. Instead, we will recognize this idiom specially,
and treat it as a kind of β-*contraction* of the function c.

6.2   Eta reduction and uncurrying

In lambda calculus the transformation $\lambda x.M(x) \rightarrow M$ can be used, providing
x is not free in M. This is called η-reduction. In continuation-passing style, the
expression M must be quite simple if it is applied to arguments, so we have the
following transformation:

$$\mathtt{FIX}([\ldots, (f, [x_1, x_2, \ldots], \mathtt{APP}(g, [x_1, x_2, \ldots])), \ldots], B) \rightarrow$$
$$\mathtt{FIX}([\ldots, \ldots], B\{f \mapsto g\})$$

provided that $f \notin \{x_1, x_2, \ldots\}$. This just means that we can use g everywhere that
f was referred to previously, and we can drop the definition of f entirely.

As described in Section 2.2, some functions *escape*—their call sites cannot
be predicted at compile time. On the other hand, some functions are *known*—
all their call sites are known at compile time. Known functions can be called
more efficiently, since specialized parameter-passing mechanisms can be devised
for them. But what about a function that both escapes and has some known
call sites? It is not possible to specialize the parameter-passing mechanism of an
escaping function, yet we would like the known sites to be able to call the function
efficiently. The solution is to split an escaping function f into two functions f and
f'. The function f will simply call f', and f' will be a known function. This is just
an inverse η-reduction, and an early phase of the CPS optimizer will "eta split"
every function in this way.

$$\mathtt{FIX}([\ldots, (f, [x_1, x_2, \ldots], M), \ldots], B) \rightarrow$$
$$\mathtt{FIX}([\ldots, (f, [x_1', x_2', \ldots], \mathtt{APP}(f', [x_1', x_2', \ldots])), (f', [x_1, x_2, \ldots], M), \ldots], B)$$

Later, β-reductions will ensure that all of the known call sites actually call f'.

It may seem pointless to perform both η-reducation *and* inverse η-reduction.
However, there may be a cascade of several η-reductions that repeatedly rename
f_1 to f_2, f_2 to f_3, and so on, followed by just one inverse η-reduction.

It might seem that typical programmers don't often write functions— susceptible to η-reduction—that just call other functions with the same arguments. However, the match compiler and the CPS converter are so clumsy that they introduce
many opportunities for reductions.

Another useful transformation is *uncurrying*. A function $f = \lambda x.\lambda y.B$ is said
to be *curried* because it accumulates its arguments x and y one at a time; on the
other hand, $g = \lambda(x, y).B$ is *uncurried*.

Uncurried known functions that pass tuples of arguments are optimized by the
argument-flattening rule (page 70) of the constant-folding phase of the optimizer.
It is useful to identify curried functions and uncurry them in the η-phase so that
argument expansion can be applied to them later. The transformation is:

$$\text{FIX}([\ldots, (f, [x_1, x_2, \ldots, c], \text{FIX}([(g, [b, k], A)], \text{APP}(\text{VAR } c, [\text{VAR } g]))), \ldots], B)$$
$$\to \text{FIX}([\ldots,$$
$$(f, [x_1', x_2', \ldots, c'],$$
$$\text{FIX}([(g', [b', k'], \text{APP}(\text{VAR } f', [\text{VAR } x_1', \text{VAR } x_2', \ldots,$$
$$\text{VAR } c', \text{VAR } g', \text{VAR } b', \text{VAR } k']))],$$
$$\text{APP}(\text{VAR } c', [\text{VAR } g']))),$$
$$(f', [x_1, x_2, \ldots, c, g, b, k], A),$$
$$\ldots],$$
$$B)$$

Let us examine this transformation in the context of an ordinary ML function that gets compiled into continuation-passing style:

```
fun f(x) = let fun g(b) = x+b in g end
```

or, more concisely, `fun f x b = x+b`.

Now, let us imagine that there are several calls of the form `f i j` in the program. We would like to optimize those calls so they don't have to build a new function g on the application $f(i)$. One good way to simplify `f i j` is just to insert $i + j$ in place of it—this is just β-reduction! The only reason we might conceivably want to avoid β-reduction is if there are several calls to f, and if the body of g is large; because in this case we would not want to duplicate the body several times.

Here, the body of g is quite small: It is the expression $x + b$. For pedagogical purposes, we will imagine that this $x + b$ is quite a large expression, so β-reduction is not desirable.

The continuation-passing-style representation of f (in ML notation) is

```
fun f(x,c) = let fun g(b,k) = k(x+b) in c(g) end
```

The uncurrying transformation turns this into

```
fun f(x',c') = let fun g'(b',k') = f'(x',c',g',b',k')
                 in c'(g')
              end
and f'(x,c,g,b,k) = k(x+b)
```

Later, other transformations will remove the useless arguments to g', so what remains is

```
fun f(x',c') = let fun g'(b',k') = f'(x',b',k')
                 in c'(g')
              end
and f'(x,b,k) = k(x+b)
```

Consider the size of the body of f. Now it is quite small: It is just the function definition of g', which is of constant size regardless of the size of the original body of g. So this expression can get β-reduced wherever f is applied to an argument.

(See Chapter 7 for a fuller discussion of the criteria for in-line expansion of function calls.)

The expression f i j, in continuation-passing style, is

```
let fun c1(g1) = g1(j,c0) in f(i,c1) end
```

After β-reduction, it becomes:

```
let fun c1(g1) = g1(j,c0)
 in let fun g'(b',k')=f'(i,b',k') in c1(g') end
end
```

Now the local function c_1 is called exactly once and doesn't escape, so it can be β-reduced:

```
let fun g'(b',k')=f'(i,b',k') in g'(j,c0) end
```

Similarly, g' is called exactly once and doesn't escape, so it will be β-reduced:

```
f'(i,j,c0)
```

Voila! The function call has been uncurried.

This seems like a complicated set of transformations. It is important to realize that only the first transformation (described in the more formal notation above) is necessary to define "uncurrying." The other transformations—defined more formally in Section 6.1— are quite general purpose, and just "clean up" the optimization.

6.3   Cascading optimizations

Very often the result of doing one constant fold or β-contraction is an expression in which another constant fold is newly possible. It might be desirable to accomplish all of the transformations in one pass over the program, but this may not be possible. Certainly, in the general case of the λ-calculus, a program cannot be reduced to normal form in one pass. What we have is not the general case, since the only β-redexes we reduce are the functions applied just once.

Let us examine the possibility of a simple one-pass, top-down or bottom-up method. Consider the expression

$$\text{PRIMOP}(+, \; [\text{INT } 1, \; \text{INT } 2], \; [x], [\text{PRIMOP}(+, \; [\text{VAR } x, \; \text{INT } 5], \; [y], [\, B \,])])$$

which sums the integers 1, 2, and 5. We assume that x is not free in B.

Clearly a simple bottom-up method cannot do much with the inner expression

$$\text{PRIMOP}(+, \; [\text{VAR } x, \; \text{INT } 5], \; [y], [\, B \,])$$

since nothing is known about x. We will have better success with a top-down rewrite that considers the outer expression

$$\text{PRIMOP}(+, \; [\text{INT } 1, \; \text{INT } 2], \; [x], \; [C])$$

and yields $C\{x \mapsto 3\}$, and then

$$\text{PRIMOP}(+, \; [\text{INT 3, INT 5}], \; [y], [\; B \;])$$

which yields $B\{x \mapsto 3, y \mapsto 8\}$.

So the simple-minded top-down approach works better than the simple-minded bottom-up approach: In this way, continuation-passing style is unlike ordinary expression trees, in which the bottom-up approach is more natural. Of course, the CPS is indeed the result of traversing the original expression tree in a bottom-up fashion! The top-down traversal of the CPS corresponds closely to the way machine code is generated for it, and to the way CPS is "meant" to be evaluated.

On the other hand, consider dead-variable analysis. Assume that x and y are not free in B within the expression

$$\text{SELECT}(2, \text{VAR } a, \; x, \; \text{SELECT}(4, \text{VAR } x, \; y, \; B))$$

Then the inner SELECT can be removed, since y is dead. Now, x is dead and the outer SELECT can be removed, leaving just the expression B. But this is bottom-up! And a top-down approach could not work easily; x cannot be removed before y. Of course, this is not surprising; in conventional dataflow optimizers[1], dead-variable analysis is done "backwards" along control-flow edges.

Clearly, a completely top-down pass can do all the arithmetic constant folding, and a completely bottom-up pass can cascade the dead-variable elimination. Now, consider the expression

$$\text{SELECT}(2, \text{VAR } r, \; a,$$
$$\text{PRIMOP}(-, \; [\text{INT 3}, \text{INT 3}], \; [z], \; [$$
$$\text{PRIMOP}(*, \; [\text{VAR } z, \text{VAR } a], \; [x], \; [\; B \;])])))$$

The variable a is live until a constant folding is done that yields $z = 0$ and therefore $x = 0$. Assuming a is not free in B, then a is now dead and the SELECT can be removed. This demonstrates that dead-variable elimination is dependent on constant folding. It is also possible to make examples using only RECORDs and SELECTs, if the multiplication-by-zero optimization seems too contrived.

On the other hand, consider

$$\text{FIX}([(f, \; [x, c], \; \text{PRIMOP}(+, [\text{VAR } x, \; \text{VAR } x], [y], \; [\text{APP}(\text{VAR } c, \; [\text{VAR } y])])))],$$
$$\text{RECORD}([(\text{VAR } f, \; \text{OFFp } 0)], \; r,$$
$$\text{APP}(\text{VAR } f, \; [\text{INT 4}])))$$

In this expression, the function f cannot be β-contracted because it is used in more than one place. But after dead-variable analysis removes the record r, then f can be contracted and the constant folding of $x + x$ can take place. This demonstrates that constant folding is dependent on dead-variable analysis.

The interdependence of these kinds of optimizations, some of which cascade naturally from the bottom up and others that cascade top down, makes an algorithm that operates in a constant number of passes unlikely. We have chosen a multipass approach that, in each pass, makes as many transformations as is convenient. We keep repeating the contraction passes until no more contractions are obtained. (In fact, to avoid pursuing diminishing returns, we usually adjust the compiler to stop after any pass that finds fewer than 15 contractions.)

The contractions performed in the β-contraction and constant-folding pass do not lead to η-redexes, so it is unnecessary to include η-reduction in the cycle of repetitive contractions; one pass of η-reduction suffices before commencing β-contraction. However, β-contractions can lead to redexes of the "uncurry" optimization. We have found that exactly two passes of β-contraction are necessary before the η phase (which also performs uncurrying), in order to uncover all the uncurry redexes (see figure 15.7).

6.4   Implementation

Each pass of the contraction phase is preceded by a data-gathering pass that collects information about the definition and use of each variable. The usage information of interest are the following quantities: *used*, the number of times a variable is referred to (not including its definition); and *escapes*, the number of times a variable is passed as an argument or stored in a record (etc.).

Useful facts about the definition of each variable are stored, but the kinds of facts depend on the kind of definition:

- For functions, we record the formal parameters (a variable list) and the body (a continuation expression). We also record the "arity" of each call; that is, whether any of the actual parameters are in fact RECORDs, and the size of those records. We also note any conditions that prevent the β-contraction of the function; these will be discussed below.

- For records, we remember the components (fields) of the record; this is a list of *value* × *accesspath* pairs.

- For variables bound by SELECTs, we record the variable denoting the record selected from, and the integer offset.

- For variables bound as formal parameters of functions, we record the highest field number guaranted to be selected (if any) on all paths. This is for the "liberal" function-argument flattening, as discussed in Section 6.1.

- For variables bound by integer arithmetic primops, we record upper and lower bounds for the possible range of values. This helps to fold some comparisons, though we do a very primitive job at present.

- For other variables (e.g., variables bound by other primops, free variables of the entire expression, etc.) we record nothing.

There are several conditions that can prevent a function application from being contracted in this phase. The simplest is that a function used in more than one place cannot be contracted because that would require copying the body; such copying is reserved for the β-expansion optimizer.

Another situation is related to the inverse-η optimization described in Section 6.2. When the inverse η-reduction has just been performed, splitting a function $f(x, y) = B$ into two functions $f(x', y') = f'(x', y')$ and $f'(x, y) = B$, the function f' is used in exactly one place. But we don't want a β-contraction to occur here, as that will just undo the inverse-η transformation before anything useful has come of it. (The useful consequences of the inverse-η are that the applications of f to arguments will be replaced by applications of f'.) To prevent this harmful β-contraction, whenever there is an escaping function f whose body is just the application of another function f', we mark f' as irreducible. (Of course, we can perform contractions within the body of f'; irreducible just means that we won't reduce applications of f'.)

Similarly, the *uncurrying* optimization leads to a situation containing a function whose reduction would defeat the purpose of the optimization. To avoid this, in any situation such as

$$\text{FIX}(f, [a, c], \text{FIX}([(h, [b, k], B)], \text{APP}(\text{VAR } c, [\text{VAR } h])))$$

where the body B is just a chain of selections followed by the application of a known function g, we mark g as irreducible.

It is a simple matter to collect all of this information by a single pass over the program. Then the actual transformation pass is just a tree traversal that goes top down and then bottom up; we illustrate with an example—the (simplified) fragment of the **reduce** function that optimizes the **SELECT** operator:

```
reduce(SELECT(i,v,w,e)) =
if not(used w) then (click(); reduce e)
else case (get(rename v))
        of {info=RECinfo vl,...} =>
                (click();
                 newname(w,rename(nth(vl,i)));
                 reduce e)
        | _ => SELECT(i, rename v, w, reduce e)
```

This is not quite right, because it pretends that record fields are simple values (without accesspaths), but it illustrates the important points. The **newname** function binds a variable to a value; any occurrence of that variable is to be replaced by the value. (In this case, w is to be replaced by the ith field of the record.) The calls to **rename** are just looking up variables to see if they have been bound to values (constants or other variables) by previous calls to **newname**. The **click** function records the fact that an optimizing transformation has been found; this will help decide whether another pass of the constant folder is worthwhile.

Two different optimizations are applied here. The first one (if not (used w)) tests whether the variable w is dead, in which case the **SELECT** can be dropped entirely and replaced by e. The second tests whether v is bound directly by a

RECORD operator, in which case the ith value used in making the record can be used directly. If neither optimization applies, then the SELECT is preserved intact; but in any case, the subexpression e must be reduced.

So there is a top-down component of the algorithm that renames variables, and a bottom-up component that rebuilds the transformed expression tree.

The η-phase (which performs η-reduction, inverse η-reduction, and uncurrying) is separate from the constant-folding phase (which performs β-contractions, dead-variable elimination, and so on). This is because the different kinds of variable-renaming that take place in the two different phases interact in a complicated way that was a source of many bugs when they were combined into one pass. For the inverse-η phase, it is not necessary to gather information in a pre-pass, since the η-redexes are self-contained and independent of context. In this phase, as in the constant-folding phase, a rename function—implemented using a hash table—is used to perform variable substitutions.

CHAPTER SEVEN

BETA EXPANSION

In-line expansion of functions—substitution of function bodies for function calls, otherwise known as β-reduction—is a useful but dangerous optimization. Because each expansion makes a copy of the function body, the size of the program can grow with each transformation. Although each in-line expansion makes the program faster—in principle—by reducing the number of function calls executed, a larger program in a finite-size memory may actually run slower than a smaller program that does more operations, because it may incur more page faults or cache misses. Furthermore, in-line expansion of recursive programs can increase the program size infinitely—in effect, "executing" the program at compile time; or worse, "optimizing" parts of the program that might never be executed (because of control-flow decisions dependent on runtime input).

On the other hand, in-line expansion is most useful indeed. Many constant-folding optimizations are expressed in terms of static binding: "if a variable r, bound by a RECORD operator, is the operand of a SELECT," and so on. It is often the case that a variable r_1 is bound in one function, passed as an argument to a formal parameter r_2, where it is used in an interesting way. There must be some way for the compiler to connect r_1 with r_2. Ordinary dataflow analysis is usually inadequate, because the formal parameter r_2 will be associated with many different actual parameters from the several calls to the function. The interesting information about r_1 is not likely to be valid for all the other variables bound to r_2 by function calls. What is necessary is a *specialization* of the function body for this call site, so r_2 is equivalent to r_1. The simplest way to achieve this is by in-line expansion, or β-reduction of the CPS.

To see the utility of β-reduction, consider an example. A general-purpose list-mapping utility, count, takes a predicate p and a list l as (curried) arguments, and counts the number of elements of l that satisfy p. We wish to count the number of zeros in a list of integers:

```
fun count p = let fun f (a::r) = if p a then 1+f(r) else f r
                    |  f nil = 0
              in f
              end
fun curry f x y = f(x,y)
val countzeros = count (curry (fn (w,z)=> w=z) 0)
```

This program is explained in detail in Section A.4.

In continuation-passing style, it looks roughly like this:

```
fun count(p,c) =
   let fun f(l,k) =
           case l
            of (a::r) =>
                 let fun j b = if b=true
                               then let fun h n = k(1+n)
                                    in f(r,h)
                                    end
                               else f(r,k)
                 in p(a,j)
                 end
             | nil => k(0)
   in c(f)
   end

fun curry (f,d) =
   let fun e(x,g) =
           let fun m(y,q) =
                   let val s = (x,y)
                   in f(s,q)
                   end
           in g(m)
           end
     in d(e)
   end

let fun eq(w,z) = if ieql(#1 w, #2 w)
                  then z(true)
                  else z(false)
 in curry(eq, fn u => u(0, fn v => count(v, c0)))
end
```

This may look verbose; but, in fact, the direct output of the CPS conversion algorithm is even more verbose. All the optimizations short of β-expansion have already been done, reducing the expression to its present state (we are assuming that count and curry are referred to from other places besides the one shown here, or else a β-contraction could have been done).

Note that the = function must return a Boolean result as the argument of its continuation; this Boolean is then tested inside the count function. This is exactly the kind of idiom recognized and optimized by the constant folder, if only the entire idiom were inside the same function. As it is, since there may be other calls to count, the optimizer can't be sure that p always refers to =.

Now let us do a β-expansion of the application of curry:

```
fun count(p,c) = let  . . .  end
fun curry (f,d) = let  . . .  end

let fun eq(w,z) = if ieql(#1 w, #2 w) then z(true)
                                      else z(false)
    fun e(x,g) = let fun m(y,q) = let val s = (x,y)
                                  in eq(s,q)
                                  end
                 in g(m)
                 end
 in (fn u => u(0, fn v => count(v, c0))) (e)
end
```

Now there are several β-contractions (β-reductions of functions called only once, which are guaranteed not to expand the program size) that can be performed. Then the SELECT operators (#1 and #2) can be constant-folded inside m. Here is the result:

```
fun count(p,c) = let  . . .  end
fun curry (f,d) = let  . . .  end

let fun m(y,q) = if ieql(0,y) then q(true) else q(false)
 in count(m, c0)
end
```

At this point we are stuck again, unless we perform a β-expansion of the call to count:

```
let fun m(y,q) = if ieql(0,y) then q(true) else q(false)
 in let fun f(l,k) =
          case l
          of (a::r) => let fun j b =
                               if b=true
                               then let fun h n = k(1+n)
                                    in f(r,h)
                                    end
                               else f(r,k)
                       in m(a,j)
                       end
           | nil => k(0)
    in c0(f)
    end
end
```

Now there are several contractions and constant folds that can be performed:

```
let fun f(l,k) =
            case l
            of (a::r) => if ieql(0, a)
                            then let fun h n = k(1+n)
                                   in f(r,h)
                                 end
                            else f(r,k)
             | nil => k(0)
  in c0(f)
end
```

The resulting program is much more efficient than the original one. Most of the memory traffic has disappeared; continuation closures need not be constructed, 2-tuple arguments need not be boxed, Booleans need not be represented in registers, and so on. All of these are optimizations across procedure boundaries that become intraprocedural after the β-expansion.

On the other hand, consider the recursive call to f in the following program:

```
fun f(i,s,k) =
      if i < Array.length(a)
        then f(i+1, s + (a sub i), k)
        else k(s)
```

An in-line expansion of this function call is just "loop unrolling":

```
fun f(i,s,k) =
      if i < Array.length(a)
        then let val i' = i+1
                 val s' = s + (a sub i)
              in if i' < Array.length(a)
                    then f(i'+1, s' + (a sub i'), k)
                    else s'
             end
        else k(s)
```

Now, when $i + 1 < \text{length}(a)$, the function f will examine the next element without jumping back to the "top" of the loop. There is not much to be gained by this transformation: The jump instruction itself is not extremely costly; perhaps (on an exposed-pipeline machine) the calculation of a_i and $s + a_i$ can be executed in parallel with testing $i' < \text{length}(a)$. On the other hand, there are many cases where a little bit of loop unrolling gives more substantial benefits than in this example. What we need is a general heuristic for deciding about expansion.

7.1 When to do in-line expansion

It is unwise to use every possible opportunity for in-line expansion, since this can lead to nontermination of the compiler. For example, expanding the call to f in the program above leads to a new call to f, which can then be expanded, ad infinitum. We need an objective criterion for deciding which expansions to do; actually performing the expansion itself is the easy part, requiring just some variable substitution and renaming.

Unfortunately, no computable criterion will lead to optimal results. We can define an optimal sequence of β-reductions as the one that leads to the smallest β-equivalent program, or the one that leads to the fastest β-equivalent program under a certain size. But optimizing programs subject to these criteria is easily seen to be equivalent to the halting problem. Consider

$$(\lambda x.0)(B)$$

where B is a possibly terminating calculation in a strict lambda calculus. The smallest β-equivalent program is either 0 or $(\lambda x.xx)(\lambda x.xx)$, depending on whether B halts, and to determine the answer requires solving the halting problem for B.

Our approach—which must be taken by any "optimizing" compiler— is to find a good, but suboptimal, program in a reasonable length of time. To this end, we have some heuristics that are all embellishments of a simple rule.

Simple rule: If the body of a function f is smaller than the overhead required for a function call, then f may be in-line expanded with no danger of increasing the program size.

This rule is obviously reasonable: If each transformation makes the program smaller, then no sequence of transformations can expand the size of the program unduly. And this rule, suitably modified, will prove quite useful. But it is interesting to note that it is almost vacuous, as written. In an "ordinary" compiler, a procedure call has a lot of overhead: storing the arguments into the stack frame, saving registers, generating a return address, jumping to the procedure; inside the called procedure, fetching the arguments, storing the result, fetching the return address, jumping to the return point. But in the CPS language, the procedure call itself is nothing more than a jump with arguments; all notions of return address are encoded into the continuation, which is just one of the arguments. And the arguments themselves are passed in registers; good register targeting by the final code generator can ensure that the arguments are already in the right registers by the time of the call. So the "overhead" of a procedure call is just a *jump* instruction. Since the body of f must have an APP node in it (i.e., a *jump* instruction), there is no function f satisfying the premise of the rule.

However, the simple rule expresses the intuition behind the heuristics we use, so the reader is asked to suspend disbelief and imagine that a function call has some nontrivial expense.

Now, after a function f is expanded, its formal parameters have been replaced by actual parameters, some of which may be constants. The constant folder will go to work on these variables, contracting the body of f. For example,

$$\text{FIX}([(f, [x, y], \text{PRIMOP}(>, [x, \text{INT } 0], [], [B, C]))], \ldots$$
$$\ldots \text{ APP}(\text{VAR } f, [\text{INT } 5, \text{VAR } c]) \ldots)$$

After f is β-reduced, INT 5 will be substituted for x, leading to a contraction of the comparison that shrinks the body of f by perhaps more than half. Here's another example:

$$\text{FIX}([(h, [x, y], \text{SELECT}(0, x, w, B))], \ldots$$
$$\ldots \text{ RECORD}([(\text{VAR } a, \text{ OFFp0}), \ldots], r,$$
$$\text{APP}(\text{VAR } h, [\text{VAR } r, \text{VAR } c])) \ldots)$$

In this case, after r is substituted for x, then the SELECT can be folded, with a substituted for w in B. Better yet, if this is the only remaining use of r, then the RECORD itself will disappear.

We can modify the simple rule to take into account the shrinkage of the in-line-expanded function:

Unattainable rule: If the body of f, after expansion, will shrink by further optimizations to be smaller than the overhead required for a function call, then f may be in-line expanded.

This is unattainable, of course, because we cannot predict (using a computable function) whether future reductions will sufficiently shrink f. But we can estimate, and this is our approach.

It is useful to introduce the notion of a *nontrivial definition* and a *nontrivial use*. A binding (definition) of a variable is *nontrivial* if there is some constant-folding optimization that can contract variables similarly bound. Informally, a nontrivial definition is one that tells us something concrete about the structure of the variable; so a formal parameter of a function tells us nothing, and is *trivial*, but a variable bound as the result of a RECORD operation tells us the sources of the components of that record, so is *nontrivial*.

Trivial definitions include: formal parameters of functions; variables bound by SELECT and OFFSET operators; variables bound as the result of the primops !, subscript, ordof, alength, slength, gethdlr, *, +, -, div, ~, fadd, fsub, fdiv, and fmul.

Nontrivial definitions include: the names of functions bound by FIX operators, and variables bound by RECORD operators.

One might wish to consider variables bound by makeref to be nontrivial, if one were optimizing operations on the store. Also, some of the arithmetic operations might be considered to bind nontrivial results, to the extent that the properties of the results can be analyzed at compile time.

A *nontrivial use* of a variable x is one which might lead to constant folding if x has a nontrivial definition. Variables used nontrivally are: arguments of the SELECT, OFFSET, and SWITCH operators; the function applied by an APP; arguments of the arithmetic primops *, +, ~, -, div, fadd, fsub, fdiv, fmul; arguments of the primops alength, slength, boxed; and arguments of the integer and real comparison primops.

Trivial uses are those that just store into data structures or pass as parameters: arguments of RECORD, actual parameters of APP, the argument of makeref or :=, and so on.

A *value* in the CPS language is either a variable or a constant. We define a *value* to be nontrivial if it is a constant or a nontrivial variable.

We can use these concepts to estimate the effect of β-reducing a call to a function f. If there are actual parameters of the call that are nontrivial; and the corresponding formal parameters have nontrivial uses within f, then there is likely to be some constant folding within the expanded body of f.

The amount of constant folding likely depends on the nature of the nontrivial definitions and uses. For example, if the definition is an integer constant, and the use is a comparison against another constant, then a large chunk of code (one branch of the comparison) will drop away. On the other hand, if the use is a comparison against another variable, then no shrinkage will occur—though the function body will be "more ripe" for future contraction. If the definition is by a RECORD operator, and the use is a SELECT, then one operation can quite predictably be removed; but perhaps that will have been the last use of the record, which can now be removed by dead-variable elimination, or perhaps the selected value can participate in further constant folding.

Thus, it's complicated to predict *exactly how much* shrinkage we can expect from the matching of nontrivial definitions to nontrivial uses. But by computability theory, we knew in advance that accurate predictions are impossible. We can simply improve the heuristics.

7.2   Estimating the savings

Our more refined heuristic uses the notion of the *savings* S that might be obtained from a particular match of nontrivial argument a to nontrivial formal parameter p. S is measured in units of "operations," where we count a SELECT or an add as one operation, the creation of a record of size n as $n+2$ operations, and so on. Operations are meant to correspond roughly to RISC-machine instructions.

We can measure the size of a function body in operations as follows:

$\mathcal{O}(\text{RECORD}(\vec{v}, w, B)) = |\vec{v}| + 2 + \mathcal{O}(B)$, because each of the fields of the record must be stored, and there are a couple of instructions of overhead in record creation.

$\mathcal{O}(\text{SELECT}(v, w, B)) = 1 + \mathcal{O}(B)$

$\mathcal{O}(\text{OFFSET}(v, w, B)) = 1 + \mathcal{O}(B)$

$\mathcal{O}(\text{APP}(f, \vec{a})) = 1 + |\vec{a}|$, because the arguments must be marshaled into the right registers before the call. In fact, the arguments are likely to be in the right registers already; but on the other hand, the closure-introduction phase may add more arguments to hold free variables of the function. So it's not easy to predict the cost of a function application.

$\mathcal{O}(\text{FIX}([(f_1, v_1, B_1), (f_2, v_2, B_2), \ldots], E)) = \sum(\mathcal{O}(B_i) + 1) + \mathcal{O}(E)$. The cost of entering a function is independent of the number of arguments it has, since arguments are passed in registers; but each function is likely to appear in a closure (if it is not a *known* function), requiring an operation for closure building. In general, we will not try to take account of the cost incurred for representing free variables in closures.

$\mathcal{O}(\text{SWITCH}(v, [B_1, B_2, \ldots])) = 4 + \sum(\mathcal{O}(B_i) + 1)$. A few instructions are required to set up the indexed jump; the jump table contains one address per case.

$\mathcal{O}(\text{PRIMOP}(p, \vec{v}, \vec{w}, [c_1, c_2, \ldots])) = |\vec{v}| + |\vec{w}| + \sum \mathcal{O}(c_i)$; a crude estimate of the cost of a primop is to add up the number of arguments and results. It would seem that an integer add would not require three instructions; but the implementation is likely to have to strip tags from arguments and/or add tags to results. In any case, this is an approximation.

Given this notion of size, we can estimate the savings $\mathcal{S}$ of a particular match of an actual parameter a with a formal parameter p when expanding a function f:

- If a is a function that escapes just once (at the current call, of course), and p does not escape (it is just applied to arguments, if anything), then six operations are saved. This is because an expansion of f will cause a to escape no longer. Escaping functions (after the inverse η-reductions) are just calls to corresponding known functions; when the last call to a is replaced by a call to the known function (via another in-line expansion), then the definition of a can disappear. The size of a simple function such as a that just calls another function is about six operations.

- If a is a record and p is used in n different SELECT operations, then n operations are saved.

- If a is a record that escapes just once (at the current call), and p does not escape, then the saving is the size (number of fields) of a plus two; because after expansion, SELECT optimizations will cause a to become dead, and the record creation won't be necessary. (A record "escapes" if any operation other than SELECT is applied to it, e.g., if it's passed as an argument to a function, put in another record, etc.)

- If a is an integer constant, and p is the argument of a SWITCH (with n possible continuations c_i) or comparison against a constant (with $n = 2$ continuations), then the saving is $k + ((n-1)/n)(\sum \mathcal{O}(c_i))$; that is, all but one of the continuations will drop away and so will the cost of doing the indexed jump ($k = 4$) or comparison ($k = 2$).

- If a is a numeric constant, and p is a two-argument primop with one argument constant, or p is a one-argument primop, then the saving is the size of the primop (number of arguments plus number of results).

- If a is a numeric constant, and p is a two-argument primop with the other argument nonconstant, then the saving is the size of the primop discounted

by a factor of 0.25. The factor is somewhat arbitrary, and expresses the like-
lihood that the other argument will eventually become constant and enable
future folding. Similar discounting (of a much bigger potential savings) is
done for comparisons against nonconstant arguments.

If more than one of these savings applies to an actual–formal pair, the savings
are cumulative.

There is another opportunity for savings: if a function f is called in just one
place, then the definition of f can be eliminated after the call is expanded. Of
course, such functions are expanded by our "constant-folding" phase, not by the
β-expansion phase. But what about a function called in just two or three places?
If that function gets expanded in all the places it is called, then the definition will
go away. So, in estimating the savings for expanding a particular function, we
should take into account the probability that all the calls will be expanded. The
fewer calls there are to a function f, the more willing we should be to do in-line
expansion.

Suppose we are considering the expansion of $f(\vec{a})$. Let b be the size of the
body of f, let $\mathcal{S}$ be the estimated savings for this call to f (i.e., the predicted
shrinkage of the body using the criterion above), and let k be the cost of the APP
node that we are considering expanding. Then the program as a whole will grow
by $b - \mathcal{S} - k$ if this node is expanded. But if we consider that there are only m calls
to the function and that the body will go away if we expand them all, then we
can pretend that $1/m$ of the body will disappear for each call, so the cost becomes
$b - \mathcal{S} - k - b/m$.

Our estimate of the savings is mostly conservative; we are counting savings that
will predictably happen right away. But the result of doing one β-expansion might
be a cascade of further optimizations that is difficult to predict. So we can err on
the optimistic side by adding a "fudge factor": We will perform a β-expansion even
if it appears to have a positive net cost, or, in particular, if $b - \mathcal{S} - k - b/m < C$
for some constant C. We can then fine-tune C experimentally to see what value
leads to best results.

The savings estimate is not invariant under β-contraction and constant folding,
and the estimate is quite speculative. For this reason, we perform as much β-
contraction and constant folding as possible *before* trying any β-expansion. There
may be several passes of the constant folder—until few or no more constant fold-
ings can be found—and then a pass of hoisting (see Chapter 8), a pass of common-
subexpression elimination (see Chapter 9), and a pass of expansion. This will
lead to more redexes for the constant folder; we will perform several more passes
of constant folding until quiescence is reached, and then another pass of the expander, and so on. We call each sequence—of several passes of contraction (until
quiescence) followed by a pass of expansion—a "round" of optimization.

7.3   Runaway expansion

With luck, after several rounds of optimization, the β-expansion phase will find
no more optimizations to do. The heuristics that estimate future contraction
attempt to prevent, for the most part, any runaway expansion. However, since
the estimates of constant folding within an expanded function are not completely
accurate, there are programs for which infinite expansion will result. For example,
a recursive function f might, according to the estimate, be worth expanding; but
then in each expanded version there is another call worth expanding.

It is essential that a compiler must terminate on all inputs: on legal inputs
with a correctly translated program and on illegal inputs with an appropriate error
message. Since the front end of our compiler detects all errors before conversion
into continuation-passing style, we expect the CPS optimizer to terminate in every
case with a continuation expression equivalent to the input. We don't require that
the output expression be optimal in any sense, or even that it be more efficient
than the input (though these qualities are to be hoped for as much as possible).

Therefore, we adjust the heuristics in two ways to guarantee termination. First,
we make the expander very reluctant to β-expand any function application within
the body of another expansion. That is, if we replace $\text{APP}(f, \vec{a})$ by the body B of
f (with appropriate substitutions), we should be more reluctant to expand other
applications within the new copy of B.

We can formalize this as follows: Let n be the nesting level of β-expansion,
with all APP nodes in the program at the beginning of the expand phase having
$n = 0$, the APP nodes in the expressions substituted for depth-zero nodes having
$n = 1$, and so on. We introduce a constant D and introduce it into the formula
for evaluating the "goodness" of a β-expansion:

$$b - S - k - b/m \; < \; C - nD$$

Thus, applications at depth zero are evaluated by the original formula, but at high
depth an expansion must look astonishingly good to satisfy the criterion.

There are two justifications for this "fudge factor." The first is that it will work:
At sufficiently high depth n_h it will become impossible to satisfy the criterion, and
the number of possible redexes at depth less than n_h is bounded. (Note that n_h
is not constant but depends on the input program.) The second justification is
that after one expansion, it is really worth doing some contractions to improve the
accuracy of the estimation function.

The parameter D guarantees that each round of β-expansion will terminate.
But it could be that each round of β-expansion finds something to do, which leads
to another round of optimization, ad infinitum. To solve this problem we introduce
another fudge factor E; let r be the number of rounds so far (with the first round
having $r = 0$); then the new criterion is

$$b - S - k - b/m \; < \; C - nD - rE$$

After enough rounds, r will become sufficiently high that the criterion will be
difficult (and after more rounds, impossible) to satisfy.

CHAPTER EIGHT

HOISTING

Often it is useful to narrow or broaden the scope of a variable in the continuation-passing-style representation. Narrowing the scope of a variable means moving its definition "down" in the CPS expression, nesting it deeper within the scopes of variables bound by other operators. Broadening the scope of a variable means moving the operator that defines it "up" in the CPS expression, or "hoisting" it. We will call all of these scope-changing transformations "hoisting."

These transformations are useful because they can reduce the dynamic frequency of execution of an operation. For example, if an operation is within a loop (or a function executed many times), hoisting it up can move it outside the loop (or the function) so it is executed only once. Or, if an operation produces a value that's used only inside one branch of a conditional, hoisting it down inside that branch will avoid executing the operation when the other branch is taken.

8.1 Merging FIX definitions

There is another use for hoisting transformations. Recall that closures—the data structures that implement functions with their free variables—are represented with the closed function in the first slot of a record and the free variables in the other slots. We can play an interesting trick with this representation if two functions have the same free variables. Consider the functions f and g in this example:

```
fun h(a,b) = let fun f(x,y) = x*a+y*b
                 fun g(i) = i+a+b
             in . . .
             end
```

The "ordinary" representation of f and g would be as two separate closures:

```
fun h(a,b) = let fun f'((f'',a,b),x,y) = x*a+y*b
                 val f = (f',a,b)
                 fun g'((f'',a,b),i) = i+a+b
                 val g = (g',a,b)
             in . . .
             end
```

93

Since the functions f and g have a compatible set of free variables, they can share
a closure, as follows:

```
fun h(a,b) = let fun f'((f'',g'',a,b),x,y) = x*a+y*b
                 fun g'((g'',a,b),i) = i+a+b
                 val f = (f',g',a,b)
                 val g = f+1
             in . . .
           end
```

This abuse of notation is meant to indicate that the value g is derived by offsetting
the pointer f by one word. The variables f'' and g'' are just the "code pointers"
(closed functions) for f and g; the record (g'', a, b) is the same object as (f'', g'', a, b)
but seen starting at the second field. The variable g is implemented as a pointer
into the middle of the f record. From the point of view of any caller of g, the
closed function g' is obtained by fetching at location g, just as with an ordinary
closure.

Closure sharing saves time (for building closures) and space, and will be discussed in much more detail in Chapter 10. For the moment, we just consider
the conditions required for closure sharing. A closure c for a function f can be
constructed at the point in the CPS program where the function definition FIX
is encountered. More generally, the closure can be constructed in any scope in
which all the free variables of f are defined. If the free variables are all defined
much earlier than the place where f is defined, then the definition of f (the closure
creation) could be hoisted upward to that point.

On the other hand, if a function f is defined early and not used until a much
more deeply nested scope, the function definition could be "hoisted downward"
toward the point of first use.

Two functions can share the same closure if there is any scope before the first
use of either in which all of their free variables are defined. Clearly this is the
case for functions in the same set of mutually recursive functions (in the same FIX
of the CPS language). (For reasons to be explained in Chapter 10, the names of
functions defined in the same FIX need not count as free variables.) So we will
say that functions defined by the same FIX will definitely share a closure, and
functions not defined by the same FIX will not; and one of the jobs of the hoist
phase is to bring functions into the same FIX.

To return to the example above, we could write f and g as mutually recursive
(using an **and** in ML instead of another **fun**), even though they don't actually have
any recursive calls:

```
fun h(a,b) =
    let fun f(x,y) = x*a+y*b
        and g(i) = i+a+b
    in . . .
    end
```

Now f and g are guaranteed to share a closure, since they are in the same FIX.

In summary, each occurrence of a FIX operator in the CPS language may create a closure; if different FIXes can be merged together, the number of closure creations will be reduced; the criterion for merging FIXES is a simple free-variable analysis.

One complication involves the *known* functions, which do not usually require a closure. Any FIX that contains only *known* functions will not require a closure, unless the functions have so many free variables that they won't fit in registers. Thus, the cost of elaborating such a FIX is zero. Thus, our hoist phase sometimes finds it useful to split a FIX into two or more sets of mutually recursive functions (though there can be no mutual recursion between the different sets). This is for the following reason: It may be that all the escaping functions (that require closures) can be hoisted up or hoisted down to merge with other FIXes; but perhaps some of the known functions cannot (because of scope rules involving their free variables). In this case, splitting the FIX allows the closure-requiring escaping functions to be merged with other closures, leaving only the known functions in a FIX that requires no closure at all.

8.2 Rules for hoisting

Given that the goal of the hoist phase is to move CPS operators up or down in the expression tree to minimize the dynamic frequency of execution, or to minimize the number of distinct FIX definitions, what are the rules that must be followed? When is it appropriate to move one operator above another? The rules for hoisting can be expressed in terms of free variables of subexpressions.

We start with something simple:

$$\text{SELECT}(i_1, v_1, w_1, \text{SELECT}(i_2, v_2, w_2, E)) \rightarrow$$
$$\text{SELECT}(i_2, v_2, w_2, \text{SELECT}(i_1, v_1, w_1, E))$$
$$\textbf{if } w_1 \neq v_2$$

That is, we can interchange the two SELECT operators as long as the second one does not use the value produced by the first. Note, however, that if $w_1 = v_2$ then the right-hand expression violates the scope rules for the CPS given in Section 2.3. So we can summarize this rule by saying that two different SELECT operators may be interchanged as long as that does not cause scope rules to be violated.

Indeed, this is the situation for any pair of "purely functional" operators (those that don't change or examine the store, or raise exceptions). Let each of $\textbf{op}_1(E)$ and $\textbf{op}_2(E)$ be any of the following:

$$\text{SELECT}(i, v, w, E)$$
$$\text{OFFSET}(i, v, w, E)$$
$$\text{PRIMOP}(p, \vec{v}, \vec{w}, [E]), \quad p \in \{\texttt{alength}, \texttt{slength}\}$$
$$\text{PRIMOP}(p, \vec{v}, \vec{w}, [E, F]), \quad p \text{ any comparison operator}$$
$$\text{PRIMOP}(p, \vec{v}, \vec{w}, [F, E]), \quad p \text{ any comparison operator}$$
$$\text{SWITCH}(p, \vec{v}, \vec{w}, [F_1, \ldots, E, \ldots, F_n])$$
$$\text{FIX}(\vec{f}, E)$$
$$\text{FIX}([(f_1, v_1, B_1), \ldots, (f_i, v_i, E), \ldots, (f_n, v_n, B_n)], F)$$

Then $\mathbf{op}_1(\mathbf{op}_2(E)) \to \mathbf{op}_2(\mathbf{op}_1(E))$, provided that scope rules are not thereby violated.

Furthermore, purely functional operators may be exchanged with "impure" operators:

$$\mathtt{PRIMOP}(p, \vec{v}, \vec{w}, [\mathbf{op}_1(E)]) \to \mathbf{op}_1(\mathtt{PRIMOP}(p, \vec{v}, \vec{w}, [E]))$$

$$\mathbf{op}_1(\mathtt{PRIMOP}(p, \vec{v}, \vec{w}, [E])) \to \mathtt{PRIMOP}(p, \vec{v}, \vec{w}, [\mathbf{op}_1(E)])$$

for any primop p, provided that scope rules are not violated.

Finally, function-definition sets can be merged together, again providing that scope rules are not violated. Let $\mathcal{H}$ be the list of mutually recursive function definitions $(g_1, \vec{w}_1, C_1), \ldots, (g_n, \vec{w}_n, C_n)$. Then the transformations are:

$$\mathtt{FIX}([(f_1, \vec{v_1}, B_1), \ldots, (f_n, \vec{v_n}, B_n)], \mathtt{FIX}([\mathcal{H}], E)) \to$$
$$\mathtt{FIX}([(f_1, \vec{v_1}, B_1), \ldots, (f_n, \vec{v_n}, B_n), \mathcal{H}], E)$$

$$\mathtt{FIX}([(f_1, \vec{v_1}, B_1), \ldots, (f_i, v_i, \mathtt{FIX}([\mathcal{H}], D)), \ldots, (f_n, \vec{v_n}, B_n)], E) \to$$
$$\mathtt{FIX}([(f_1, \vec{v_1}, B_1), \ldots, (f_i, v_i, D), \ldots, (f_n, \vec{v_n}, B_n), \mathcal{H}], E)$$

Scope violations are not difficult to check. Assuming the the left-hand side of a rewrite rule does not violate scope rules, the right-hand-side expression can be checked by a constant number of free-variable-set operations. For example, the last transformation described is legal provided that $v_i \notin \mathrm{fv}(C_j)$ for all j. Clearly, it is necessary to know what the free variables of each subexpression are; and as transformations are performed in the hoist phase, the free-variable information must be kept current. In fact, maintaining free-variable sets is the most tedious part of the implementation of this phase.

8.3   Hoisting optimizations

Given these ground rules, which hoisting transformations actually improve the code? We have taken a conservative approach: An operator will be hoisted (down or up) only when the transformation is guaranteed to reduce execution time.

For operators other than FIXes, we will attempt to push the operator inside of a SWITCH or branching PRIMOP. That is, in an expression

$$\mathbf{op}_1(\mathbf{op}_2(\mathbf{op}_3(\mathbf{op}_4(\cdots(\mathtt{SWITCH}(v, [C_1, \ldots, C_i, \ldots, C_n]))\cdots))))$$

if the scope rules will allow, we will push $\mathbf{op}_1$ inside the ith branch of the SWITCH or comparison, resulting in

$$\mathbf{op}_2(\mathbf{op}_3(\mathbf{op}_4(\cdots(\mathtt{SWITCH}(v, [C_1, \ldots, \mathbf{op}_1(C_i), \ldots, C_n]))\cdots)))$$

The resulting program will be faster whenever the ith branch is not taken, and will be no slower when it is taken. This ignores issues of instruction scheduling, an optimization performed in a later phase (Section 14.3.2), which might render the preceding sentence untrue.

If $\mathbf{op}_1$ can modify the store, then this optimization is impermissible. Obviously, an assignment operation (:= or `update`) must be evaluated no matter which branch is taken, if the program so specifies. But the same is true of arithmetic operators! Consider the program

```
let val j = i*i
  in if x then j else i
end handle Overflow => 0
```

This program will return 0 if $i^2 >$ maxint; otherwise it will return i if $x =$ false or i^2 if $x =$ true. If the optimizer rewrites the program as

```
(if x then i*i else i)
handle Overflow => 0
```

then its behavior will be different. We are careful to avoid doing any optimization that changes the behavior of the program.

Perhaps it would be a good idea to hoist variables out of function bodies, that is,

$$\texttt{FIX}([(f_1, \vec{v_1}, B_1), \ldots, (f_i, v_i, \mathbf{op}_1(E)), \ldots, (f_n, \vec{v_n}, B_n)], F) \rightarrow$$
$$\mathbf{op}_1(\texttt{FIX}([(f_1, \vec{v_1}, B_1), \ldots, (f_i, v_i, E), \ldots, (f_n, \vec{v_n}, B_n)], F))$$

provided that scope rules allowed. If f_i is evaluated more than once, on average, then this optimization will probably save time (unless f_i gains another free variable, which must be fetched from the closure; but we will ignore this effect). But we can have no guarantee of f_i's evaluation, so we have not made such optimizations. Thus, loop-invariant operations are in general not hoisted because the loops are not known to execute for at least one iteration. However, in-line expansion and common-subexpression elimination may partially solve that problem, as will be discussed in Chapter 9.

Finally, we will hoist `FIX` operators up or down as necessary to merge with other `FIX`es, thus saving on closure creation. We take a greedy approach: We consider expressions bottom up, and for each `FIX` we first attempt to push it down to join another `FIX` (or go inside one branch of a conditional); if that fails, we pull the `FIX` up as far as its scope will allow, hoping that it will eventually merge with a `FIX` at an outer scope.

CHAPTER NINE

COMMON SUBEXPRESSIONS

When the same computation is performed twice in the execution of a program, the second computation can be eliminated and the result of the first used instead. This is called "common-subexpression elimination." Of course, to implement this as an optimization it must be possible to identify statically a sequence of operations with a repeated computation.

We will say that if an operator $\mathbf{op_2}$ binds a variable v_2 within the scope of a variable v_1 bound by operator $\mathbf{op_1}$, and we can calculate at compile time that v_2 will always have the same value as v_1, then we can eliminate $\mathbf{op_2}$ and substitute v_1 everywhere for v_2. Thus, our version of common-subexpression elimination (CSE) requires that the eliminated expression must be lexically dominated by an equivalent expression.

As an example, consider the ML expression

```
val z = a*b*c+a*b*c
```

This will be translated into CPS as

```
PRIMOP(*,[VAR a, VAR b], [u], [
 PRIMOP(*, [VAR u, VAR c], [v], [
  PRIMOP(*, [VAR a, VAR b], [w], [
   PRIMOP(*, [VAR w, VAR c], [x], [
    PRIMOP(+, [VAR v, VAR x], [z], [ ...
```

Now, the operator PRIMOP(*,[VAR a, VAR b],[w]...) is in the scope of the variable u that is bound by an identical computation. So that operator can be removed, and uses of w can be replaced by u:

```
PRIMOP(*,[VAR a, VAR b], [u], [
 PRIMOP(*, [VAR u, VAR c], [v], [
   PRIMOP(*, [VAR u, VAR c], [x], [
    PRIMOP(+, [VAR v, VAR x], [z], [ ...
```

Now, of course, the binding of x is redundant, and x can be replaced by uses of v:

```
PRIMOP(*,[VAR a, VAR b], [u], [
 PRIMOP(*, [VAR u, VAR c], [v], [
   PRIMOP(+, [VAR v, VAR v], [z], [ ...
```

99

An eminently satisfactory result!

According to the scope rules for CPS, if a variable w contains a FIX operator in its scope, then the bodies of the functions defined by the FIX are also in the scope of w. This means that common subexpression elimination can take place across function boundaries:

```
SELECT(i,v,w,
   . . .
   FIX([(f,[a,c], SELECT(i,v,u,B))],E)
```

The selection of the ith field from v is performed outside the function f, then repeated within it. The inner SELECT can be removed, and w substituted for u within B. This means that each time f is called (from E or recursively from B), there will be some savings. We ignore the fact that w might have to be fetched from the closure of f, which is just as expensive as the SELECT just eliminated! Of course, if f is a known function, there will be no such expense, unless the extra value w in registers causes a spill.

Our scope rule for CSE optimizations is a bit restrictive. Sometimes there are common subexpressions, neither of which dominates the other:

```
SWITCH(VAR v, [
   PRIMOP(+, [VAR a, VAR b], x, A),
   B,
   PRIMOP(+, [VAR a, VAR b], y, C)])
```

Here the operation $a + b$ is performed in two different branches of the SWITCH. We might like to lift the PRIMOP above the SWITCH, and use the result both in A and C. However, there are two problems with this (as described in the discussion of hoisting, in Chapter 8):

1. This will waste time if the branch B is taken most often; and

2. The add might overflow, yielding an erroneous result if B would have been taken.

Of course, problem 2 is not an issue for "pure" operators such as SELECT and RECORD.

However, consider the following example:

```
FIX([(f, [a,c], PRIMOP(+, [VAR x, VAR y], [z], [
                  PRIMOP(+, [VAR z, VAR a], [u], [
                     APP(VAR c, [VAR u])])])])],
      PRIMOP(+, [VAR x, VAR y], [w], [
         APP(VAR f, [VAR w, VAR k])]))
```

There are two copies of the addition $x + y$, and neither is in the scope of the other. However, the *add* that binds w can quite legitimately be hoisted above the FIX:

```
PRIMOP(+, [VAR x, VAR y], [w], [
  FIX([(f, [a,c], PRIMOP(+, [VAR x, VAR y], [z], [
                    PRIMOP(+, [VAR z, VAR a], [u], [
                      APP(VAR c, [VAR u])])])])],
      APP(VAR f, [VAR w, VAR k]))])
```

This is permissible because any control path that leads to the FIX will inevitably lead to the first instruction of its body; so, since scope rules permit in this case, we can hoist the instruction from the body of the FIX to just above it. (The only way that this would be prohibited by scope rules is if the instruction in question referred to one of the functions defined by the FIX.)

Now, the binding of z is within the scope of w, so a CSE optimization is possible:

```
PRIMOP(+, [VAR x, VAR y], [w], [
  FIX([(f, [a,c],  PRIMOP(+, [VAR w, VAR a], [u], [
                    APP(VAR c, [VAR u])])])],
      APP(VAR f, [VAR w, VAR k]))])
```

To see the power of this kind of optimization, we consider loop-invariant hoisting: that is, taking a computation within a loop that computes the same value each time, and moving it above the loop so it executes only once. We take the loop

```
let fun loop(0,s) = s
  | loop(i,s) = loop(i-1,a+b+s)
 in loop(n,0)
end
```

This translates (with some optimization) into CPS as:

```
FIX([(loop, [i, s, c],
        PRIMOP(ieql, [VAR i, INT 0], [
          APP(VAR c, [VAR s]),
          PRIMOP(-, [VAR i, INT 1], [j], [
          PRIMOP(+, [VAR a, VAR b], [x], [
           PRIMOP(+, [VAR x, VAR s], [y], [
            APP(VAR loop, [VAR j, VAR y, VAR c]
                                 )])])])])])],
    APP(VAR loop, [VAR n, INT 0, VAR k]))
```

We would like to hoist the loop-invariant computation $a + b$, but we can't be sure that $n > 0$, so this transformation is not possible. However, the β-expansion phase is likely to unroll the first iteration of the loop:

```
FIX([[(loop, [i, s, c],
            PRIMOP(ieql, [VAR i, INT 0], [
             APP(VAR c, [VAR s]),
              PRIMOP(-, [VAR i, INT 1], [j], [
               PRIMOP(+, [VAR a, VAR b], [x], [
                PRIMOP(+, [VAR x, VAR s], [y], [
                 APP(VAR loop, [VAR j, VAR y, VAR c])])])])])]],
  PRIMOP(ieql, [VAR n, INT 0], [
   APP(VAR k, [INT 0]),
   PRIMOP(-, [VAR n, INT 1], [j'], [
    PRIMOP(+, [VAR a, VAR b], [x'], [
     PRIMOP(+, [VAR x', INT 0], [y'], [
      APP(VAR loop, [VAR j', VAR y', VAR k])])])])]))
```

Now, several operations—including the comparison—can be hoisted above the FIX; also the addition $x + 0$ can be simplified:

```
PRIMOP(ieql, [VAR n, INT 0], [
 APP(VAR k, [INT 0]),
 PRIMOP(-, [VAR n, INT 1], [j'], [
  PRIMOP(+, [VAR a, VAR b], [x'], [
   FIX([[(loop, [i, s, c],
              PRIMOP(ieql, [VAR i, INT 0], [
               APP(VAR c, [VAR s]),
               PRIMOP(-, [VAR i, INT 1], [j], [
                PRIMOP(+, [VAR a, VAR b], [x], [
                 PRIMOP(+, [VAR x, VAR s], [y], [
                  APP(VAR loop, [VAR j, VAR y, VAR c])])])])])]],
        APP(VAR loop, [VAR j', VAR x', VAR k]))])])])
```

Finally, the binding of x is in the scope of x', so a CSE optimization can be performed:

```
PRIMOP(ieql, [VAR n, INT 0], [
 APP(VAR k, [INT 0]),
 PRIMOP(-, [VAR n, INT 1], [j'], [
  PRIMOP(+, [VAR a, VAR b], [x'], [
   FIX([[(loop, [i, s, c],
              PRIMOP(ieql, [VAR i, INT 0], [
               APP(VAR c, [VAR s]),
               PRIMOP(-, [VAR i, INT 1], [j], [
                PRIMOP(+, [VAR x', VAR s], [y], [
                 APP(VAR loop, [VAR j, VAR y, VAR c])])])])]],
        APP(VAR loop, [VAR j', VAR x', VAR k]))])])])
```

Thus the loop-invariant computation $a + b$ has been safely hoisted out of the loop. The interesting thing is that none of the individual transformations—β-expansion, code hoisting, CSE elimination— know anything about loops!

CHAPTER TEN

CLOSURE CONVERSION

Continuation-passing style is meant to approximate the operation of a von Neumann computer; each operator of the former corresponds to one (or at most a few) instructions of the latter. Selecting the ith field of a record in the CPS is like a fetch with constant offset on a computer, and so on.

A "function" in machine language is just an address in the executable program, perhaps with some convention about which registers hold the parameters—very much like a "jump with arguments." The notion of function in the CPS is almost the same: The structure of CPS expressions is that an APP is the last thing a function does; the result of an APP is always the result of its parent expression. Thus the APP is also a "jump with arguments." If a "return" from a procedure (in the usual sense) is desired, then a *continuation function* must be made: One of the arguments to the called function will itself be a function c; the called function is expected to call c with its result.

However, the function definitions of continuation-passing style are a bit more powerful than those of conventional computers. FIX definitions in CPS have nested static scope; if the function f is statically nested inside the function g, then f can refer to the variables of g. The notion of a function as a machine-code address does not provide for free variables. The problem is solved in Algol-like languages by the method of *access links*, meaning that the activation for the function f contains a pointer to the activation record for g. Furthermore, if it is desired to pass f as an argument to another function (that need not be statically nested within g), then a pair comprising the machine-code address for f and the activation record for g is passed.

Such a pair is called a *closure,* though there are other ways to represent closures. A function with free variables is said to be *open;* a *closure* is a data structure containing both the machine code address of an open function, and bindings for all the free variables of that function. The machine-code implementation of the function knows to find the values of free variables in the closure data structure.

When the function f can be returned as the result of g, or stored into a data structure and invoked after g returns, then the variables in the activation record of g may now be used after g has returned. This means that activation records can no longer be stored on a stack, but must instead be allocated on a heap. The idea of heap-allocated closures to implement higher-order functions dates back to the Landin's implementation of a strict λ-calculus in the early 1960's [57].

In many implementations, the notion of *closure* is divorced from that of *activation record*, so activation records may still be stack allocated whereas closures are heap allocated *and do not point into the stack*. Instead, copies of the free variables of a function *f* are put into *f*'s closure, which therefore does not need to point to any activation record. To make copies of variables, it must be that the variables are *immutable* (i.e., cannot be modified after they are created); otherwise, assignments to one copy would not be seen by users of the other copies. In ML, of course, this is the case; Section 10.5 discusses how this approach works for other languages.

In a compiler that uses continuation-passing style, it is usual to dispense entirely with the notion of *activation record*, and use closures exclusively. The context of the currently executing function is held in registers; and in CPS, there is never any other function context "suspended" and still live. Instead, there is the "closure of the continuation function."

10.1   A simple example

Let us consider the simplest possible example: a curried addition function.

```
val add = fn x => fn y => x+y
```

The closure for `add` is trivial, since `add` has no free variables; there is just a "code pointer" for the function:

$$add \longrightarrow \boxed{\ \bullet\ } \longrightarrow \text{machine code for } \lambda x.\lambda y.x + y$$

Now, when `add` is applied to the argument 5

```
val g = add 5
```

the closure for `fn y => x+y` must provide the free variable `x`:

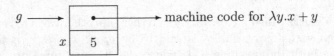

$$g \longrightarrow \boxed{\begin{array}{c} \bullet \\ \hline x \quad 5 \end{array}} \longrightarrow \text{machine code for } \lambda y.x + y$$

When `g` is applied to the argument 10, the function `fn y => x+y` executes with y bound to 10. But the closure pointer must also be accessible to the function while it executes, so the value `x` can be fetched when needed. The caller of `fn y => x+y` must provide this closure pointer. Now, the caller may have been passed `fn y => x+y` as an argument, in which case all it gets is the closure pointer. To invoke the function, the code pointer is fetched out of the closure, the argument

10 is provided, and the closure pointer is put in a "standard" place. But the caller does not need to know the format of the closure, or how many free variables there are, or what their values are.

We will represent closure creation and closure access explicitly in the CPS notation; we will call this *closure-passing style*. Let us first translate the *add* example into continuation-passing style:

```
fun add(x, k) = let val g(y, c) = c(x+y)
                in k(g)
                end
```

Now, for closure-passing style, each function will be passed *its own closure* in addition to its other arguments. To pass a function as an argument (or store it into a data structure), one passes *the closure only*. To invoke such a closure *c*, one fetches the first field *f* and applies *f* to its arguments *including c*. To construct a closure for a function *g*, one makes a record containing a modified version of *g* and all the free variables of *g*. To extract a free variable from a closure, one simply uses SELECT. Here's the add example:

```
fun add'(add'', x, k) = let val g'(g'', y, c) =
                            let val x' = #1(c)
                                val c' = #0(c)
                            in c'(c,x'+y)
                            end
                        val g = (g',x)
                        val k' = #0(k)
                    in k'(k,g)
                    end
```

When add is invoked, its first argument will be a closure pointer add''. Since add has no free variables, it has no use for a closure; but the caller of add had no way of knowing this. The other arguments are an integer x and a continuation closure k. The first thing it does is define a closed function g', and then a closure record g containing g' and the value x. When g is invoked from some other context, what will happen is that g' will be entered with its formal parameter g'' bound to the closure g.

An example of a closure call is the invocation of k. The closed function ("code pointer") k' is fetched from the zeroth field of k; the other fields of k might contain free variables but we don't know or care about them. Then we pass to k' the closure k and the argument g.

Once g' is invoked, it fetches the free variable x from its closure by #1(c). Note that the format of g's closure must be known by the creator of the closure (val g=(g',x)) and by the implementation of g' itself. But the creation of the closure can always take place right after the definition of the function.

After this *closure-passing* transformation, it will be the case that no function has free variables; clearly this is the case with add' and g' in our example.

10.2   A bigger example

```
fun h(x) = x * w

fun f(g,y) = g(y) + h(z)

val i = (f,1)

let fun m(n) = n+t
    val p = f(m,1)
 in ...p+m(e)...
end
```

Figure 10.1. An example: ML source code.

For the remainder of this chapter, we will discuss closure representations in the context of a somewhat larger example, shown in figure 10.1. The *escaping* function f calls a *known* function h and also calls its argument g, which of course escapes. In our example, the actual parameter m in the call to f corresponds to the formal parameter g.

Figure 10.2 shows the translation of this program into continuation-passing style. We will use an informal ML notation here, as the `cexp` datatype notation would get too cumbersome. Note that in ML, a multiple-argument function such as f is really considered to take a single n-tuple argument, so g and y are really just fields of some variable *arg*.

Now, the function m is passed as an argument to f; the function k is passed to h, and so on. Each of these functions has free variables (t is a free variable of m, a and c are free variables of k, etc.). The implementation must represent k using some data structure that contains the machine code for computing $a+b$ (etc.) and also contains the values for a and c.

When g is called from within f, the machine-code pointer must be extracted from the closure, arguments y and j must be put in registers, and the jump (i.e., to m) must be made. But m must also be able to access its closure; so it is important that the closure pointer g (e.g., m) be placed in a standard register before the jump—in effect, the closure pointer is an extra argument to the function. Then m can extract free variables through this pointer. The format of the free variables in the closure need not be standardized: The creator of the closure (at `fun m(n,r)...`) and the code that extracts free variables (at `n+t`) need to know the format, but the caller (at `g(y,j)`) need not know where they are, or indeed how many there are. However, the location of the code pointer within the closure must be standardized so the caller can find it and jump to it. A typical representation puts the code pointer at field 0 of the closure record, and the free variables at other offsets from the closure pointer, perhaps in a linked list of closures.

```
fun h(x,d) = let val t1 = x * w
                in d(t1)
                end

fun f(arg,c) =
    let val g = #0(arg)
        val y = #1(arg)
        fun j(a) =
            let fun k(b) =
                    let val t2 = a+b
                    in c(t2)
                    end
                in h(z,k)
                end
        in g(y,j)
    end

val i = (f,1)

let fun m(n,r) =
        let val q = n+t
        in r(q)
        end
    fun s(p) = ...p...m...e...
    val u = (m,1)
in f(u,s)
end
```

Figure 10.2. An example: CPS code.

Notice that h is never passed as an argument; it appears in the expression $h(z, k)$ in *function position*. Since we know all the call sites, we can choose the representation of h more freely; for example, we could require all the callers to pass the free variable w as an extra argument, so no closure at all is required.

In general, *escaping functions* must be compiled using a standard closure mechanism; *known functions* can use cheaper, more specialized representations [83].

One interesting trick [54, 13] is to let several functions share a single closure. The functions m and s might ordinarily be represented like this:

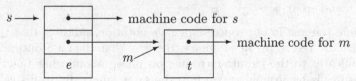

The closure for m has the value for the free variable t; the closure for s has free variables m and e.

Now consider this data structure:

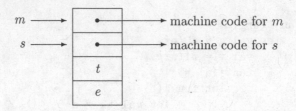

The value s is really a pointer to the middle of the closure record! The caller of s does not know this, however, and when it extracts what it thinks is field 0, it gets (correctly) the code pointer for s. Of course, the machine-code functions m and s must know the closure format; in particular, s derives the closure value m by subtracting from its own closure pointer, without a fetch! (This is the use of the mysterious OFFSET primitive of the CPS.) Since there is some overhead for record creation—creating a record of size n costs $Bn + C$ operations, for some B and C—the closure-sharing trick is quite useful; in this case there is a savings of $B + C$ per instance of m/s.

The data structure shown here is built by the lines

```
val m = (m',s',t,e)
val s = offset(m,1)
```

of figure 10.3.

Closure sharing is particularly useful with mutually recursive functions. Consider two such functions f and g. In a representation without closure sharing, the closure f must contain the closure g as a free variable, and vice versa. This is therefore a cyclic data structure, which is inconvenient to construct at runtime.

In the Standard ML of New Jersey compiler, we will perform closure sharing exactly on functions defined by the same FIX operator. Thus, nonnested mutually recursive functions will share a closure. Functions with compatible free-variable sets (such as m and s in our example) that do not appear in the same FIX will not share a closure. However, the *hoist* phase will bring such functions into the same FIX, so in our example they would appear as

```
    fun m(n,r) =
      let val q = n+t
      in r(q)
      end
    and s(p) = ...p...m...e...
```

where the and in our source-language notation indicates that they are pro forma mutually recursive. In summary, the way that the CPS optimization phase communicates to the closure-introduction phase about what functions should share closures is by grouping them into the same "mutually recursive" definition.

10.3 Closure-passing style

Some compilers [83, 26, 54] perform these closure analyses as part of their translation from lambda calculus or continuation-passing style into machine code. But the representation of closures is not at all machine dependent; furthermore, closure representations can get quite complicated, and it is useful to have a clean notation in which to express them [52, 11]. Therefore, we separate closure introduction from machine-code generation, and we use CPS notation to express closure creation and use. The reader should note that representing closures as explicit records does not require the use of continuations; it has been done in compilers based on ordinary lambda calculus [32].

Our example—as transformed into closure-passing style—is shown in figure 10.3

After closure conversion, the function k is now a closure record; k' is a function without free variables, which can thus be represented as just a machine-code pointer; the formal parameter k'' will be bound to k by any caller.

The function h is known, so does not need a closure; however, its free variable w must be passed as an extra argument w'; this in turn means that w is a free variable of f. If f is known, w would become an extra argument; but since f escapes, w goes into its closure.

10.4 The closure-conversion algorithm

The closure-conversion algorithm must produce a CPS-expression in which no function defined by any FIX operator has free variables other than the names of functions defined by all the FIXes.

We first describe closure conversion with single-variable continuations, that is, without the callee-saves convention described in Section 10.6. These are the strategies that will be employed:

- Functions that escape will require a closure of a standard form; the function pointer (the variable defined by the FIX operator for the closed function) will be at field 0 of the closure, and free variables, or pointers to other records and closures containing free variables, will be at other fields of the closure. The closure itself will be passed as the first argument to the escaping function.

- All the functions defined in the same FIX will share a closure.

- A known function will not, in general, require a closure; instead, its free variables will be passed as extra arguments to the function. This means that any function g that calls a known function f will effectively have its free-variable set augmented by the free variables of f.

- No function may have more than N arguments, where N is the number of registers on the target machine (but see Section 13.4 for a more precise bound). This means that if a known function has a arguments and b free variables, and $a + b > N$, then the free variables cannot all be passed as

```
fun h(x,d,w') =                         let
let val t1 = x*w'                         fun m'(m'',n,r) =
    val d' = #0(d)                        let
 in d'(d,t1)                                val t = #2(m'')
end                                         val q = n+t
                                            val r' = #0(r)
fun f'(f'',arg,c) =                       in r'(r,q)
let                                        end
  val g = #0(arg)
  val y = #1(arg)                        fun s'(s'',p) =
                                         let
  fun j'(j'',a)=                           val e=#2(s'')
  let                                       val m=offset(s'',-1)
    fun k'(k'',b)=                         in ...p...m...e...
    let                                    end
      val a = #1(k'')
      val t2 = a+b                       val m = (m',s',t,e)
      val c''=#2(k'')                    val s = offset(m,1)
      val c'= #0(c'')                    val u = (m,1)
     in c'(c'',t2)                      in f'(f,u,s)
    end                                 end

    val c'''= #1(j'')
    val k = (k',a,c''')
    val z' = #2(j'')
    val w'' = #3(j'')
   in h(z',k,w'')
  end

  val w = #2(f'')
  val z = #1(f'')
  val j = (j',c,z,w)
  val g' = #0(g)
 in g'(g,y,j)
end

val f = (f',z,w)
val i = (f,1)
```

Figure 10.3. Closure-passing style.

extra arguments. Instead, a closure will be made, and passed as a single extra argument. This closure need not contain a function pointer (i.e., the name of the closed function defined by the FIX operator), since all the callers will know which function to pass the closure to.

- If a known function f calls an escaping function g defined in the same FIX, or calls a known function h in the same FIX that requires a closure, then f will use the same closure as g or h instead of having its free variables passed as extra arguments. This is because a closure is required for that FIX anyway, so it costs little for f to share that closure. As described above, the closure need not contain the function pointer for f.

There are at least two kinds of circularity here. First consider the known functions f, g, and h, where f calls g and g calls h. Then the free-variable set of g must be augmented by the free variables of h, and the free variables of f must be augmented by those of g (including the ones from h). But what if h calls f?

Fortunately, this circularity converges quite simply; in fact, the analysis is exactly the same as "live-variable" dataflow analysis [1] in a conventional compiler. There is a close correspondence between free variables in the CPS and statically live variables in the flowgraph of a conventional compiler. We may write the dataflow equations as follows: Let the initial free variables of f be $\mathcal{V}_0(f)$, let $\mathcal{E}(f)$ be the set of functions applied in the body of f, and let $\mathcal{K}$ be the set of known functions in the program. We desire a minimal mapping $\mathcal{V}$ such that

$$\mathcal{V}_0(f) \cup \left(\bigcup_{g \in \mathcal{E}(f) \cap \mathcal{K}} \mathcal{V}(g) \right) \subset \mathcal{V}(f)$$

One way to calculate $\mathcal{V}$ given $\mathcal{V}_0$ is to iterate, that is, repeatedly calculate $\mathcal{V}_i$ using

$$\mathcal{V}_i(f) = \mathcal{V}_{i-1}(f) \cup \left(\bigcup_{g \in \mathcal{E}(f) \cap \mathcal{K}} \mathcal{V}_{i-1}(g) \right)$$

When $\mathcal{V}_i(f) = \mathcal{V}_{i-1}(f)$ for all f, then $\mathcal{V}_i = \mathcal{V}$, and the iteration is finished. Since each iteration where $\mathcal{V}_i(f) \neq \mathcal{V}_{i-1}(f)$ must add at least one variable to at least one known function's set, the number of iterations is bounded by the number of variables times the number of functions. In practice, the fixed point is usually found much sooner. A fuller description of this technique may be found in almost any book on dataflow optimization [1].

There is another kind of circularity. Consider known functions f, g, h such that f calls g and g calls h. The free variables of f are augmented by those of g, and then g's are augmented by h's; in the next iteration f's will be augmented again. But suppose that f has by now acquired more free variables than the machine has registers, so it needs a closure. And then suppose in the next iteration that g acquires so many free variables that it too needs a closure. Since g will use a closure, the free variables of f no longer need to include those of g; this means that f might not need a closure.

Rather than try and solve this problem optimally, we will use an approximation: Let $\mathcal{C}_i$ be the set of functions that seem to require a closure in iteration i; this includes all escaping functions and some known functions. We will say that $\mathcal{C}_i \subset \mathcal{C}_{i+1}$; that is, if f seems at any point in the iteration to require a closure, then we will never reverse that decision.

If f calls any function defined in the same FIX that requires the closure, we will make f use the closure. Let $\mathcal{F}(f)$ be the set of functions defined by the same FIX as f; let N be the number of registers on the target machine.

$$\mathcal{V}_i(f) = \mathcal{V}_{i-1}(f) \cup \left(\bigcup_{g \in \mathcal{E}(f) - \mathcal{C}_{i-1}} \mathcal{V}_{i-1}(g) \right)$$

$$\mathcal{C}_i = \mathcal{C}_{i-1} \cup \{f \mid N < |\mathcal{V}_{i-1}(f)|\} \cup \{f \mid \mathcal{C}_{i-1} \cap \mathcal{E}(f) \cap \mathcal{F}(f) \neq \phi\}$$

This simple algorithm determines which functions require a closure.

10.5   Closure representation

Once it is decided whether a function must have closures, there remains the question of how its free variables are to be arranged in the closure record. There are two fundamental approaches, which we shall call *flat* and *linked:*

- A *flat* closure representing the free variables v_i of a function f is a single record containing each of the values v_i. In addition, for an escaping function, the closure record contains the function pointer.

- A *linked* closure for a function f statically nested inside a function g is a record containing the free variables of f that are not free in g (e.g., that are bound by g), and also containing a pointer to the closure for g. For an escaping function, of course, the function pointer for f will also be present, occupying the zeroth field.

The method of linked closures is very much like the method of *static links* (also called *access links*) [1] in implementations of block-structured languages such as Algol or Pascal. The variables free in f but not free in g are a subset of the parameters and local variables of g; so the closure for f is very much like the activation record of g.

Why might one method be preferable over the other?

- With the flat method, the same variable may appear in several different closures. In a language where variables may be modified after their creation, this will lead to incorrect results, as the modification of one copy of the variable will not be seen by holders of the other copy. Fortunately, variables in ML are immutable, so this is not an issue. And in other languages, it is usually possible to tell statically which variables cannot be modified after creation. The mutable variables can then be put in memory (in "cells") [52], and pointers to these variables can be copied freely.

- The linked method may lead to smaller closures than the flat method; if a function has many free variables that are also free in the enclosing function, then all of these variables take up just one word in the closure. This leads to faster closure creation, and perhaps faster garbage collection.

- The flat method has faster access time, since the value of any free variable of the currently executing function can be obtained with just one fetch. With the linked method, the access time of a variable is proportional (at worst) to the level of static nesting of the executing function.

- The flat method remembers a parsimonious set of values. With the linked method, there is the danger that a large data structure, which will never again be used, will be pointed to by an outer function. Consider:

```
fun f(x) =  let val y = very_large_object
                fun g(z) = let fun h(w) = w+x+z
                           in j(y); h
                           end
            in g(3)
            end
```

Using flat closures, a closure for h is of size 3—one word for the function pointer and one word each for x and z. Using linked closures, each h closure is also of size 3—one word for the function pointer, one word for z, and one word for the pointer to a closure for g. But unfortunately, the closure for g contains a pointer to a huge data structure y, which is quite useless to h. As long as h is live, y cannot be reclaimed, as it could if flat closures were used. This is a serious disadvantage of linked closures; see Chapter 12.

There are many variations on flat and linked closures [12]:

- **Linked as necessary**: Like *linked*, except that the link (the pointer to the enclosing closure) is omitted if it is not necessary. This will be the case if none of the function's free variables are free in the statically enclosing function.

- **Grouped functions**: Several functions can share a closure, as described on page 107.

- **Optimally linked**: When a closure is created, there may be several other closures in scope that together contain many of the desired variable bindings. The compiler can take advantage of this, and represent the new closure as a record of pointers to the minimal set of other closures that will cover the set of free variables. A variant of this, in which we minimize the product of closure size times maximum link depth, is provably NP-complete. Note that the "optimality" takes no account of the space-reclamation problems mentioned above.

- **Skip lists:** In linked closures, each closure could include a link not only to the immediately enclosing function, but to a closure several levels up. By clever arrangement of these extra links, we could guarantee that no more than $\log n$ fetches are required to access a variable n nesting levels up. This would increase the size of each closure by approximately 1 pointer.

- **Path compression:** In any strategy using links, there may be a link to a closure f from which we need only one element x. Instead of including f in the new closure, we could include x directly. This costs no extra space, but now each reference to x will be faster, at the expense of an extra fetch when we construct the closure.

- **Heuristic path compression:** Flat closures economize on access time at the expense of closure-building time; linked closures economize on closure size at the expense of access time. Heuristic path compression is a compromise between these two approaches. A value is copied into each scope where it is directly used, but other free variables—those free in a given function only because they are free in internally nested functions—must be accessed by static links.

Clearly, there is an infinite variety of closure-representation strategies.

10.6   Callee-save registers

The original function f made two subroutine calls, to g and h. Neither of these was a tail call, so each call requires a continuation to be made, respectively, j and k. Each continuation requires a closure. Thus the implementation of f requires the construction of two closures of size 3 and 4, for a total cost of $7B + 2C$, assuming B instructions are required to store each word, and there are C instructions of overhead for each record creation. It would be nice if j and k could use the closure-sharing trick, but they cannot: The variable a is free in k but bound by j, so it cannot yet exist when the closure for j is made but must exist when k is created.

A conventional compiler on a conventional machine will often use registers to hold local variables and temporaries (e.g., internal nodes of expression trees). When one procedure calls another, both procedures may use the same registers for different purposes, and there must be some convention for saving the registers and restoring them. For example, it could be that the calling procedure (the "caller") must assume that the procedure it calls (the "callee") may put any values in registers without preserving the original values; therefore the caller must save registers (copy them into memory) before the call, and restore them (copy them from memory) after the call. This is a "caller-saves" convention. On the other hand, it could be that the callee is responsible for leaving registers exactly as it found them; therefore, if the callee wants to use some registers for temporary values, it must save them prior to use and restore them before returning. This is a "callee-saves" convention.

Which approach is preferable? Consider temporaries that hold the internal nodes of expression-tree evaluation. Since most procedure calls occur outside of expression trees, the registers that hold these temporaries are "idle" at the time of a procedure call—the caller does not care if their contents are lost. Therefore, a caller-saves convention is best for such registers.

On the other hand, consider a small "leaf" procedure—one that does not call other procedures, and which uses very few registers before returning. If the caller wanted to preserve several local (register) variables across the call, then under a caller-save convention they would have to be written to memory before the call and read from memory afterward, even though the leaf procedure does not modify them. In this case, a callee-saves convention seems best, since any registers not used by a leaf procedure are can be considered "automatically" callee-saved.

The main advantage of callee-saved registers is for procedures that make two or more calls (either statically or dynamically, e.g., a single call within a loop counts as more than one call). If a register is to be preserved across the call, then a caller-saves convention would save it and restore it at each call; a callee-saves convention will avoid the save and restore if the callee does not happen to use the register.

In practice, compiler writers have opted to have some of each. The Berkeley C compiler for the VAX, for example, uses six caller-saves and six callee-saves registers (in addition to four special-purpose registers such as the stack pointer, frame pointer, etc.). With a mixed caller/callee-saves convention like this, variables not needed after the call can be put in caller-saves registers and not saved at all; leaf procedures can use caller-saves registers to the extent possible.

Consider again the example of figure 10.1: The function f calls two other functions, g and h. When f calls g it saves all the registers it might need after the call in the closure j. This is clearly like a caller-saves convention. It might be nice to have some callee-saves registers where values could be stored; the trick is to express this kind of convention in continuation-passing style.

What we will do is to give every function n extra arguments. We will require that each "user" (noncontinuation) function f must pass these arguments to its continuation c, when f (or some function that f calls) eventually calls c. Thus, these extra arguments will behave like callee-saves registers.

Another way to look at our new callee-saves convention is that each user function will be passed a continuation, as before, but now a continuation is represented using $n + 1$ actual parameters. One of these parameters will be the code pointer; the others will be free variables of the continuation. Let us consider the function f from our previous example, letting $n = 3$:

```
fun f(w'',g,y,z,c0,c1,c2,c3) =
    let . . . c0(v,c1,c2,c3) . . . end
```

```
fun h(x,d0,w',d1,d2,d3) = let t1 = x*w'
                          in d0(t1,d1,d2,d3)
                          end

fun f'(f'',arg,c0,c1,c2,c3) =
     let val g = #0(arg)
         val y = #1(arg)

         fun j0(a,j1,j2,j3) =
                let val z' = #3(j1)
                in h(z',k0,j2,j1,a,j3)
                end
         and k0(b,k1,k2,k3) =
                let val t2 = k2+b
                    val c0' = #0(k1)
                    val c1' = #1(k1)
                    val c2' = #2(k1)
                in c0'(t2,c1',c2',k3)
                end
         val w = #2(f'')
         val z = #1(f'')
         val u = (c0,c1,c2,z)
         val g' = #0(g)
     in g'(g,y,j0,u,w,c3)
     end
```

Figure 10.4. Using three callee-saves registers.

Instead of a single continuation argument c, now f gets four arguments c_0, c_1, c_2, c_3, of which c_0 is the machine-code pointer. When f eventually "returns" (actually, it is k that calls the continuation function c), the variables c_1, c_2, c_3 are passed as extra arguments to c_0, along with the "result" v of the computation. Thus, the caller of f can put values into the arguments c_1, c_2, c_3 that it will need after f returns; it need not put those values into a closure record in memory, with the expense of **fetch** and **store** instructions.

This is the entire essence of our callee-saves representation. What remains is our method for organizing the closure-conversion algorithm to make use of this convention to best advantage. The main advantage is enhanced closure-sharing.

Figure 10.4 shows our new representation for f and h. Now the value w— needed by h—is passed as an argument (in a register) to g, from there to j_0 (where it's called j_2), and then to h, without ever being stored into a closure. The variable a is passed from j_0 to h and then to k_0 in a register, so now k and j can share a closure u. Note that some of the variables passed as callee-save arguments

are ordinary variables (such as w and a), and some are closure-records (such as u);
the compiler has great flexibility in using one or more of the callee-save registers
to pass closure records if necessary.

What we have achieved is that the functions j and k now share a closure, for a
cost of $4B + C$ instead of $7B + 2C$. The fact that a is free in k and bound in j is
no longer a problem, since a is passed from j to k in a callee-save argument (k_2).

Actually we can do even better than above. Since z and w are also free variables
of function f, continuations j and k can directly grab the closure f'' so we only
need build a closure with c_0, c_1, and c_2. Thus our cost is only $3B + C$:

```
fun f'(f'',arg,c0,c1,c2,c3)
    let ......
        val u = (c0,c1,c2)
        val g'= #0(g)
    in g'(g,y,j0,u,f'',c3)
    end
```

In general, the new representation for continuations will save time and space
when one function makes two or more nontail calls. In the CPS representation,
the continuations for these calls will be nested. The callee-saves convention allows
the continuation functions to be unnested and to share a closure. Since all continuation functions are nested in some other user functions, the new representation
for continuations can take advantage of the closure of the enclosing user functions
if they happen to have some free variables in common, thus decreasing the cost of
closure-record constructions.

This optimization depends on the fact that most noncontinuation functions
take a continuation argument, that each escaping function is either a "standard"
user function or a "standard" continuation, etc. These assumptions are defined in
Section 2.2.

However, this mechanism will not work if we have first-class continuations such
as those introduced by `callcc` and exceptions. A continuation may be put into
a record, registered as an exception handler, stored into some reference cell, or
passed as a "noncontinuation" argument of an escaping user function. In the CPS
code before closure conversion, we say a continuation variable is *well behaved* if all
of its occurrences appear at the following positions:

- the second argument of escaping user functions;

- any argument of known functions;

- in function position, such as g in $g(y)$.

All continuation variables that are not *well behaved* are called *strange continuation
variables*. In the example in figure 10.2, all continuation variables are well behaved.

To make our new schemes work correctly, we'll eliminate all strange continuation variables by transforming them into well-behaved continuation variables.
First by using a classical dataflow algorithm we can easily identify all continuation
variables. Then for every strange occurrence v as in

1. `val r = (...,v,...)`, where v is put in a record;

2. `k(v)` , where an escaping continuation function k is applied to v;

3. `f(v,k)` , where an escaping user function f is applied to (v, k);

4. `sethdlr(v)` , where `sethdlr` is the primop that registers v as an exception handler;

we define a new function u as `fun u(x,c) = v(x)` and substitute u for v, that is,

1. `let fun u(x,c) = v(x)`
   `in val r = (...,u,...)  end;`

2. `let fun u(x,c) = v(x) in k(u) end ;`

3. `let fun u(x,c) = v(x) in f(u,k) end;`

4. `let fun u(x,c) = v(x) in sethdlr(u) end;`

so v is now well behaved and u is just treated as an escaping user function.

For every strange occurrence v in

A. `val v = #i(r);`

B. `fun k(v) = ...` , where k is an escaping continuation function;

C. `fun f(v,k) = ...` , where f is an escaping user function;

D. `val v = gethdlr()` , where `gethdlr` is the primop that grabs the current exception handler;

we substitute v by u and redefine v as a well-behaved continuation function by `fun v(x) = u(x,0)`, that is,

A. `val u = #i(r); fun v(x) = u(x,0) ;`

B. `fun k(u) = let fun v(x) = u(x,0) in ...;`

C. `fun f(u,k) = let fun v(x) = u(x,0) in ...;`

D. `val u = gethdlr(); fun v(x) = u(x,0) .`

Here since the second argument of u will never be used, we simply supply it to be 0. So v is well-behaved at these occurrences.

We can use similar methods to make all known functions have at most one continuation argument. Thus we obtain *well-formed CPS expressions* that satisfy the following conventions:

- All escaping user functions will have two arguments, the first one is the standard noncontinuation argument and the second is always a well-behaved continuation variable.

- All escaping continuation functions have only one, noncontinuation, argument.

- Each known function has an arbitrary number of arguments but at most one of them is a continuation variable.

The well-formed CPS expression will be fed into the closure-conversion phase.

Now that we know all continuation variables can only appear at certain places, we can simply use K actual parameters to represent each one as long as this number is consistent throughout the whole program.

10.7 Callee-save continuation closures

To call a function, the actual parameters of the call must be put in registers first. Known functions' free variables can all be treated as part of the actual parameters since their call sites are all known (there is one exception, if the number of free variables is bigger than the number of registers available in the target machine then we have to spill part of them into closures). We can do such transformations at compile time.

The behavior of an escaping user function is not known at compile time. Because it might be put into and extracted from records (and manipulated in other ways), we can only use one single value (i.e., the closure) to represent both the code pointer of the function and all its free variables. There are many ways to structure the closure record, as discussed earlier in the chapter. For escaping continuation functions, their call sites are not all known but they must be *well behaved* in the sense defined in the previous section.

We can now add a fixed number of parameters to each continuation-function definition. The continuation-function closure now is represented by one code pointer plus n extra variables (n must be same throughout the program but could be arbitrary from 1 to the maximum number of registers available in the target machine). These n extra variables behave just like the callee-save registers. We denote them as $r_1, r_2, \ldots, r_n$.

Now every escaping continuation function will have $n + 2$ arguments and every escaping user function will have $n + 3$ arguments (one is the closure record for the function itself, one is the original (source-language) argument, and $n + 1$ represent the continuation). All escaping functions use the same calling conventions: A fixed set of $n + 1$ registers will thus correspond to those $n + 1$ parameters for continuations.

These techniques will let two nested continuation functions such as j and k in figure 10.2 share a closure. However, we should be more careful when we deal with a continuation function that is not nested within any other continuation functions. For the source program `fun f(g,x,y) = g(x)+y` we have the CPS code

```
fun f(arg,c) = let val g = #0(arg)
                   val x = #1(arg)
                   val y = #2(arg)
                   fun k(t) = let val u = t+y
                               in c(u)
                              end
               in g(x,k)
               end
```

If we use our new representations for continuations, it will be (suppose $n = 3$)

```
fun f(f',arg,c0,c1,c2,c3) =
   let  . . .
       fun k0(t,k1,k2,k3) =
           let val u = t+y

            . . .

            in c0(u,c1,c2,c3)
           end
       . . .
   in g(x,k0,?,?,?)
   end
```

The set of free variables for the continuation k_0 is $\{c_0, c_1, c_2, c_3, y\}$. There are only three callee-save arguments, so we need a closure; but this closure will occupy one of the callee-save arguments. So two variables can go in callee-save arguments and three must go into the closure; though it seems that it doesn't matter which three. But this is not true. Remember we are using the same set of callee-save registers so $c1$ and k_1, c_2 and k_2, c_3 and k_3 will be mapped to registers r_1, r_2, r_3. If we put c_1, c_2, c_3 into closures,

```
fun f(f',arg,c0,c1,c2,c3) =
   let . . .
       fun k0(t,k1,k2,k3) =
           let val u = t+k3
               val c1' = #0(k1)
               val c2' = #1(k1)
               val c3' = #2(k1)
           in k2(u,c1',c2',c3')
           end
       val k1' = (c1,c2,c3)
   in g(g',x,k0,k1',c0,y)
   end
```

there will be a lot of extra *callee-save register shuffling*. Now c_0 and y have to be moved into those callee-save register r_2 and r_3 which originally held c_2 and c_3. However, if we use a more conservative approach by putting c_0, c_1, and y into closures then this shuffling could be eliminated:

```
fun f(f',arg,c0,c1,c2,c3) =
   let . . .
      fun k0(t,k1,k2,k3) =
         let val y = #1(k1)
             val u = t+y
             val c0' = #0(k1)
             val c1' = #2(k1)
         in c0'(u,c1',k2,k3)
         end
      val k1' = (c0,y,c1)
   in g(g',x,k0,k1',c2,c3)
   end
```

Note that c_2, c_3 stay in r_2, r_3 throughout.

The previous strategy is called "conservative" because we'll at least not get worse performance than the old closure representation on those continuations that are not nested within another continuation. However, we don't get too much benefit on those nested continuation functions either. In the example in figure 10.2, continuation k is nested inside the continuation j. The set of free variables for j is $\{c_0, c_1, c_2, c_3, w, z\}$ and the set of free variables for k is $\{c_0, c_1, c_2, c_3, a\}$. Intuitively we want to put w and z in the callee-save registers because they are no longer needed when we try to set up the callee-save registers for k. If w and z are put into the closure made for j, we have to build another closure record $k2'$ for k:

```
fun f'(f'',arg,c0,c1,c2,c3) =
   let . . .
      fun j0(a,j1,j2,j3) =
         let val z' = #3(j1)
             val w' = #2(j1)
             val k2' = (a,j2)
         in h(z',k0,w',j1,k2',j3)
         end
      and k0(b,k1,k2,k3) =
         let val t2 = k2+b
             val c0' = #0(k1)
             val c1' = #1(k1)
             val c2' = #2(k1)
         in c0'(t2,c1',c2',k3)
         end
      . . .
      val u = (c0,c1,w,z)
      val g' = #0(g)
   in g'(g,y,j0,u,c2,c3)
   end
```

Therefore before we decide which free variables will be put into the closure record of the continuation function (such as j), we'll look through the free variable set of all continuation functions nested inside. Outer continuation functions (such as j) are called earlier than inner ones (such as k). So we can simply compare their free-variable sets and put those variables that are free in outer functions but not free in inner ones (such as w,z) into callee-save registers. In cases where such variables don't exist, we could use either the conservative approach or a more aggressive method.

Clearly there are many variations on this "callee-saves" closure idea, just as there are many variants for closure representation. In fact, the callee-saves technique is really just a way of putting the first level of the representation of continuation closures in registers instead of memory; the rest of the representation can be flat, linked, or anything in between.

10.8   Stack allocation of closures

Some closures have an *extent* predictable at compile time; that is, the compiler can determine when the last reference to a closure will disappear, and can explicitly deallocate the closure [83]. If the closure is allocated on the heap, in a system with copying garbage collection, then there is no advantage to deallocating it; deallocation of arbitrary records leads to fragmentation, which is otherwise avoided by a copying (compacting) collector. However, if the lifetimes of certain closures (and perhaps other records as well) are *nested* in a simple way, then those closures can be allocated on a stack. And if stack allocation/deallocation is much faster than heap allocation with garbage collection, then this is a good optimization to perform.

We will first assume that continuations do not share closures, and that *call with current continuation* is not permitted. Now, any *continuation closure* can be de-allocated as soon as it is first invoked (applied to arguments); no continuation is ever invoked more than once. Furthermore, the most recent continuation-closure created will be the first one invoked (and deallocated); this means that continuation closures can be allocated on a stack.

Furthermore, some user-function (noncontinuation) closures can also be allocated on the same stack. Consider a nonescaping function f:

```
FIX(g, [x, k], ...
    FIX([(f, v⃗, B)], ...
        ... APP(VAR f, a⃗) ... APP(VAR f, b⃗) ... APP(VAR k, [VAR r]) ...))
```

The closure for k will be at the top of the stack when g is entered. Then the closure for f can be pushed on the stack. Then f can be invoked a few times; eventually the continuation k is about to be invoked. Just at that point, it is clear that f can never again be called; for we are leaving its static scope *and* it does not escape. Thus f can be popped from the stack just before k is invoked; after k is entered it can pop itself from the stack.

The condition that f does not escape is stronger than necessary. In fact, it is sufficient that f does not *escape upward*. We say that a function *escapes downward* if it is passed as an argument to another user function, and it *escapes upward* if it is returned as the result of a function (i.e., passed as an argument of a continuation) or if it is stored into a data structure (record or **ref** cell). These properties are transitive: If f is passed into formal parameter j of function h, and j escapes upward then f is considered to escape upward.

We can use static dataflow analysis to approximate these properties. If f is passed as an argument to a known function, we can propagate the escaping properties backward from the properties of that function. If f is passed as an argument to a function variable, then we know nothing about the function that will be bound to this variable and we must assume the worst—that f escapes upward.

Now, any function f that escapes downward, or does not escape, may be stack-allocated. By the time we leave the static scope of f all functions into which it has downward escaped will have returned, and the f will never again be used.

It is interesting to note that all functions in Pascal programs escape downward (or don't escape); therefore, this analysis will successfully stack allocate *all* closures, rendering the heap necessary only for records explicitly created by the programmer. Thus, a continuation-based Pascal compiler need not rely on a garbage collector [52].

Let us now revisit the two assumptions made earlier. If two functions share a closure, it is still not difficult for the compiler to determine when the closure should be deallocated; the details are straightforward to work out.

But *call with current continuation* (`callcc`) causes big problems. Now, any continuation or downward-escaping function may have an arbitrary extent. Consider this program:

```
fun f(x) = callcc(fn k => (g := k; x))
```

which translates into (simplified):

```
FIX([(f,[x,k], PRIMOP(:=, [VAR g, VAR k],[],[
              APP(VAR k, [VAR x])]))],
    . . .)
```

Now suppose there are several continuations on the stack, and f is called. The topmost continuation k on the stack will be saved in a global reference variable, and then invoked. Normally, the invocation of a continuation causes it to be popped from the stack; but now there is still a reference to it!

If a stack is used, then `callcc` must have a more complicated implementation that moves the entire contents of the stack into the heap. The deallocations—generated by the compiler—of these closures must somehow be disabled. This means that not only are things much more complicated, but the cost of `callcc` is proportional to the height of the stack, instead of constant-time as it is in the stackless version.

To ameliorate this problem, one might copy the stack into the heap whenever it reaches some not-too-large size. Then the time taken by any `callcc` is bounded by this size. There are many variations on this theme [47], but they all complicate the runtime system in one way or another.

It is not at all clear that stack allocation is worthwhile. Garbage collection need not be particularly expensive (see Chapter 16.1), so the difference in cost between stack allocation and heap allocation is not large. Furthermore, it turns out that the very same downward-escaping closures that can be stack allocated are exactly the ones for which the *callee-save-register* optimizations reduce the number of separate heap allocations. For these reasons, we do not use a stack in the implementation of Standard ML of New Jersey; and we still get very efficient performance.

10.9   Lifting function definitions to top level

Since functions no longer contain free variables after closure conversion, their definitions may be lifted to top level. The result is a program that is just one large FIX definition, containing no internal FIX operators. Furthermore, all references to variables defined as functions by these FIX operators will be via the LABEL constructor, not the VAR constructor that is used for other variables (e.g., formal parameters of functions, results of RECORD, SELECT, and PRIMOP). This is mainly to simplify the free-variable analysis in the spill and code-generation phases, since LABELs don't need to be considered as "free" variables for most purposes.

CHAPTER ELEVEN

REGISTER SPILLING

Variables in the CPS language are intended to correspond to registers of the target machine. This is only approximately true in the phases before closure conversion, because many of the CPS variables are free variables that are really contained in closures; thus, these CPS variables correspond to memory locations. But after closure conversion, free variables are rewritten so that they are explicitly extracted from closures. Also, both the CPS optimization (constant folding and β-expansion) and the closure-conversion phase are careful never to produce any function that has more arguments than the machine has registers.

Inside a function body, however, there are variable bindings and variable uses—most of the CPS operators bind variables and take variables as arguments. Thus, at any point within a function the number of free variables may be more or less than the number of arguments to the function. Of course, at the root ("top") of the function body, the set of free variables is a subset of the formal parameters; this is a consequence of closure conversion. In all cases, we are not considering the names of functions defined by FIX operators (and referred to by the LABEL constructor) as "variables," since these are effectively constant addresses in the machine-language program, they do not need to occupy registers.

The *spill* phase of the CPS compiler comes after closure conversion; its job is to produce a CPS program obeying the rule that every subexpression has fewer than N free variables, where N is the number of registers on the target machine. In Section 13.4 it will be shown that this rule guarantees that a register can easily be found in which to generate each newly bound value. The name of the phase is chosen by analogy with conventional compilers, which "spill" the contents of registers into the stack frame (memory) when they run out of registers.

How is the bounded-register invariant accomplished? Just as in a conventional compiler, we must generate code that writes values from registers into memory, and fetches them back when needed. However, we do not have a "stack frame" in which it is convenient to write them. Instead, our only way of writing values to memory is to create records on the heap (we could also write to the mutable store, but we prefer to avoid the mutable store whenever possible).

So, when we accumulate N live (free) variables, we can create a record containing some or all of them; now we need only one variable to hold the pointer to this record. All the uses of these variables may be replaced with new variables fetched (SELECTed) from the spill record; this means that the variables stored in the record are no longer live (free in the subexpression).

A conventional register-spilling algorithm[1] has a bit more flexibility, since registers may be spilled *individually* into the stack frame. In principle, this flexibility leads to faster programs. However, on modern machines (that have many registers) spills do not occur often enough for the details of the spilling algorithm to matter much.

An example will help to illustrate. Let $N = 5$ (the maximum allowable number of free variables). The following expression selects several values from the record a and adds them together. To the left of each line is shown the set of free variables of the subexpression beginning at that line:

```
am      SELECT(0, VAR a, b,
abm     SELECT(1, VAR a, c,
abcm     SELECT(2, VAR a, d,
abcdm     SELECT(3, VAR a, e,
abcdem     SELECT(4, VAR a, f,
abcdefm     SELECT(5, VAR a, g,
bcdefgm      PRIMOP(+, [VAR b, VAR c], [h], [
defghm        PRIMOP(+, [VAR d, VAR e], [i], [
fghim          PRIMOP(+, [VAR f, VAR g], [j], [
hijm            PRIMOP(+, [VAR h, VAR i], [k], [
jkm              PRIMOP(+, [VAR k, VAR j], [l], [
lm                APP(VAR m, [VAR l])])])])])])))))))
```

After the fourth line, the number of free variables is more than N, which is impermissible. Thus, we will create a "spill record" after the third line, and fetch values from it as needed:

```
am      SELECT(0, VAR a, b,
abm     SELECT(1, VAR a, c,
abcm     SELECT(2, VAR a, d,
abcdm     RECORD([(VAR a, OFFp 0), (VAR b, OFFp 0),
                  (VAR c, OFFp 0), (VAR d, OFFp 0),
                  (VAR m, OFFp 0)], r,
abr      SELECT(3, VAR a, e,
aber      SELECT(4, VAR a, f,
abefr      SELECT(5, VAR a, g,
befgr       SELECT(2, VAR r, c',
bcefgr       PRIMOP(+, [VAR b, VAR c'], [h], [
efghr         SELECT(3, VAR r, d',
defgh          PRIMOP(+, [VAR d', VAR e], [i], [
fghir           PRIMOP(+, [VAR f, VAR g], [j], [
hijr             PRIMOP(+, [VAR h, VAR i], [k], [
jkr               PRIMOP(+, [VAR k, VAR j], [l], [
lr                 SELECT(4, VAR r, m',
lm                  APP(VAR m', [VAR l])])])])])])))))))))
```

All free variables are spilled into the record r. Then, for example, when d is needed later, it is SELECTed into the new variable d', which is used in place of d (to avoid duplicate variable bindings). The treatment of a and b deserves explanation. A naive approach would be to fetch a from r each time it is needed. But our spilling algorithm realizes that using a directly, though it increases the number of free variables of the subexpression starting right after the RECORD operation, does not increase this number above N. So it uses the original value of a, and similarly for b, thus saving several fetches. In fact, there is no need to write a and b to the record at all, but our one-pass algorithm is not smart enough to realize that.

Unfortunately, the resulting expression still has six free variables at one point, which is greater than N (in this example). Thus, another spill record must be created:

```
am      SELECT(0, VAR a, b,
abm     SELECT(1, VAR a, c,
abcm    SELECT(2, VAR a, d,
abcdm     RECORD([(VAR a, OFFp 0), (VAR b, OFFp 0),
                  (VAR c, OFFp 0), (VAR d, OFFp 0),
                  (VAR m, OFFp 0)], r,
abr       SELECT(3, VAR a, e,
aber        SELECT(4, VAR a, f,
abefr         SELECT(5, VAR a, g,
befgr           RECORD([(VAR b, OFFp 0), (VAR e, OFFp 0),
                        (VAR f, OFFp 0), (VAR g, OFFp 0),
                        (VAR r, SELp(2,OFFp 0)),
                        (VAR r, SELp(3,OFFp 0)),
                        (VAR r, SELp(4,OFFp 0))], s,
befs              SELECT(4, VAR s, c',
bcefs               PRIMOP(+, [VAR b, VAR c'], [h], [
efhs                  SELECT(5, VAR s, d',
defhs                   PRIMOP(+, [VAR d', VAR e], [i], [
fhis                      SELECT(3, VAR s, g',
fghis                       PRIMOP(+, [VAR f, VAR g'], [j], [
hijs                          PRIMOP(+, [VAR h, VAR i], [k], [
jks                             PRIMOP(+, [VAR k, VAR j], [l], [
ls                                SELECT(6, VAR s, m',
lm                                  APP(VAR m', [VAR l])
                    )])])])))])])))))))))))
```

Now there are never more than five free variables at any point. Although it was not so illustrated, our spilling algorithm would actually introduce both of the spill records in one pass through the expression.

Note that our spilling algorithm maintains at most one spill record at a time. When the spill record s is created, all the values from r are copied into it. Of course, in an expression with a huge number M of free variables, the time spent in copying spill records will be quadratic in M. One could imagine having several spill records live at the same time; or making the record r a component of s so there was a linked list of spill records. Then spill-record creation would be efficient, but to look up all the variables would take quadratic time. By structuring large spill records as trees, however, it is possible to spill (and refetch) M variables in arbitrary order in only $\log_N(M)$. Such elaborations have not proven necessary, for reasons discussed below.

The copying of r into s is expressed using the "access path" notation (SELp and OFFp) of the CPS. There is an important reason for this. The CPS notation allows for the creation of arbitrarily large records. A single record can have $M > N$ fields, each of which is a different variable. Without the path notation in record fields, there is absolutely no way to rewrite the record expression so it has fewer than M free variables. With the path notation, one can make a record containing N different values, then make another record, copying the N values from the first record and including $N - 1$ more values, and with approximately M/N RECORD operators, create the large record.

11.1   Rearranging the expression

The astute reader will have noticed that there is no need to spill variables in the example given; a simple rearrangement of the expression will suffice:

```
am    SELECT(0, VAR a, b,
abm    SELECT(1, VAR a, c,
abcm    PRIMOP(+, [VAR b, VAR c], [h], [
ahm      SELECT(2, VAR a, d,
adhm      SELECT(3, VAR a, e,
adehm      PRIMOP(+, [VAR d, VAR e], [i], [
ahim        PRIMOP(+, [VAR h, VAR i], [k], [
akm          SELECT(4, VAR a, f,
afkm          SELECT(5, VAR a, g,
afgkm          PRIMOP(+, [VAR f, VAR g], [j], [
akjm            PRIMOP(+, [VAR k, VAR j], [l], [
lm                APP(VAR m, [VAR l])])])])))])])))])))
```

Unfortunately, the problem of reordering directed acyclic graphs for optimal register allocation is NP-complete [78]. That does not rule out an implementation of some good heuristics that might in many cases avoid the need to create spill records. But our measurements have shown this to be unnecessary, as discussed below.

11.2   The spilling algorithm

Since the spill phase is applied after the closure-conversion phase, all function definitions are at top level, never nested. The spill algorithm is applied to the body of each function, and will never encounter a FIX operator.

The function $\mathcal{F}$ implements spilling. It takes several arguments describing an expression e and its context, and returns an expression e' that uses no more than N free variables in the context. The context has several parts:

- The results R bound by the immediately previous operator. This is a set of variables; given that each operator binds no more than one variable, R has cardinality 0 or 1.

- The current spill record, if any. Initially (at the top of a function) there is no spill record; one is created when the free-variable count is about to exceed N. The spill record S consists of the set S_c of variables contained in the the the spill record, and the variable S_v that names the record.

- The uniquely bound variables U. These are variables possibly free in the subexpression e, but which are not in the current spill record, if any. It must be that $|U| \leq N$, and if $S_c \neq \phi$ then $|U| < N$ to allow a register to hold the pointer to the spill record.

- The duplicate variables D. These are variables "still in registers" that are also contained in the spill record. D can be any subset of S_c such that $|D| + |U| \leq N$, and if $S_c \neq \phi$ then $|D| + |U| < N$.

So, here is the function $\mathcal{F}(R, U, D, S_c, S_v, e)$:

The expression e may use some values, bind some variables, and possibly continue with the evaluation of a subexpression.

- Let A be the set of arguments—variables used as operands of the "root" (the first operator) of e,

- let W be the set of variables bound by the root operator of e,

- and let C be the set of continuation expressions with which the root of e might continue.

These are straightforward to compute; note that for some primops W is empty, for APP nodes C is empty, and so on.

We now compute the sets V_{before} of variables free in the expression e, and V_{after} of variables free right after the root operator of e has executed. That is,

$$
\begin{aligned}
V_{\text{before}} &= \text{fv}(e) \\
V_{\text{after}} &= \bigcup_{c \in C} \text{fv}(c)
\end{aligned}
$$

Let $S_{\text{before}} = \{S_v\}$ if there is a spill record ($S_c \neq \phi$), and $S_{\text{before}} = \phi$ otherwise.

If there is a spill record, we decide whether it will still be useful after the root operation. If $S_c \cap V_{\text{after}} = \phi$, then the spill record contains no useful variables after the operation, and can then be discarded. Let S_v^{after} be the empty set if no spill record is required after the operation (or if none is present before), and $S_v^{\text{after}} = \{S_v\}$ otherwise; similarly for S_c^{after}.

We now calculate the number of registers available to hold duplicate variables (those also present in the spill record) before the operation:

$$N_{\text{dup}} = N - |S_{\text{before}}| - |(U \cap V_{\text{before}}) \cup R|$$

This requires some explanation. We have N registers, of which one may be holding the pointer to the spill record. Some of the other registers may be holding unique values (those that can't be refetched from the spill record) that are still live (free in e). Furthermore, the previous operation may have produced a result and bound it to a variable. Even if this variable is not live, we must reserve a register for it; on many machines, when an instruction is executed the result must be put somewhere![1] Now, any remaining registers can hold duplicate values; presumably the duplicate values are already sitting in registers. If $N_{\text{dup}} < |D|$, then we must discard one of the duplicates. Presumably, the previous operator has produced a value in some register that must overwrite a duplicate value; we have delayed until now the decision about which value to discard.

So, we calculate some maximal set D' such that $D' \subset D$ and $|D'| \leq N_{\text{dup}}$. We choose to discard that member of D that is first used most distantly; that is, whose first use is most deeply nested within the expression e. Of course, we start by discarding those elements of D that are not used at all, that is, we start with $D \cap V_{\text{before}}$.

Next, we calculate whether it is time to make a new spill record. If

$$|A \cup (U \cap V_{\text{after}})| > N - |S_v^{\text{after}}|$$

we must spill because we cannot simultaneously hold all of the arguments to the current operator and all the irreplaceable values (those that are live after the operation but not in the spill record). Or, if

$$|W \cup (U \cap V_{\text{after}})| > N - |S_v^{\text{after}}|$$

we must spill because there is not room to hold both the results of the current operation and the irreplaceable values needed afterward.

If a spill is necessary, the new contents of the spill record will be V_{before}. We create a new variable name S_v' to denote the new spill record. We calculate the new duplicates $D'' = (U \cup D') \cap V_{\text{before}}$, that is, that subset of the new contents that is currently in registers. Then the result of $\mathcal{F}$ is

$$\begin{aligned}
\mathcal{F}(R, U, D, S_c, S_v, e) = {} \\
\texttt{RECORD}(\text{get}(V_{\text{before}}), S_v', \mathcal{F}(\phi, \phi, D'', V_{\text{before}}, S_v', e)).
\end{aligned}$$

The function **get** makes a list of record fields out of the variables of V_{before}; for each variable in D' or U it makes a field of the form $(v, \texttt{OFFp}\ 0)$, and for the other

---

[1] Needless to say, this subtle point was not at first appreciated by the author.

variables in S_c it makes a field of the form $(S_v, \text{SELp}(i, \text{OFFp } 0))$. The recursive call to $\mathcal{F}$ is guaranteed not to spill at the root, because its parameter U is empty; there can be at most one spill per operator in the expression e.

If no spill is necessary, it may still be necessary to fetch some variables from the current spill record if they are operands of the root operator and not already in registers. Let $F = A - (U \cup D')$ be the set of variables that must be fetched back from the spill record. Then there are three cases: $|F| = 0$, $|F| = 1$, and $|F| > 1$. In the first case, no fetching is necessary, and we have

$$\mathcal{F}(R, U, D, S_c, S_v, e) =$$
$$\text{root}_e(A, W, \{\mathcal{F}(W, U \cap V_{\text{after}}, D', S_c^{\text{after}}, S_v^{\text{after}}, c) : c \in C\})$$

where root_e is the root operator of e applied to the given arguments, result variables, and continuation expressions. (This is perhaps an abuse of notation, since root_e should take lists not sets: It would probably like to know in what order the operands appear!)

If $|F| = 1$, then we must fetch; but there is also the possibility that this is the very last fetch from this spill record, and we can now discard it: $S_c^{\text{after}} = \phi$ in this case. Then

$$\mathcal{F}(R, U, D, S_c, S_v, e) =$$
$$\text{SELECT}(i, S_v, v', \mathcal{F}(\phi, U \cap V_{\text{before}}, D' \cup \{v'\}, S_c^{\text{after}}, S_v^{\text{after}}, e\{v \mapsto v'\}))$$

Finally, if $|F| > 1$, we cannot use S_c^{after}, because we still must fetch from S_c before evaluating the root operator. We have in this case

$$\mathcal{F}(R, U, D, S_c, S_v, e) =$$
$$\text{SELECT}(i, S_v, v', \mathcal{F}(\phi, U \cap V_{\text{before}}, D' \cup \{v'\}, S_c, S_v, e\{v \mapsto v'\}))$$

If all this seems tricky, that's because—unfortunately—it is. The program was difficult to get right. Fortunately, the simplicity of the CPS interface between the closure-conversion phase and the spill phase, and between the spill phase and the next phase, mean that once the spill phase is right, it can be left alone.

Spills are rare. On a modern machine with 32 registers, perhaps 10 of them are reserved for special uses, leaving $N = 22$ "general-purpose" registers. When N is this large, one can expect about one spill for every several thousand lines of code compiled. The rarity of spills is not a phenomenon peculiar to ML; it is also noted in conventional C compilers [40]. Furthermore, in Standard ML the places where there tend to be huge numbers of free variables—causing spills—are at structure-creation time. Since structures are static objects, evaluated once per program, the effect of spills on execution time is trivial indeed. This means that the fancier heuristics mentioned earlier in this chapter are unnecessary.

Our spiller operates in one pass. This is almost obvious from our description of the recursive, top-down algorithm. There are certain aspects of our presentation— such as the renaming of variables within the subexpression e when fetching is required—that appear to require separate traversals of subexpressions. However, in the actual implementation these are computed on the fly.

Though it is a one-pass algorithm, it is still rather expensive. It is much faster to check a function body to see if it ever requires more than N free variables than it is to execute the spill transformation. Since spills are rare, we check each function body first, and apply the spill function $\mathcal{F}$ only if necessary.

CHAPTER TWELVE

SPACE COMPLEXITY

When writing a program, one often wants to calculate its efficiency. The tools of asymptotic complexity analysis allow us to reason about the time complexity and space complexity of programs as a function of the size of their inputs. This kind of reasoning is easier in some languages than others, however. Perhaps in languages with lazy evaluation—where the compiler attempts to shield the programmer from the knowledge of exactly which parts of the program are evaluated—reasoning about time complexity may be particularly difficult [91]. However, most nonlazy (call-by-value) languages (Algol, Scheme, ML, etc.) pose relatively well-defined problems for those who wish to analyze time complexity.

Let us consider space complexity: For a program P running on input N, what is the maximum memory required at any time, as a function of N (ignoring constant factors)? In a language without automatic garbage collection, this is also a relatively well-defined question. But the presence of a garbage collector complicates the issue, since the purpose of the collector is to relieve the programmer from any analysis of when memory is reclaimed. We cannot simply count the number of allocations since the beginning of the program and say that that represents the memory required, since many of the allocated cells will have been collected. A useful measure of space complexity must include reasoning about the behavior of the collector.

It turns out that there are few, if any, language definitions that adequately address this issue—that provide enough useful axioms to characterize the asymptotic space complexity of programs. Most typical is a statement that some subset of the inaccessible data will be reclaimed:

> *No Scheme object is ever destroyed. The reason that implementations of Scheme do not (usually!) run out of storage is that they are permitted to reclaim the storage occupied by an object if they can prove that the object cannot possibly matter to any future computation.* (Scheme [69])

> *There are no rules concerning disposal of inaccessible addresses ("garbage collection"). (Standard ML [65])*

> *A member of a traced reference type is traced by the garbage collector; that is, the implementation stores its referent in a system-managed*

133

storage pool, determines at runtime when all traced references to it are gone, and then reclaims its storage. (Modula-3 [27])

What remains unsaid is mostly left so intentionally....
(Oberon [96], in which garbage collection is left unspecified.)

Of the language reference manuals quoted above, the first two include a formal definition and the last two do not. But none of them give sufficient rules for reasoning about the space complexity of programs.

The Scheme report adds a mysterious injunction about tail recursion:

Implementations of Scheme are required to be properly tail recursive. This allows the execution of an iterative computation in constant space, even if the iterative computation is described by a syntactically recursive procedure [69].

However, the denotational semantics of Scheme in the same report does not attempt to express this rule formally.

Let us now consider a simple program P:

```
fun s(0) = nil | s(i) = 0 :: s(i-1)

fun f(n,x) =
   let val z = length(x)
       fun g() = f(n-1,s(N))
   in if n=0 then 0 else g()
   end


val result = f(N,nil)
```

What is the space complexity of this program? Each call to g computes a list of length N that is passed as an argument to f; the function f then calls g, perhaps discarding this list. There are clearly N recursive calls of g.

Consider a "naive" implementation. In the Nth call to g, there are N calls to f suspended, waiting for subroutines to return. Each of these activations of f has a different copy of the list x. Therefore, there are N^2 list cells active at the same time, for a space complexity of $\Theta(N^2)$.

There are two different ways that an implementation might be more clever. One might notice that when f calls g, it is a "tail call," so the activation record for f can be discarded before entry into g. This is a more general case of the "tail recursion" that the Scheme report alludes to [69]. In that case, only one version of x will ever be live at any time, so the space complexity is $\Theta(N)$.

On the other hand, an implementation might not bother with tail call optimization, but might notice that x is not live in f after the call to g. Then the garbage collector, when invoked while several activations of f are suspended, can reclaim the storage for all instantiations of x in suspended activations of f. (This is done in the Göteborg Lazy-ML compiler [17], which also performs tail-recursion optimizations.) Then the space complexity is also $\Theta(N)$.

Let us adjust the example very slightly, and make f non-tail recursive:

```
fun s(0) = nil | s(i) = 0 :: s(i-1)

fun f(n,x) =
    let val z = length(x)
        fun g() = f(n-1,s(N))
    in if n=0 then 0 else g()+1
    end

val result = f(N,nil)
```

When f calls g, g must return back to f so 1 can be added. For this program P', the naive compiler still uses space $\Theta(N^2)$. So does the compiler that optimizes tail calls, because the call to g is no longer a tail call. However, the compiler that analyzes the liveness of variables after procedure calls may still use only $O(N)$ space.

Let us consider a third program Q:

```
fun h(n) = if n=0 then 1 else h(n-1)

val result = h(N)
```

For this simple example, liveness analysis does not help—an implementation without tail-call optimization will take $\Theta(N)$ space, but an implementation with tail-call optimizations will take $\Theta(1)$ space.

Thus, both liveness analysis and tail-call optimizations are necessary for optimal memory consumption. To make it easier for programmers to calculate the asymptotic memory consumption of their programs—independently of any particular implementation— it is useful to formalize these notions. It turns out that one of the simplest ways to formalize both notions is using continuation-passing style:

- A variable is *statically live* after a procedure call if and only if, in the CPS representation of the program, it is *free* in the continuation passed to the call. An implementation can ensure that the representation (closure) of a function or continuation f contains pointers only to the free variables of f.

- A program compiled using CPS is fully tail recursive if its CPS representation is reduced to η-normal form before evaluation. This is reached by performing all η-reductions, that is, replacing all expressions of the form $\lambda x.f(x)$ by f (see Section 6.2).

Another advantage of continuation-passing style for reasoning about garbage collection is that there is no "runtime stack" of activation records. Only the local variables of the current procedure (the procedure executing when the collector is invoked) are "roots" of garbage collection. Variables that, in conventional compilation, would be in activation records of "suspended" procedures are, in the CPS version, free variables of continuation closures. But the continuation closures are just ordinary records reachable from the local variables of the current procedure.

Thus, the compiler, the collector, and the programmer can characterize more precisely which storage must be preserved.

This is true even for CPS compilers that use stack allocation for continuation closures. Such compilers [83, 54] use compile-time analysis to see which closures have a sufficiently predictable extent that they can be allocated on a stack and deallocated explicitly. These closures must certainly be considered "live" by the garbage collector; but the point is that this compile-time analysis will stack allocate only those closures that the garbage collector would have preserved anyway.

12.1   Axioms for analyzing space

We have asserted that the free-variable rule and the η-normal-form rule are useful for programmers to use in estimating the memory usage of their programs. Let us now state the rules of memory usage:

- If a record value is reachable, then all of its components are reachable.

- If a constructed (datatype) value is reachable, then the value it carries is reachable.

- If a function value is reachable, then all of its free variables are reachable. The free variables of a recursive function include all of the free variables of function defined in the same mutually recursive definition (`val rec`).

- If an array or ref is reachable, then so are all of its components.

- Each reachable record, constructed value, function value, or number takes one unit of storage. Each array or string value takes storage equal to the number of elements or characters.

- Upon entry to a function $f(\vec{x})$, the value f is reachable, and the variables of $\vec{x}$—one of which may be the "continuation" —are reachable.

- Values not reachable by the above rules are unreachable.

- Memory usage is proportional to the number of distinct reachable values.

There are two approaches a programmer might use in calculating the variables free in the continuation. The first, obviously, is to learn the basics of continuation-passing style—a well-founded, precise, and not-too-complicated notion—and to understand how her program will look after conversion into CPS. The second is to have an idea that it means "values needed after the function call." In general, these are variables mentioned in the text of the calling function after the function-call subexpression, but with the exception that if the function call occurs within one branch of a `case` or `if`, the other branches need not be considered. If the programming language has a loop construct, then things are a bit more complicated, but not terribly so.

It may seem a bit severe to require "ordinary programmers" to know about continuations. But at least we now have a precise definition to use in calculating space usage; programmers can use the "rough-and-ready" rule most of the time. In the same way, the "ordinary programmer" does not usually refer directly to *The Definition of Standard ML* [65] to clarify a semantic point, but it's available when necessary.

What do we mean by "distinct reachable values?" Two values are distinct if the program can tell them apart by some sequence of operations. In most languages, two structured (record) values created at different times are always distinct, since they can be distinguished by "pointer equality." In ML, there is no "pointer equality": two values of a structured type are equal if their components are equal, and cannot be distinguished in any way. Thus we might say that they are not "distinct reachable values."

But all implementations of ML known to the author keep separate copies of "equal" records if they are (re-)created at different times. This means that the definition of "distinct" value given in the previous paragraph will not realistically characterize the space-consumption behavior of ML implementations.

There are two solutions to this problem: One is to give a different definition of "distinct," so values created at different times are considered distinct; this can be done formally by augmenting the semantics of the language to put a unique counter value into each record. The other is to implement an ML garbage collector that does "hash consing"—that identifies indistinguishable records (using a hash table) so only one copy is kept. This hashing approach is consistent with the semantics of the language, and combined with modern techniques of generational garbage collection (i.e., to hash-cons only the older generations) might even be efficient.

Rather than prescribe one of these solutions, we will note that all of the theorems alluded to in the subsequent discussion can be proved in either model.

12.2   Preserving space complexity

For programmers wishing to understand how much memory is being used, continuation-passing style might or might not be the best approach. But for an optimizing compiler, continuation-passing style is a concise and easily manipulable representation that quite precisely characterizes liveness properties for garbage collection. The optimizer can preserve the correct asymptotic space complexity of programs without even realizing that it is doing so. All we need to do is prove that the transformations used are *conservative*: that they preserve asymptotic upper bounds on space complexity.

We can prove these properties using the denotational semantics of the CPS augmented with a "space-usage counter." The proofs are quite technical; they require few, if any, brilliant insights, and many arguments about reductions, free variables, environments, contexts, and so on. In this chapter we will argue informally about these program transformations rather than proving their properties formally.

β-reduction

Let us first consider β-reduction. We have a CPS expression P_1 of the form

$$\text{FIX}([\ldots,(f,\vec{v},B),\ldots],\ldots\text{APP}(\text{VAR } f,\ \vec{a})\ldots)$$

Now, we replace the function application by the body of the function, substituting the actual parameters for the formal parameters, yielding P_2:

$$\text{FIX}([\ldots,(f,\vec{v},B),\ldots],\ldots B\{\vec{v}\mapsto\vec{a}\}\ldots)$$

We must argue that if some value x is reachable at any time during the execution of P_2, then it is also reachable at the corresponding time in P_1. Clearly this is true up to the time when execution reaches the APP node (or the substituted body of B, respectively). (The converse is not true, because f is free (and therefore reachable) in some subexpressions of P_1 whereas it might not be free in the corresponding subexpressions of P_2.) At the subexpression $B\{\vec{v}\mapsto\vec{a}\}$ in P_2 the reachable variables are precisely those reachable from the free variables of the current subexpression:

$$\text{fv}(B\{\vec{v}\mapsto\vec{a}\})$$

This is equivalent to

$$(\text{fv}(B)-\vec{v})\cup\text{fv}(\vec{a})$$

The reachable variables of the APP expression are just those reachable from the free variables of that expression:

$$\text{fv}(\text{APP}(\text{VAR } f,\ \vec{a}))=\{f\}\cup\text{fv}(\vec{a})$$

Now, the variables reachable from f are, by definition, the free variables of f; these are the variables free in the body but not including the formal parameters: $\text{fv}(f)=\text{fv}(B)-\vec{v}$. Thus the variables free at the APP node include

$$\{f\}\cup(\text{fv}(B)-\vec{v})\cup\text{fv}(\vec{a}).$$

This is a superset of the variables free at the corresponding point in P_2 (the closure for f is reachable in P_1 whereas perhaps it is not reachable in P_2), and thus this transformation is conservative.

Dead-variable elimination

Now consider dead-variable elimination. Each binding rule of the CPS has its own dead-variable-elimination transformation rule; we will consider just a couple of simple ones:

$$\text{FIX}([(f,\vec{v},B)],E)\ \rightarrow\ E\quad\text{if } f\notin\text{fv}(E)$$
$$\text{SELECT}(i,v,w,E)\ \rightarrow\ E\quad\text{if } w\notin\text{fv}(E)$$

In either case, the free variables of the right-hand side are (at any point in the program) a subset of the free variables of the left-hand side, and therefore the same must hold for the reachable values.

Elimination of unused arguments of known functions is very similar to dead-variable elimination, and can similarly be shown to be conservative. Flattening of a single record argument into several separate arguments is conservative: Essentially, the operators that SELECT from the record are moved from the interior of the function to just before the call, so the record selected from may be "less reachable" after the optimization, and no value will be "more reachable."

Constant folding

Constant folding of SELECT operations is conservative. Consider

$$\text{SELECT}(i, v, w, E)$$

where v is statically bound by a RECORD operator. The variable w is live (after the optimization) only where v or w was live before the optimization; but if v is live, then w is reachable (it is a component of the record). Thus the reachability of the value w is not changed. However, the liveness (and therefore reachability) of the record v will either decrease or stay the same.

Spilling

Register spilling (see Chapter 11) is conservative. Records introduced by the spiller have bounded extent—they must disappear before the next procedure call, and in the CPS each procedure is like an extended basic block without loops. Even though the spill record may keep some values reachable beyond the point where they are dead in the untransformed program, it can do so during the creation of only a bounded number of new values; so the space complexity is increased by at most a constant increment.

Common-subexpression elimination

General common-subexpression elimination is not conservative of space complexity. Consider the program

```
fun s(0) = nil | s(i) = 0 :: s(i-1)

fun f(n) = if n=0 then 0
           else let val x = s(N)
                    val y = f(n-1)
                    val z = s(N)
                in y+length(z)
                end

val result = f(N)
```

The space complexity of this program is N, because at most one list of length N will be live at one time. But if the common subexpression is eliminated, we have

```
fun f(n) = if n=0 then 0
           else let val x = s(N)
                    val y = f(n-1)
                    val z = x
                in y+length(z)
                end
```

and now, at the most deeply nested recursive call, there will be N copies of the list still reachable.

If we look at this program in (mostly) continuation-passing style, however, the common subexpression is not as obvious:

```
fun s(i,c) = if i=0 then c(nil)
                    else let fun c'(a) = c(0::a)
                         in s(i-1,c')
                         end


fun f(n,k) =
    if n=0 then k(0)
    else let fun c1(x) =
                 let fun c2(y) =
                     let fun c3(z) = c(y+length(z))
                     in s(N,c3)
                     end
                 in f(n-1,c2)
                 end
         in s(N,c1)
         end
```

Here the two calls to s have different continuations, and are not really common subexpressions; so the "duplicate" expression will not be eliminated, and the blowup is cleverly avoided. Of course, this is more a commentary on the stupidity of the CSE optimization in CPS than on its cleverness.

If we consider the simpler CSE optimization—as we have implemented it—on CPS programs, we find that it is conservative. We consider two cases (others are similar); the first is a common SELECT expression:

$$\text{SELECT}(i, v, w, \ldots \text{SELECT}(i, v, x, E) \ldots) \;\rightarrow\; \text{SELECT}(i, v, w, \ldots E\{x \mapsto w\} \ldots)$$

Even though the liveness of the variable w may increase, the reachability of the value it points to cannot, since v (which contains it) was live over the entire range between the binding of w and the binding of x. On the other hand, the record v is now perhaps less live (and certainly no more live) than it was, and therefore perhaps less reachable.

Now consider a common RECORD expression:

$$\text{RECORD}(\vec{f}, w, \ldots \text{RECORD}(\vec{f}, x, E) \ldots) \;\rightarrow\; \text{RECORD}(\vec{f}, w, \ldots E\{x \mapsto w\} \ldots)$$

In the new program, the record w is live for a possibly longer period; it might have been dead at some time between the binding of w and that of x. Thus, at such a point, the absolute number of reachable values will be higher in the new program than the old.

Though this transformation might increase the absolute space complexity of the program, it cannot increase the asymptotic complexity. To see this, we ask: How many instances of w can exist simultaneously? Each time the RECORD operator is executed, another instance is created. Each previous instance, if it is still reachable, must be contained in a closure somewhere; and each closure can contain at most one instance of w. Therefore, the space complexity can increase by at most one unit per closure. Since the number of closures is no more than the number of memory units allocated, the space complexity cannot grow by more than a factor of two. But this is, of course, a constant factor—thus, each instance of a RECORD CSE transformation will increase space complexity by at most a constant factor. Thus, any sequence of K such transformations will only increase space complexity by at most 2^K. And since the number of transformations is a computable function g of the size S of the program (since the optimizer always halts), the increase in space complexity can be at most $2^{g(S)}$. But since S is independent of the size of the input to the program, the asymptotic space complexity is not changed.

In practice, of course, we expect that this transformation will not increase space complexity by any large amount, and will save enough time to be worthwhile; if that turns out not to be the case, we could always disable the optimization.

Hoisting

A *hoisting* transformation is one that interchanges the order of variable bindings in a continuation-passing style program. For example, if $\{f, \vec{x}\} \cap \mathrm{fv}(C) = \phi$ then

$$\mathtt{FIX}([(f, \vec{x}, B)], \mathtt{FIX}([(g, \vec{y}, C)], E)) \; \rightarrow \; \mathtt{FIX}([(g, \vec{y}, C)], \mathtt{FIX}([(f, \vec{x}, B)], E))$$

Hoisting transformations have no effect on asymptotic space complexity. In this case (the interchange of two function definitions), the closure for f has exactly the same free variables that it had before the transformation, and similarly for g, so reachability is unaffected. Similar arguments can be made for other hoisting transformations.

The only dangerous hoisting transformations are those that pull bindings out of function bodies, since these change the free-variable sets—and therefore the size of closures—of functions. Here there is a strong analogy with common-subexpression elimination: It is all right to hoist small operations (individual record creations) out of functions, but not large ones (function calls that create large data structures). And, just as with CSE, the CPS representation is a bit "too stupid" to hoist large operations.

12.3   Closure representations

The good news so far has been that many of the interesting transformations and partial evaluations of continuation-passing-style programs do not increase space complexity. However, the choice of closure representations can have a great effect.

Flat closures

Thus far in the analysis of space complexity, we have assumed that each function closure is like a record that holds only the free variables needed by the function—we call this a "flat" representation; it was used in Cardelli's ML compiler [26].

A disadvantage of the flat representation is that variables can be copied many times from one closure to another. Consider

```
fun f(u,v,w,x,y,z) =
 let fun g() =
     let fun h() =
        let fun i() =
           let fun j() = u+v+w+x+y+z
             in j
           end
         in i
       end
     in h
   end
 in g
end
```

Each of the variables u, v, w, x, y, z must be copied from the arguments of f into the closure of g, and from there into the closure for h, and then into the closures of i and j. This can be quite expensive; to avoid this problem the method of *linked* closures [57] is usually used instead.

Linked closures

With linked closures, the closure of each function h is a record containing

- the values of all variables free in h but not free in the statically enclosing function g, and

- a pointer to the closure for g.

The variables free in h but not in g are, of course, a subset of the parameters and locals of h; some implementations put all of these variables in the closure, which is unnecessary.

It is easy to see that linked closures may save a lot of copying. In the example above, the closure for g is large (containing u, v, w, x, y, z); but the closure for h

contains just a pointer to g's closure, and i's closure contains just a pointer to h's, and so on. Of course, when j tries to access its free variables, lots of pointer traversal may be necessary.

Another advantage of linked closures is that side-effectable variables must not be copied; linked closures never create more than one copy of a variable. This advantage does not pertain to implementations of ML, where variables are immutable; and in implementations of languages such as Scheme, a simple compile-time analysis can identify which variables are side effected and handle them using a pointer to a memory cell [55]—the pointer can be copied as necessary.

Using linked instead of flat closures can lead to an increase in asymptotic space complexity. Consider this program:

```
fun s(0) = nil | s(i) = 0 :: s(i-1)

fun f() = let val x = s(N)
              fun g() = let val z = length(x)
                            fun h() = z
                        in h
                        end
          in g
          end

fun t(0) = nil
  | t(i) = f()() :: t(i-1)

val result = t(N)
```

With flat closures, each evaluation of $f()()$ yields a closure for h that contains just an integer z. With linked closures, each closure for h contains a pointer to the closure for g, which contains a list x of size N. Since this program keeps N closures for h simultaneously, the complexity with linked closures is N^2.

In contrast, the asymptotic complexity of flat closures can never be greater than that of linked closures. Even though the individual closure records in a flat implementation may be larger than those in a linked implementation, the increase in size (i.e., extra pointers to free variables) is a factor related only to the size of the program, not to the size of the input.

Merged closures

Another strategy used by the Standard ML of New Jersey compiler is *merging of closures*. When two functions are adjacent (or can be made adjacent by hoisting), and have consistent sets of free variables, then both functions can share the same closure record.

The compiler arranges for all the functions defined in the same mutually recursive definition to share the same closure (see sections 8.1 and 10.2). When a mutually recursive definition A is nested directly inside another mutually recursive definition B, then A and B can be merged into one mutually recursive definition. The same is true if A is inside the body of one of the functions defined by B, as long as none of the free variables of A are bound by B.

Unfortunately, closure sharing can increase the asymptotic complexity of programs. Consider the program:

```
fun s(0) = nil | s(i) = 0 :: s(i-1)

fun f() = let val x = s(N)
              fun g() = let val z = length(x)
              fun h() = 0
          in h
          end

fun t(0) = nil
  | t(i) = f() :: t(i-1)

val result = t(N)
```

With the closure-sharing "optimization," the function f looks like:

```
fun f() = let val x = s(N)
              fun g() = let val z = length(x)
              and h() = 0
          in g
          end
```

When the closures for g and h are shared, the closure for h is saddled with the value x, which it does not need. The result is N^2 space consumption instead of N.

The danger of linked or merged closures—that some programs will use far too much space, without the programmer being able to figure out why—is a very serious disadvantage. Unless there is a counterbalancing advantage—which there isn't, as our measurements in Chapter 15 show—linked and merged closures *should not be used*. This does not apply to functions written as mutually recursive by the programmer, however, which must have some sort of interlinked or merged closures in any implementation.

12.4   When to initiate garbage collection

Though we have given the definition of "reachable values" (Section 12.1) we have not explained how the garbage collector implements this definition. Starting with some "root set" of variables, the collector traverses all values reachable from those variables, reclaiming the storage of the unreachable values. But what is the "root set?" The definition of reachable values states the base case of the induction:

- Upon entry to a function $f(x)$, the value f is reachable, and the values $\vec{x}$ are reachable.

In continuation-passing style, this is sufficient, since the function f can allocate only a finite number of records and closures before entering another function; so we don't need a definition of the reachable variables during the execution of a function.

This definition implies that it is permissible to invoke the collector only at the beginning of a function, and indeed, that is what Standard ML of New Jersey does. In the CPS representation (after the spill phase), each variable will correspond to a machine register; the collector can just use the registers as roots of the reachable graph. At the beginning of each function, a test can be made for exhaustion of the free space, and the garbage collector can be conditionally invoked.

There is a minor problem, however. Suppose some function f, rarely invoked, uses register r; but the other functions of the program do not. Then if the garbage collector is invoked in some other function g, the register r is reachable even though the computation no longer has any use for it. The data preserved by the collector will be a superset of the reachable data.

This cannot affect the asymptotic space complexity of the program. If there is a finite number K of registers, then at worst the space complexity will worsen by a factor of K, which is a constant. (The argument is quite simple and won't be expounded here.)

However, factors of K are to be avoided where possible. Standard ML of New Jersey uses a descriptor associated with each function, telling the collector which registers are live; so the collector can implement the definition of Section 12.1 more faithfully.

The garbage collector cannot be run on every function call—that would waste too much time. Thus, at any point there will be unreachable records that occupy memory. The following rule will lead to the right asymptotic behavior, for any constant $R > 1$:

- When current memory use is more than R times the amount of reachable data preserved by the previous garbage collection, start a new garbage collection.

Then the maximum memory usage will be at most R times the maximum amount of reachable data, and asymptotic space complexity will be conserved.

CHAPTER THIRTEEN

THE ABSTRACT MACHINE

After the spill phase, a CPS expression is in a form where it is very easy to translate into machine code for a conventional, von Neumann machine. It is useful to define an abstract machine that generalizes the notion of von Neumann machine; we can translate CPS into *abstract-continuation-machine* instructions and then translate the abstract-machine instructions into the machine code of a particular concrete machine.

The abstract machine has a *state* comprising several parts: memory, integer registers, floating-point registers, and a program counter. Thus, it is similar to most modern machines, and this similarity is intentional. The abstract-machine *program* is a linear sequence of instructions, labels, and literal data; it is essentially an assembly-language program.

13.1 Compilation units

A *compilation unit* is a program that is parsed in one batch, translated and optimized in one batch, and then turned into one contiguous piece of target-machine code. A compilation unit can be as small as a single `val` declaration or function, or as large as a group of several modules. Typically it is a single module.

A compilation unit in the source language may make free references to variables declared in previous compilation units. For the convenience of the CPS optimizer, and of the target-machine code generator, it is desirable that all compilation units be *closed*, that is, make no free references to variables bound elsewhere.

Each compilation unit makes some of its variables available for reference from other compilation units. For example, in the two compilation units

```
structure S : sig  val x : int  val z : int  end
 = struct val z = 4   and y = 3  and x = 2  end;

local fun f(x) = x+x
  in fun g(y) = y*f(S.z)
     fun h() = g(0)
  end;
```

147

the first compilation unit "exports" only the lambda-language variable S, which is a record of two fields x and z (y is omitted because of the signature). The second compilation unit makes use of S, and "exports" only g and h.

In the interactive ML system, we have an internal table holding each lambda-language variable that has been "exported" from a compilation unit; the variable name is mapped to its runtime value. Let us call this table *lookup*. Then each compilation unit can be "closed" by generating lambda-language calls that will call *lookup* at runtime. For example, consider a third compilation unit C that refers to S and g. We can wrap some bindings around its body as follows:

```
fn lookup =>
  let val S = lookup "S"
      val g = lookup "g"
   in      body of C
  end
```

The only free variables of C were S and g, and now these are bound. (In practice, instead of literal strings "S" and "g" we use numerical indices.)

When each compilation unit is executed, it is applied to the *lookup* function, which then performs runtime "linkage" to connect variable uses to their definitions in other compilation units. But each compilation unit is a formally closed λ-expression, with no globally free variables.

This closure property simplifies the CPS optimization phases. But it also simplifies the code generator and the garbage collector! There is never a need for the machine code of one compilation unit to contain a pointer to another. And, since all pointers *within* a compilation unit's machine code can be made program-counter relative, machine-code objects *never contain pointers*. Thus, no link-loader is needed, and no link-loader interface format is needed either.

Where did the pointers go? In fact, when executing the body of C described above, the pointers to S and g are available in the *closures* of whatever functions require them. Thus, the closure mechanism for managing free variables of functions generalizes to handle free variables of compilation units as well.

13.2   Interface with the garbage collector

The machine allocates records and arrays in memory. A garbage collector is occasionally invoked that traverses the data structure in memory, using the general-purpose registers as roots of the graph of pointers, to see which records and arrays are unreachable from registers—these are garbage. In doing so, it may move reachable records to eliminate fragmentation; whenever a record is moved, all the (reachable) pointers to it must be adjusted. This means that the garbage collector must be able to understand which of the general-purpose registers are pointers, and which are just integer values (or other nonpointers).

There are three approaches to this problem. The first approach, called "conservative garbage collection [18, 24]," treats all registers as pointers, even though some registers might be integers that merely look like pointers. Conservative collection must avoid moving any object pointed to by a register, when that register might just be an integer whose value is coincidentally the address of an object, since "adjusting" the integer value will cause the program to go wrong. (Adjusting a pointer value is all right, since the program will continue to get the same results when the pointer is dereferenced; but conservative collection doesn't know how the program is using the register.)

The second approach is to assume that a garbage collection might happen at any time—perhaps the collector is invoked by a timer interrupt that might occur between any adjacent instructions. Then the registers must be divided into two disjoint sets, one set containing only pointers and the other containing only nonpointers. Maintaining this invariant is troublesome, especially in the middle of the allocation of a new record; but it can be done [4].

The third approach is to have periodic "safe points," at which the contents of registers are clearly explained to the garbage collector. At a safe point, every pointer (and only pointers) must be in the pointer registers. We have chosen a more flexible approach: Instead of using disjoint pointer and nonpointer registers, we have a "register mask" at each safe point that indicates exactly which registers contain pointers. This is advantageous because it prevents previously used, dead registers (those which will be written before they are next read) from causing useless records to be retained by the garbage collector (see Section 12.4). Garbage collections can occur only at safe points; between safe points, the contents of registers and the format of pointers are unrestricted. Each safe point has a test to see whether the collector must be invoked.

This third approach is the one we are using at present, after some years of using the "always-safe" second approach. We abandoned the "always-safe" approach because it greatly complicates the implementation of peephole optimizations in the target-machine-specific phase of the compiler: Arithmetic on pointers often leads to "unsafe" temporary values.

We have avoided the "conservative" approach entirely, because of the burden it places on the garbage collector. Since ML programs allocate records so frequently, the collector must be as efficient as possible. Also, copying or compacting garbage can maintain large contiguous free regions (instead of a "free list"), which makes allocation of new records more efficient. This is more difficult (though still possible [18]) with conservative collection.

We put a safe point at the beginning of each CPS function. Since functions in the CPS language do not contain loops, a function can execute for only a bounded amount of time—and allocate a bounded number of records—before calling another CPS function (and reaching another safe point). The first instruction of each function tests to see if the allocation region (from which records and arrays are allocated) is almost exhausted, and if so invokes the garbage collector. Immediately before this instruction, there is a register mask, embedded in the machine-code program. This mask is never "executed," even though it sits in the instruction stream, since the function is always entered via a **jump** to an address following the mask.

The test for exhaustion of the allocation region is implemented by a comparison of the current **data pointer** (which indicates the next free address that can be used for allocating a new record) with the **data-limit** (which indicates the last address that can be allocated). If the difference is less than the amount of data allocated in the current CPS function, the collector must be invoked.

It is easy to compute an upper bound on the amount of data allocated by a CPS function. Each CPS operator allocates a fixed amount of data; one can traverse the expression tree from the root to a leaf (an APP node) and sum these amounts to see how much data is allocated along the path. Then one can take the maximum over all paths (there will be more than one path only if a branch or SWITCH operator is present).

Let the last allocatable address be L. For efficient implementation of the heap-limit check in machine language (on most machines), we put in the **data limit** register a value $L' = M - L + K$, where M is the maximum integer representable on the machine, and K is a small constant (we use 4096, arbitrarily). Let D be the current value of the **data pointer**. Then, for any CPS function that allocates less than K bytes, the implementation of the heap-exhausted test is quite simple: we compute $D + L'$, discard the result, and test for overflow. This can be done in one instruction on most machines. If the heap is exhausted, an overflow will occur and a machine interrupt will be generated; the interrupt handler will invoke the garbage collector. On some machines, it is more convenient (and certainly more straightforward) to use a compare-and-trap-on-greater-than instruction.

For functions that may allocate more than K bytes, a more complicated test is required. Let B be the amount to be allocated; as a conservative approximation we compute $D + B + L'$ and initiate collection if that overflows. The function that allocates arrays (whose size is not known at compile time) is an external, assembly-language function that also makes a more elaborate test for heap exhaustion.

Loop unrolling and in-line expansions will reduce the dynamic frequency of safe points, and will therefore reduce both the overhead of checking for heap exhaustion and the overhead of periodically constraining the representation of data in registers to be "safe."

13.3   Position-independent code

One minor complication is that each compilation unit must be position independent, because the garbage collector may move machine code from one place to another.

There are two ways that one could implement position independence. The first is to use program-counter-relative instructions where necessary, both for the targets of jumps, and for reference to literals (strings and reals) embedded within the program. This usually suffices. The second way is to give up on PC-independent code, and just have the garbage collector adjust addresses in programs whenever machine code is moved; we have not had to do this.

On all machines we have compiled for, it is possible to implement PC-relative jumps without too much difficulty. However, some recent RISC machines (e.g., the MIPS and the SPARC) do not have a PC-relative addressing mode for loading the addresses of literals. What we do on those machines is to use a branch-and-link instruction (that branches to the next instruction!) to load the program counter into a register P; then we add an appropriate offset to the result. There are two variations on this theme: We can have P point to the beginning of the compilation unit (or some fixed offset from the beginning, to allow smaller offsets embedded in instructions), or we can have P point at an arbitrary place (which we must keep track of). Either scheme has its advantages: For each scheme there is a different subset of functions for which reloading of P is not necessary.

On some machines, the instruction cache does not track stores into the instruction stream. Thus, when the garbage collector moves a block of machine code, it must flush a portion of the instruction cache before executing the moved code. This is easily accomplished in the runtime system and is not a problem relevant to the code generator.

13.4 Special-purpose registers

Five of the integer registers are reserved for special purposes, and at least four "general-purpose" registers must be available to hold values of the CPS language. Thus, the target machine must have at least nine registers, or must simulate some of the registers in memory. On machines with more registers, CPS code is more efficient because more registers may be used in passing arguments to known functions, and there are fewer spills. The number of registers is an input to the CPS optimization and transformation phases, which use it to limit the number of free variables of CPS expressions. Otherwise, CPS expressions are independent of the target machine.

The special registers are:

- The **data pointer**, which holds the address of the beginning of the free region, where the next record will be allocated on the heap.

- The **data limit**, which indicates the end of the free region. When the data pointer reaches the end of the free region, either a garbage collection must be done or another free region must be found.

- In some implementations, a **store pointer**, which points to the *modified set* (see Section 16.3), a list of heap locations that have been updated since the last garbage collection.

- The **exception pointer**, which holds the current exception handler.

- On the Motorola 68020 processor, which has separate address and data registers, we use the address registers as "general-purpose" registers. We designate one of the data registers as an **arithmetic temporary** in which certain arithmetic operations must be performed. (This is no fun at all!) On other machines, it is still handy to have an arithmetic temporary for certain limited purposes, so we use one of the general-purpose registers.

Some of the general-purpose registers have conventional meanings for calls to escaping functions (those whose call sites are not all known, and which must therefore use standard calling conventions). The escaping functions fall into a small number of classes (usually two, as explained in the next paragraph, though languages such as Prolog might have three), and all of the functions within a class must have the same calling sequence. We can arbitrarily say that for an N-argument escaping function, the first formal parameter will be passed in the first general-purpose register, the second parameter in the second register, and so on.

The different classes of escaping functions are related, however. For the implementations of conventional single-threaded languages (including ML, Scheme, Lisp, Pascal, etc.) there are two classes of functions: "user functions" and "continuations." An escaping user function takes three arguments: its closure, its "user argument" (the actual parameter written explicitly in the source language), and its continuation (which may actually occupy several registers, as explained in Section 10.6). An escaping continuation (and almost all continuations do escape) takes two arguments: its "user result" (the one returned explicitly by the source program) and its closure (which may occupy several registers). In fact, the closure of a continuation is often the same thing as the continuation argument of a recently called user function. Thus, it is important that the parameter-passing conventions for escaping functions assign the continuation argument of a user function to the same register as the closure argument of a continuation.

Thus, for parameter passing to escaping functions, we use the following conventions:

- GP-register 1 is the **standard closure** register; when calling an escaping user function, the closure argument is put here. Register 1 can also be used for other purposes, between calls to escaping functions.

- GP-register 2 is the **standard argument** register; when calling an escaping user function, the source-language argument is put here. Also, when calling an escaping continuation, the source-language result is put here. For source languages that (unlike ML) permit several arguments to be passed, one would reserve several GP-registers for this purpose.

- GP-registers $3 \rightarrow 3+K$ are used for passing the continuation to escaping user functions, and (equivalently) to pass the closure of an escaping continuation. The constant $K \geq 0$ is the number of callee-save registers (see Section 10.6), and must be fixed in advance for all functions.

For calls to known functions, any of the GP registers (including the ones listed above) may be used. This is because (by definition) all the call sites are known, and the compiler can arrange the marshaling of actual parameters, and the use of formal parameters, as it chooses. Also, all bindings of variables inside functions (e.g., the results of SELECTs, RECORDs, and PRIMOPs) may be put in any of the general-purpose registers.

How many registers?

It is instructive to see how the registers of real machines are used to implement our abstract machine.

- On the Vax, there are 14 registers, not including the stack pointer and the program counter. Even though we do not use a stack, we cannot use the stack pointer as a general-purpose register because the Unix operating system dumps information about Unix signals onto the stack. We use five of these for our "special" registers, leaving nine "general" registers.

- On the MC68020, there are seven "address" registers, not including the stack pointer which is treated specially by the operating system. We need one of the address registers as a "pointer temporary" because of the infelicities of the 68020 instruction set. We use the "data" registers of the 68020 for the arithmetic temporary, the store pointer, the exception handler, and the data limit. Unfortunately, the **data pointer** must go in an address register since it is frequently used as the address for **store** instructions. This leaves five address registers to be used as "general-purpose" registers.

- The MIPS has 32 registers, of which one is always zero, one is used as a special link register, one is reserved for the "assembler," two are reserved for the operating system, one is the stack pointer, one is the "global pointer" for C programs (including, particularly, the runtime system for ML!). We need one register for a "pointer temporary" and five for our special registers, leaving 19 as "general-purpose" registers.

- The SPARC Has 32 registers; instead of reciting a similar litany we will note that about 20 are available as "general" registers. We do not use the register windows on the SPARC.

Given that there are N "general" registers, for $N \in \{5, 9, 19, 20\}$ (etc.), we must observe the following rules:

- The input to the abstract-machine code generation phase must be an expression of which no subexpression has more than N free variables.

- The spill phase, therefore, must ensure that any subexpression has at most N free variables.

- The closure phase must ensure that any function has at most N arguments, including the K "callee-saves" arguments.

- The β-reduction and argument-flattening phase must ensure that any function has at most $N-1-K$ arguments, where $K \geq 0$ is the number of callee-saves registers. A function with A arguments (before the closure-conversion phase) may need one additional argument for its closure, and K additional callee-saves arguments, so $A + 1 + K \leq N$.

Floating-point registers

Most modern machines have disjoint sets of integer and floating-point registers. There is reason to believe that this separation will endure, since in the hardware implementation the floating registers must be physically near the floating ALU, and the integer registers must be physically near the integer ALU and memory-addressing unit. Furthermore, having two sets of registers allows integer and floating instruction streams—which are interleaved in the machine-language program—to proceed asynchronously.

The abstract-machine interface, since it is intended to reflect the realities of von Neumann machines, also has a separate set of floating-point registers. In fact, there are two disjoint sets:

- those registers not saved across interrupts and garbage collections (i.e., across *safe points*), and

- those registers saved across safe points.

Obviously, since our model puts a safe point at the beginning of every function, only the latter registers can be used for passing parameters in function calls. One can arrange for the runtime system to save more of the registers at garbage collections and interrupts, which may increase parameter-passing efficiency but would increase context-switch time.

There is no provision for passing floating-point registers to escaping functions. Thus, all floating parameters to escaping functions must be passed *boxed*, as pointers to floating-point values in memory. Calls to known functions, however, can use the floating-point parameter registers.

For machines (such as the VAX) that do not have separate floating-point registers, we invent them: We reserve a region of memory to serve as a set of floating-point registers. On recent VAXes, access to the cache is as fast as access to registers for most kinds of operands [29], so simulating floating registers in memory causes some loss of performance but not too much.

13.5   Pseudo-operations

The continuation-machine interface is essentially the assembly language of a conventional von Neumann machine, and as such has several "pseudo-operations" that manipulate the assembly process but are not actual instructions. These include:

align: Generates enough zero-filled bytes to get to an "aligned" address. On a typical byte-addressable, 32-bit machine this is an address that is a multiple of four. We need to align mainly because closures can point into the middle of machine-code objects (at function entry points), and the garbage collector is confused by pointers that are not multiples of four.

mark: Generates an embedded descriptor, so if the garbage collector ever finds a pointer to the immediately following address, it will be able to find the beginning of the machine code for this compilation unit. The descriptor contains an integer offset from this address to the beginning of the compilation unit.

emit long(i): Generate a literal integer i in the machine program. This is mainly used for descriptors of embedded string literals.

define label(l): Associates the current point in the machine-language program with an assembly-language label l.

emit label(i, l_2): Occurring at an address l_1 in a program, emits the integer $i + l_2 - l_1$. Thus, it emits the difference (adjusted by a constant) between the current address and some other specified address. This is useful in position-independent jump tables for SWITCH operators.

emit string(s): Puts the characters of the string s into the machine-code program; this is used (obviously) for string literals.

real constant(s): Puts the floating-point constant s into the machine-code program. The argument s is an ASCII representation of the value; the "assembler" translates s into native floating format. This late translation into native floating-point format allows easy and precise cross compilation (we use large-precision integers to construct accurate floating-point literals) but—unfortunately—makes it almost impossible to do constant folding on floating-point expressions.

13.6   Instructions of the continuation machine

The continuation machine has three "addressing modes" that can be used as operands of instructions:

register direct: The value held in a machine register is used as an operand.

immediate integer: A literal integer is used as the operand.

immediate label: An address in the machine program is used as the operand. This address might be the beginning of an escaping function, the location of a floating-point literal, or the beginning of a string literal. It is typically implemented by a PC-relative addressing mode, to make the program segment easily movable by the garbage collector.

Some instructions take "target operands" to indicate where a result must be placed. Obviously, these must be register-direct operands.

Only the register-direct mode may be used for floating-point operands, but there are instructions for loading and storing floats to/from the floating-point registers.

Since the continuation-machine is just a von Neumann computer, its instructions are quite conventional, except for the first two that help implement "safe points" and PC-relative programs:

check limit(n): Ensures that at least n bytes of space remain in the allocation region; if not, give control to the runtime system. This instruction must occur at a "safe point," with a **mark** immediately preceding, and a register mask right before that. The register mask is typically one 32-bit word, in which a 1 is set for each register containing a live pointer. Other registers may contain live integers, dead pointers, or garbage; they are preserved unchanged by the collector.

beginStdFn: Begins a "standard" (escaping) function. On machines that need it, this translates into a "bogus" branch-and-link to load the program counter into a register for use in PC-relative instructions.

jump(x): Jumps to location x, where x can be an immediate label or the contents of a register.

record(l, r): Allocates a record with fields l and puts a pointer to it in register r. The operand l is a list of fields, each one of which is a pair of operand and access path. The operand of each field may be any of the three operand types; the access path is just like the one of the CPS language (page 34). This rather complicated instruction is discussed in more detail below.

select(i, v, r): Fetches the ith field of record v, putting the result in r. On a 32-bit byte-addressable machine, this can be written with the register transfer $r \leftarrow_{32} M[v + 4i]$.

offset(i, v, r): Makes r point to the ith field of record v. On a 32-bit byte-addressable machine, this is $r \leftarrow v + 4i$.

fetchindexb(x, r, z): Indexed, eight-bit fetch to get a byte from a string. On a byte-addressable machine $r \leftarrow_8 M[x+z]$. There is an unfortunate restriction (for the benefit of the MC68020) that r must not be the same register as x or z.

storeindexb(x, r, z): Stores a byte into a byte array: $M[x + z] \leftarrow_8 r$.

fetchindexl(x, r, z): Indexed, full-word fetch to get an element of an array or record. Byte addressably, $r \leftarrow_{32} M[x + z]$, subject to the restriction that r is not the same register as x or z.

storeindexl(x, r, z): Stores a word into an array.
    Byte addressably, $M[x + z] \leftarrow_{32} r$.

ashl(x, y, r): Arithmetic shift left: $r \leftarrow y \cdot 2^x$.

ashr(x, y, r): Arithmetic shift right: $r \leftarrow \lfloor y \cdot 2^{-x} \rfloor$.

orb(x, y, r): Bitwise inclusive or, $r_i \leftarrow x_i \vee y_i$, for the ith bit of r, for each i.

andb(x, y, r): Bitwise and.

xorb(x, y, r): Bitwise exclusive or.

notb(x, r): Bitwise complement.

add(x, y, r): Integer add: $r \leftarrow x + y$. This instruction may raise the overflow exception if $x + y$ does not fit in one word, but it is not required to.

addt(x, y, r): Integer add with trap: $r \leftarrow x + y$. This instruction must raise the overflow exception if $x + y$ does not fit in one word.

sub(x, y, r): Integer subtract: $r \leftarrow y - x$. This instruction may, but is not required to, raise the overflow exception when overflow occurs.

subt(x, y, r): Integer subtract with trap: $r \leftarrow y - x$, raising overflow if overflow occurs.

divt(x, y): Signed integer divide: $y \leftarrow \text{sign}(y/a) \cdot \lfloor (|y/a|) \rfloor$, raising the divide-by-zero exception if $a = 0$, and raising overflow if $a \neq 0$ and y/a is not representable.

mult(x, y): Signed integer multiply: $y \leftarrow x \cdot y$, raising overflow if the result is not representable.

bbs(x, l): Branch on bit set: Branch to location l if the number x is odd.

ibranch(c, x, y, l): Integer comparison. If the condition $x \, c \, y$ holds, where c is one of the operators $\{=, \neq, <, \leq, >, \geq, <_u, \leq_u, >_u, \geq_u\}$, then branch to address l. The u indicates an unsigned comparison.

mulf(x, y, r): Floating multiplication; all operands must be floating-point registers. Overflow exception must be raised on overflow.

divf(x, y, r): Floating division; operands must be floating registers. Divide-by-zero and overflow must be raised when appropriate.

addf(x, y, r): Floating add; operands must be floating registers. Overflow must be raised when appropriate.

subf(x, y, r): Floating add; operands must be floating registers. Overflow must be raised when appropriate.

fbranch(c, x, y, l): Floating comparison. If the condition $x \, c \, l$ holds, where c is one of the operators $\{=, \neq, <, \leq, >, \geq\}$, then branch to address l.

loadfloat(x, r): The contents of memory addressed by integer register x are loaded into floating register r.

storefloat(x, r): The contents of floating register r are stored into memory addressed by integer register x.

13.7   Register assignment

The structure of a CPS expression after the spill phase is sufficiently close to the structure of a abstract continuation-machine program that there's not much to do in translating from one to the other. One important part of this translation is the mapping of CPS variables to machine registers. There is never a danger of running out of registers (the spill phase has assured that), but a good choice of mapping can minimize the number of register–register **move** instructions required.

There are just a few constraints on register assignment:

1. The formal parameters of an escaping function are prescribed by convention, and must be mapped to a specified list of registers.

2. The formal parameters of a known function may be chosen at will, but all the callers of that function must use the same assignment.

3. At any CPS expression that binds a variable w and continues with a subexpression E, the register chosen for w must be different from all the registers chosen for variables free in E.

We use some simple greedy heuristics to minimize **move** instructions; these are essentially the same as those used in the ORBIT compiler [55]. A most important heuristic is to delay the choice of registers for formal parameters of a known function until one of the calls to that function is found. We start generating code with the first ("outermost") escaping function. Instructions will be generated top down starting with the operator closest to the root of the expression tree representing the body of this function.

At any point in code generation, the assignment of variables to registers is already decided for all variables whose scope contains the current subexpression. At the beginning, for example, the only variables whose scope contains the current subexpression—the body of the first escaping function—are the formal parameters of that function. Their assignment is already predetermined (by rule 1 above).

Now, assume we have some operator that binds a variable w and continues with a subexpression E, such as $\mathtt{SELECT}(i, v, w, E)$. We now choose a register for the variable w. We can choose any register except those bound to variables free in E. Since E must have fewer than N free variables (after the *spill* phase), there must be some variable we can choose for w. Now we recur on the expression E.

We can continue this until we reach a leaf of the continuation expression. This will be a node of the form $\mathtt{APP}(f, \vec{x})$. Now, there are two cases:

1. $f(\vec{v})$ is an escaping function, or is a known function whose parameter assignment has already been decided (because at least one call to it has been examined already). In this case, the registers associated with $\vec{x}$ must be moved to the registers associated with $\vec{v}$, using **move** instructions. To the extent that some values are already in the right registers, fewer moves will be necessary. If $\vec{x}$ overlaps with $\vec{v}$, then it may be necessary to use an extra temporary register to accomplish the permutation.

2. $f(\vec{v})$ is a known function whose parameter assignment has not yet been decided. Then we are free to choose that the assignment of registers for $\vec{v}$ can be just the same as that of $\vec{x}$, and no moves at all will be necessary!

In either case, some of the values $\vec{x}$ may be constants, not variables; so they won't already be in registers. In this case, some sort of load-constant instruction will be required instead of a move, but this cannot be avoided in any case. For the first call to a known function, we simply pick an arbitrary register in which to place the constant, and make this the register assignment for the formal parameter.

Thus at least one of the calls to each known function will be accomplished without any **move** instructions. And we can use the heuristic of *targeting* to reduce the number of moves in the other calls. Consider again a nonleaf operator such as $\texttt{SELECT}(i, v, w, E)$. We can examine the expression E to see if it contains a node $\texttt{APP}(f, [\ldots, \texttt{VAR } w, \ldots])$ that uses w as an argument. If so, and if the parameter assignment for f is already determined, then we should try to place w in the right register when it is first bound, so no **move** will be necessary later. Of course, that register may still be occupied by a variable free in E, in which case *targeting* cannot be applied.

We can also use a kind of *antitargeting*. In choosing a register for w, we might find a leaf $\texttt{APP}(f, \vec{x})$ where w and $\vec{x}$ are disjoint. This means that we should probably avoid putting w in any of the registers that are formal parameters of f, so targeting is more likely to be successful as we bind the rest of the variables $\vec{x}$.

Neither of these heuristics guarantees an optimal register assignment, but they are simple to implement and seem to produce good results.

Optimal register targeting is NP-complete. We can show this by a reduction from *circular-arc graph K-colorability* [41]. A circular-arc graph is one in which each node is represented by a circular arc (all arcs concentric about the same point). Two nodes are considered adjacent if their arcs overlap. A graph is K-colorable if each node can be given a color (from a set of K colors) so adjacent nodes never have the same color.

Given a circular-arc K-coloring problem, we can transform it into a register-targeting problem as follows. Pick an arbitrary point on the circle, and "cut" all the arcs crossing that point. Number each such arc with a register (from a set of K registers). These represent the registers assigned to the formal parameters of a function. Now, as we travel around the circle, the ending of an arc represents a variable no longer live, and the beginning of the arc represents a new binding. When we reach the end (i.e., the beginning) of the circle, the arcs that cross the "cut" have registers already assigned to them; these represent the actual parameters of a call to some other function that has registers already assigned to its formal parameters. Our register-targeting algorithm can assign registers and avoid generating any **move** instructions if and only if the circular-arc graph was K-colorable.

To finish the proof of NP-completeness, we must also show that the problem is in NP; clearly a solution can be generated and checked in polynomial time by a nondeterministic automaton.

Of course, targeting within one CPS function is a "small" problem. The larger, and more interesting, problem is the global assignment of formal parameters (of all functions) to registers, to globally minimize the number of **move** instructions. But consider a recursive function $f(\vec{v})$; we are required to choose registers for the formal parameters $\vec{v}$ that will optimize the number of moves. No matter what registers are chosen for $\vec{v}$, the problem is reduced to the targeting problem previously described. Therefore, optimal global register assignment is clearly intractable.

Given that optimal solutions are not possible in polynomial time, and that we have easy heuristics that give good results, clearly we should be satisfied with the heuristics.

13.8   Branch prediction

The targeting and antitargeting heuristics need to find an APP node likely to be executed after the "current" operation. Since the CPS tree for a given function may include comparison primops and SWITCH operators, there may be several such APP nodes to choose from. Presumably, the heuristics will perform better if the most likely taken APP node is used. This requires compile-time estimation of branch frequencies.

Also, some target machines have conditional-branch instructions that take a different amount of time for taken and untaken branches. Compile-time branch-frequency estimation is also useful for these machines, so the most-often-taken path will be the faster one.

In "conventional" compilers, it is assumed that "loop" branches will usually be taken. We can phrase this heuristic in the context of continuation-passing style. We construct the call graph of applications of *known* functions; that is, the function names are the nodes of this graph, and there is an edge from A to B if function A contains an APPlication of function B.

Now, any cycle in this graph is a "loop." Suppose function A is in a strongly connected component, and we are considering a branch (a SWITCH or comparison) within A. One path leads to an APP of a known function B within the same strongly connected component, and the other path leads to APPs only of functions outside the component or unknown functions (those extracted from records or received as formal parameters). Then the we call the path leading to B the "loop edge," and we guess that it is more likely taken.

Other heuristics can be applied here. Suppose we have a (source-language) **if-then-else**, that leads to a (CPS-language) comparison primop. Now, both paths of the comparison will APPly the same known (continuation) function at their leaves. If one path has a shorter path to its leaf (the APP node), we will guess that this path is more frequently taken. The rationale is that if we guess wrong, the extra cost incurred by the more frequently taken path will be amortized over a larger computation anyway.

We have implemented some of these heuristics, but have not measured their performance.

13.9 Generation of abstract-machine instructions

To generate code from the CPS-converted, optimized, closure-converted, spilled intermediate representation, we make a pool of all functions whose formal parameters have been assigned to registers. Initially, this is exactly the set of escaping functions. When we generate the first call to a known function, we choose a register assignment for its formal parameters and add it to the pool.

We remove an arbitrary function from the pool, and create a table mapping CPS variables to registers. We initialize this table with the formal parameters of the function.

We then traverse the CPS expression, top down. For each operator, there will be a set of input operands; because of scoping rules and our top-down traversal, these operands will already be bound to registers in our table. There will be a set of output operands; we can bind these to registers (and add them to the table) using the targeting and antitargeting heuristics described above. We then "emit" the appropriate abstract-machine instructions with the correct registers as operands. Finally, there will be one, or (for comparisons and SWITCHes) several, subtrees; upon these the code generator recurs.

The leaves—APP nodes—are handled somewhat differently. There are two cases: known functions to which no call has yet been generated, and others, for which the assignment of formal parameters to registers has already been made. For the former case, we can choose the assignment of formals based on the current location of the *actual* parameters, so no **move** instructions are necessary, as explained in Section 13.7. Of course, if the same variable is passed to two different formal parameters (e.g., $f(x,x)$), then a **move** is necessary since two different formals cannot be assigned to the same register.

If the formals have already been bound to registers, then the actuals must be shuffled around. Permuting N registers may take up to $N+1$ **move** instructions and may require an extra register to hold a temporary value. For this reason, the number of parameters to a function must be at least one less than the number of registers on the machine. We use the "arithmetic temporary" as the extra register for shuffling.

It is also interesting to remark that on "superscalar" machines, where several instructions might be executed at once, it might be advantageous to use more than one temporary register, so there isn't a sequentially dependent chain of $N+1$ instructions, but instead several smaller chains.

After emitting the **move** instructions (if any), we generate a **jump**, either to a known label or to a destination held in a register.

13.10 Integer arithmetic

The low-order bit of each (one-word) value at runtime distinguishes pointers from integers. This works well on byte-addressable machines, where the low-order two bits of each word-aligned pointer are zero anyway. A low-order one-bit indicates an integer (or other unboxed value); the upper 31 bits provide the value.

This distinction is (almost) entirely for the benefit of the garbage-collector, which must know which objects are pointers that need to be traversed. Tag bits don't need to be "checked" at runtime, except in the polymorphic equality function; the static polymorphic type system makes such checks unnecessary. We do use the tag bits to distinguish constant data constructors from value-carrying constructors, but as explained in Section 4.1 we could just as easily do without them.

It is inconvenient to have these tag bits. They prevent users from calculating with full 32-bit integers, and the tag bits must be stripped off operands and added to results. Can we do without the tags? In fact, for statically typed languages such as ML it is possible to garbage collect without any tags, by giving the garbage collector a "road map" of the compile-time types [5]; but this has its own complications and inconveniences.

So we represent the integer i as the number $i' = 2i + 1$. To add two "represented" numbers i' and j', we simply compute $k' = (i' - 1) + j'$, which can be accomplished in two instructions. If one of the operands happens to be a constant, we can subtract one *at compile time*, so the add can be accomplished in just one instruction. Subtraction works similarly.

To multiply two represented integers i' and j' we compute $k' = (i'-1)*\lfloor j'/2 \rfloor + 1$, which takes a subtract, a shift, a multiply, and an add. If one of the operands is constant we can omit one instruction from this sequence. Division is similar.

Comparison operators need no adjustment, since $i < j$ is equivalent to $2i+1 < 2j+1$.

Some implementations of tagged languages use a low-order zero-bit for *integers* and a one-bit for *pointers*. Then **add** and **subtract** take just one instruction, and multiply takes just two. Most uses of pointers (i.e., fetches and stores) use a displacement in the machine instruction, so the fact that pointers are "off by one" can be corrected in the displacement at no cost. There are some machines where certain instructions (i.e., *jump to address contained in register*) do not permit a displacement, so an extra instruction would be required to correct a pointer before a jump. All in all, this may be a better scheme. However, in a typical Standard ML of New Jersey program (the compiler compiling itself) we estimate the cost of handling tag bits to be only 1.65 percent of total runtime [5], so the difference is not significant.

13.11   Unboxed floating-point values

Floating-point numbers are represented on the heap as pointers to boxed double-precision values. When a floating value is passed as a parameter to an escaping function, for example, it is really the pointer to the number that is passed.

A naive approach to floating-point arithmetic in this framework is to implement **add**(x, y) as follows, where x and y start out as boxed values in integer registers.

1. Fetch the eight bytes of x into a float register.

2. Fetch the eight bytes of y into a float register.

3. Add x and y in registers, yielding z'.

4. Store the eight bytes of z' into a newly allocated record on the heap.

5. Move a pointer to the new record into an integer register z.

Indeed, if x and y are formal parameters of an escaping function and z is passed to an escaping function, nothing better can be done. But in general, if we are going to do further computation with z we can keep the value z' in a floating register, without creating the boxed value z at all.

The following strategy is somewhat crude, since it does not use the floating and integer registers optimally. It is motivated by the desire to keep the CPS representation simple, without two different kinds of variables (floating and integer). But our strategy seems to be reasonably effective.

A floating-point value can be in an integer (pointer) register, a floating register, or both simultaneously. A floating value fetched from a polymorphic record, or that's a formal parameter of an escaping function, arrives in a pointer register only. Whenever a floating-point value is created (by an arithmetic operation) it is put only in a floating-point register. When necessary, a value in a floating register can be put in a pointer register (by storing it on the heap and remembering the address); a value in a pointer register can be put into a floating register (by fetching).

Arithmetic operations demand their operands in floating registers, so a fetch is necessary only for those operands not already in floating registers. Creation of records, or passing floats to escaping functions, demands boxed values, so a store is necessary only for those operands not only in integer registers. Once a value is converted from an integer to a float, or vice versa, it continues to "live" in both register banks.

The spill phase, and previous phases, have guaranteed that the program can keep all live variables (including boxed floats) in integer registers. Our method works well as long as there are as many float registers as "general-purpose" integer registers. A typical modern computer has 32 integer registers, of which we use (approximately) 16 for "general" purposes, and 16 or 32 double-precision floating registers. So our method will work, though it may not use the full complement of registers efficiently.

Floating parameters to known functions can be passed in floating-point registers without having to "box" them; but see Section 18.1 for the discussion of a minor complication.

CHAPTER FOURTEEN

MACHINE-CODE GENERATION

The instructions of the abstract continuation machine must be translated into native code for the target machine. This is done in two stages; first, from abstract-machine into "assembly" code, then from assembly code into machine code. The assembly code is not a text file suitable for processing by a stand-alone assembler; instead, it is just an internal interface at the approximate semantic level of a typical assembly language.

Translation from assembly language into machine language has several aspects: the selection of the appropriate bit patterns for each assembly-language instruction, addressing mode, and register; the resolution of references to labels; the sizing of span-dependent instructions; and (on some machines) scheduling of instructions to minimize pipeline hazards. These will all be discussed at various points throughout the chapter.

14.1   Translation for the VAX

The VAX [90] has 16 registers, of which one is the program counter and (in principle) the others may be used for any purpose. However, the stack pointer register is treated specially by the operating system; when Unix signals are sent to a process, its registers are all pushed "on the stack" (i.e., saved at the location given by the stack pointer). Thus, only 14 registers are really available for use by the target-machine-code generator. Of these, we reserve one for the allocation pointer (**dataptr**) that indicates the next free location on the heap, one for the data limit (**datalimit**) that indicates the end of the free heap space, one for the head of the store list (**storeptr**) that points to modified *ref* cells, one for the current exception handler **exnptr**, and one for an arithmetic temporary (**arithtemp**). This leaves nine "general-purpose" registers.

If the runtime system does not require a store list (e.g., because it uses virtual memory to record updates to the mutable store), then a **storeptr** is not necessary. Also, in recent VAXes, access to words in the cache is about as fast as access to registers, *for those operands that are not directly used in addressing* [29]. This means that the **datalimit**, **storeptr**, **exnptr**, and perhaps **arithtemp** could be kept in memory (probably) without slowing access to them. A convenient place to keep them would be at small offsets from the stack pointer. Then there would be

13 "general-purpose" registers. Figure 15.8 shows that there might be a modest improvement in speed from the increased number of usable registers.

The VAX has no floating-point registers; instead, a double-precision floating-point value may be kept in a pair of adjacent integer registers. However, the *spill* phase of the compiler assumes that every value takes exactly one register, and we are loath to change it. So we have two choices: We can make some "artificial" floating-point registers in memory at small offsets from the stack pointer, or we can use the "naive" approach of unboxing and reboxing floating values before and after each operation. It turns out that either approach is equally slow; our floating-point performance on the VAX is not very good.

What remains is just the translation of each of the abstract-machine instructions into VAX instructions.

Heap-limit check

The heap-limit check is implemented as described in Section 13.2: if L is the end of the free region, we put $2^{31} - L + 4096$ in the limitptr register, and perform

```
addl3 dataptr, limitptr, arithtemp
```

on entry to each CPS function. When the dataptr is within 4096 bytes of the end of the free region, this will cause an integer overflow with the program counter pointing to the beginning of the addl3 instruction; the trap handler will invoke the garbage collector and then restart the trapping instruction.

We don't really care about the result of the add, just whether it overflows. But we are forced to put the result somewhere! The only available register is the *arithmetic temporary*, since any other register might be a procedure parameter (and thus be holding a useful value across the add).

Note that the overflow trick requires that the free region be in the lower half of the address space (because signed arithmetic is used). However, in a generational garbage collector only the youngest generation uses this trick; other generations may be put in any part of memory.

Simple instructions

The **select** (and **offset**) abstract-machine instructions translate directly into VAX move (and move-address) instructions using the displacement addressing mode. Similarly, the **add** and **addt** instructions both translate into a VAX addl3 instructions. Similarly, the abstract-machine instructions **sub, subt, ashl, ashr, mult, divt, orb, andb, notb, xorb, mulf, divf, addf, subf, jump,** and **bbs** each translate using a single VAX instruction.

A conditional branch of the abstract machine translates into a compare followed by a conditional branch on the VAX.

Record creation

The most complicated instruction of the abstract machine is the one that allocates a **record** on the heap. This instruction has as operands a list of record fields; each field is either a constant, a register, or a label, sometimes with a path of displacements and fetches to be followed in gathering the field value.

The VAX can store values in memory without first moving them into registers, and we take advantage of this. Suppose the second field of a record is

```
(r5, SELp(3, SELp(2, SELp(0, SELp(6, OFFp 0)))))
```

This would translate into VAX instructions as

```
movl 12(r5), arithtemp              # SELp(3, ... )
movl *8(arithtemp), arithtemp       # SELp(2, SELp(0, ...))
movl 24(arithtemp), 8(dataptr)      # SELp(6, OFFp 0)
```

It is often the case in ML that a record A is constructed using several adjacent fields from a record B. For example,

```
fun update_b newb {a,b,c,d,e,f} =
        {a=a, b=newb, c=c, d=d, e=e, f=f}
```

The abstract-machine **record** instruction from this program might look like:

```
record([(r2, SELp(0, OFFp 0)),   #a
        (r7, OFFp 0),            #newb
        (r2, SELp(2, OFFp 0)),   #c
        (r2, SELp(3, OFFp 0)),   #d
        (r2, SELp(4, OFFp 0)),   #e
        (r2, SELp(5, OFFp 0))], #f
     r4)
```

Whenever two adjacent fields in the new record come from two adjacent source locations, this can be recognized and a single eight-byte move instruction can be generated to do both fields at once. The fields (c, d) and (e, f) can be constructed this way.

Both of these tricks are specific to the VAX; they don't work on typical RISC machines, for example, though the two-field-at-a-time trick may work on the next generation of RISC machines. Furthermore, on RISC machines there is a quite different trick that is useful, as described in Section 14.3.4. Thus, memory-to-memory operations vary sufficiently among machines to justify the quite-complicated **record** instruction as a primitive of the abstract machine.

14.1.1   Span-dependent instructions

Labels may appear in branch instructions and PC-relative load-literal instructions (etc.), and the bit patterns for these references cannot be determined until the sizes of all instructions are known. Unfortunately, most modern computers have *span-dependent* branch and load instructions; that is, the distance between the referencing instruction and the referenced label determines the *size* of the referencing instruction itself. Thus, there is a set of simultaneous equations that must be satisfied just to determine the sizes of all instructions.

An effective way of solving this problem is by iteration to convergence. Each span-dependent instruction is assumed to take the minimum possible amount of space, and the addresses of all labels are calculated. The sizes of span-dependent instructions are recomputed based on the calculated addresses of labels; then the addresses of labels are recalculated based on the new sizes of the instructions. Since it is never necessary to decrease the size of a span-dependent instruction, this process must converge, because there are only a finite number of possible sizes for each kind of instruction.

It is interesting to note that we could just as well start with maximum-size span-dependent instructions and decrease them in each iteration until convergence is reached; but the solution we obtain in this way will in general be worse than with the first approach [97].

14.2   Translation for the MC68020

The Motorola 68020 [66] has eight "address" registers (A0–A7) and eight "data" registers (D0–D7) in addition to the program counter. The address registers can be used as addresses in load and store operations, but cannot be used as operands in most kinds of arithmetic instructions. The data registers can be used in arithmetic, but not as pointers (except with some difficulty). This greatly complicates the translation of abstract-machine instructions into native code. Indeed, we have not done as good a job as we could have in instruction selection and register allocation for this machine.

To avoid the problem of "two kinds of register," we use only the A registers as "general-purpose" registers. However, the A7 register is reserved by the operating system as a stack pointer (as on the VAX, this register is used when saving state in signal handlers). We use A6 as the **dataptr**, and A5 as a *pointer temporary* (**ptrtemp**). The pointer temporary is necessary to hold intermediate values that are used as addresses, or that are generated by *load-effective-address* instructions; on the VAX we can use the **arithtemp** for these purposes because there is no distinction between address and data registers.

We hold the **exnptr**, **storeptr**, and **datalimit** in D registers, since they are rarely used directly in addressing.

This leaves only five "general-purpose" A registers that can be used to hold CPS variables and to pass parameters to CPS procedures. As figure 15.8 shows, the performance penalty for using such a limited number of registers is about 15 percent (but with a very large variance depending on the individual program).

With ML variables kept in A registers, operations such as **select** (fetch) and **jump** can be expressed very naturally in one instruction on the 68020. But to perform arithmetic, one of the operands must be moved to a D register, the operation is performed (one source is permitted to be an A register), and then the result is moved back into an A register. This is quite costly. Furthermore, the 68020 has no provision for automatically raising an interrupt on arithmetic overflow, as is necessary to satisfy the semantics of ML. So we must execute a **trapv** (trap-on-overflow) instruction after any arithmetic instruction whose overflow we need to detect. Moving operands back and forth, and extra instructions to detect overflow, combined with the overhead (required on all processors) of stripping and inserting low-order tag bits on integers, make arithmetic quite costly on this processor.

We keep the heap-limit register in its "natural" form (the end of the heap minus 4096, *not* subtracted from *maxint*). The limit check is implemented as a compare (of dataptr versus limit register), followed by a trap on minus. These are both small (16-bit) and fast instructions.

A specialized register allocator, or a good peephole optimizer, would reduce the traffic between A and D registers, but we have not pursued this.

14.3   Translation for the MIPS and SPARC

The MIPS processor [51] has 32 registers, of which one is always zero, one is used as the target of the "branch-and-link" instruction, two are reserved by the operating system, one is the stack pointer (used for signal handling), one is the "global pointer" (used by the C-language runtime system), and one is an "assembler temporary" used in constructing certain idiomatic instruction combinations (both by the standard system assembler and the SML/NJ code generator).

The SPARC [82] processor has "register windows," each with eight "input" registers (used for receiving parameters into procedures), eight "local" registers, and eight "output" registers (used for passing parameters to other procedures). There are also eight "global" registers. Upon a procedure call, the window is usually "shifted," so the output registers become the input registers of the new procedure, and the old input and local registers are saved unchanged until the window is shifted back.

Since we do not use a runtime stack for activation records, register windows do not fit naturally into our model. Therefore, we never shift windows. Instead, we treat the registers as 32 general-purpose registers, just like on the MIPS. Of these, we do not use the the stack pointer (o6), frame pointer (i6), and return address to C code (i7, and o7 for signal handlers); and we use one register for PC-relative addressing, as described in the next section.

Standard ML of New Jersey uses some of the remaining registers (on both the MIPS and SPARC) for **dataptr**, **datalimit**, **storeptr**, **exnptr**, one **arithtemp**, and two to four other **temp** registers; leaving 16–18 "general" registers to hold CPS variables. As figure 15.8 shows, this is plenty.

Since the MIPS and SPARC have such a simple and regular instruction set, translating abstract-machine instructions into target-machine instructions is quite straightforward. The only two difficulties are PC-relative references, and scheduling of load delays and branch delays.

The heap-limit check is a single-cycle instruction that adds the dataptr to the limitptr and puts the result in register 0 (i.e., throws it away); this will overflow if the limit is exceeded.

14.3.1   PC-relative addressing

Consider the abstract-machine instruction that might result from the construction of a closure for the function whose machine code starts at *Label328* and with a free variable whose value is currently in register 13:

```
record( [ (Label328, OFFp 0), (R13, OFFp 0) ], R4 )
```

To initialize the first field of this record, the address *Label328* must be constructed and then stored into memory. Since the entire block of code for this compilation unit may be moved by the garbage collector, we should encode into the program the *displacement*: the difference between the address of the instruction referring to *Label328* and and the address of *Label328* itself.

Many machines have a load-effective-address instruction that can add a constant to the program counter and put the result into a general register. Most RISC machines do not have such an instruction. The only way we can accomplish this is to execute a branch-and-link instruction, which jumps to a given target address and also puts the current PC into a register. But we don't really want to change the flow of control—we just want the PC value—so we branch to the next instruction (actually the instruction following the branch-delay slot). Then we can add a constant to the link register, to obtain the value *Label328*.

If we need several PC-relative addresses in the same function, we need only one branch-and-link instruction; we can adjust all of the additive constants by appropriate displacements.

14.3.2   Instruction scheduling

On a modern "Reduced Instruction Set Computer" (RISC), instructions are made simple so as few cycles as possible are required to execute each instruction. For example, the **multiply** instruction does not also compute addresses and fetch operands from memory. Typically, a **load** instruction adds a constant to a register, and fetches the resulting address into another register; an arithmetic instruction takes its operands in registers and puts the result into a register and so on.

The goal is to execute one instruction each cycle; or, on "superscalar" machines, to execute several instructions per cycle. However, though we can perform an **add** in just one cycle, it may not be possible to get the result of a **load** or **multiply** into a register by the end of a cycle. An attempt to use the destination register of a long-latency instruction (such as **load** or **multiply**) too soon after the instruction is issued will result in a *stall* during which no further instructions are issued. Such a situation would occur after the second instruction of this sequence:

```
add   r7 := r2+r4
load  r3 := M[r1+8]
add   r7 := r7+r3
load  r8 := M[r1+4]
```

The stall can be avoided by executing some other useful instruction that does not use the result (in this case r_3) of the long-latency instruction. For example, the first two instructions could be interchanged, or the last two instructions could be interchanged, or both. Then the destination register r_3 would never be used within two cycles of the *issue* of the **load** instruction. On most RISC machines, no stall would occur.

This example illustrates an important point about compiling for RISC machines: it's not just that each instruction is simple, so *instruction selection* is much easier than on a "Complex Instruction Set Computer" (CISC). It's that the *compiler* is expected to analyze "pipeline hazards" and rearrange instructions to prevent stalls. This will make the compiled program run much faster, and is called *instruction scheduling*.

On the MIPS, not only is the result of the **load** unavailable for two cycles after the instruction issue, but *there is no hardware stall mechanism*. If (in our example) r_3 is used in the instruction immediately following the **load**, we will (usually) get *the wrong answer*. Thus, the compiler *must* do instruction scheduling, or at least put a no-op (NOP) instruction after each **load** instruction, in the delay slot of the **load**.

On most RISC machines (including MIPS and SPARC) there is also a *delayed branch:* The transfer of control specified by a branch or jump instruction does not take place until after the following instruction has been executed. The compiler must either put a NOP in the branch-delay slot, or reschedule instructions to put a useful instruction there.

Most compilers for RISCs are arranged so that instruction scheduling occurs in a very late stage. First, a program is translated into machine instructions ignoring all pipeline hazards, and then instructions are re-arranged to avoid stalls. Standard ML of New Jersey is very typical in this respect; the abstract "assembly" code generator knows nothing about load and branch delays, and the "assembler" performs instruction scheduling.

14.3.3   Anti-aliasing

An instruction scheduler tries to rearrange a sequence of instructions to avoid runtime delays. But when can instructions be rearranged? More specifically, when can an adjacent pair of instructions be interchanged?

As long as neither instruction writes a register or memory location that the other one reads or writes, and neither instruction is a jump, they can be rearranged. It is easy to see whether an instruction writes or reads a particular register. But consider the instructions

```
load    r2 := M[r7+12]
store   M[r8+8] := r3
```

Do these two instructions refer to the same memory location? The answer depends on the possible runtime values of r_7 and r_8; this is the *aliasing* problem. Without further information, we can't know if r_7 and r_8 are aliases for the same record (with r_7 pointing into the record at a different spot, in this case). So most compilers' instruction schedulers could not perform this interchange; this restriction might increase the number of stalls or NOPs in the generated code.

In ML, Lisp, Schéme, Smalltalk, and similar semifunctional languages, the vast majority of stores are the initializations of immutable objects. This fact can be valuable to the instruction scheduler.

The creation of a new immutable object on the heap has the following form:

1. Initialization of the fields (**stores** at constant offsets from the **dataptr** register).

2. Generation of the pointer to the object (a **move** of the dataptr to a "general-purpose" register).

3. Adjustment of the dataptr, by adding a constant (the size of the record) to the dataptr.

Furthermore, any **store** at a displacement from the **dataptr** must be an initialization; any other **store** must be an update of a mutable **ref** cell or array. Therefore:

1. Any initializing **store** may be interchanged with any adjacent **store**, initializing or otherwise.

2. Any **load** may be interchanged with any adjacent initializing **store**.

3. A **load** or noninitializing **store** may not be interchanged with an immediately preceding **move** from the **dataptr**. This ensures that fetches from a newly created record don't get moved into the initialization sequence of the record.

4. An initializing store may not be interchanged with an immediately following **move** from the **dataptr**.

If the vast majority of **stores** are initializing stores, then rules 1 and 2 allow the instruction scheduler much more flexibility then it would have in a "normal" compiler. In any mostly functional language, but especially with a compiler that allocates closures ("activation records") on the heap *and does not write to them after initializing them*, there are few noninitializing stores. However, we have not attempted to measure whether this leads to significantly better stall elimination.

We can do even better (though in the present compiler we have not implemented what is described next): In ML we can use the static type system to detect at compile time which **loads** are from immutable objects. We could propagate this information into the machine-specific assembly language by marking each **load** instruction. Then we could interchange any immutable **load** with any noninitializing **store**; the rules listed above do not permit this.

If there are many noninitializing **store**s, this might provide an important measure of flexibility to the instruction scheduler.

14.3.4 Alternating temporaries

We also improve pipeline performance by alternating temporary registers. Consider the following (quite typical) **record** abstract-machine instruction:

```
record( [ (R4, SELp(7, OFFp 0)),
          (R4, SELp(9, OFFp 0)),
          (R6, SELp(0, OFFp 0)),
          (R8, SELp(2, OFFp 0)) ],  ... )
```

A naive instruction sequence to achieve this would be:

```
LOAD   t1 := M[R4+28]
NOP
STORE M[dataptr+0] := t1
LOAD   t1 := M[R4+36]
NOP
STORE M[dataptr+4] := t1
LOAD   t1 := M[R6+0]
NOP
STORE M[dataptr+8] := t1
LOAD   t1 := M[R8+8]
NOP
STORE M[dataptr+12] := t1
```

The NOP instructions are required because the result of a **load** cannot be used in the immediately following cycle. Even on the SPARC, where explicit NOPs are not required, an attempt to use the result of a **load** in the following cycle will stall the pipeline for one cycle (or more).

Unfortunately, the instruction sequence above cannot be rescheduled to avoid the NOPs. However, if we use two temporary registers **t1** and **t2** instead of just **t1**, then we can achieve a better schedule, as shown in figure 14.1. The instructions as generated by the abstract-machine-to-assembly-language translator are shown on the left, and the result after the instruction scheduling phase appears on the right. On the SPARC, of course, the NOPs need not be written explicitly but the sequence using only one temporary register will still take just as long because of pipeline stalls.

If the pipeline was deeper (so the result of a **load** could not be used for several following instructions), then it would be useful to have more than two temporary registers.

Avoiding the reuse of the same temporary register is more generally useful than just in the translation of the **record** primitive. The abstract-machine-code

```
LOAD   t1 := M[R4+28]              LOAD   t1 := M[R4+28]
NOP                                LOAD   t2 := M[R4+36]
STORE M[dataptr+0] := t1           STORE M[dataptr+0] := t1
LOAD   t2 := M[R4+36]              STORE M[dataptr+4] := t2
NOP                                LOAD   t1 := M[R6+0]
STORE M[dataptr+4] := t2           LOAD   t2 := M[R8+8]
LOAD   t1 := M[R6+0]               STORE M[dataptr+8] := t1
NOP                                STORE M[dataptr+12] := t2
STORE M[dataptr+8] := t1
LOAD   t2 := M[R8+8]
NOP
STORE M[dataptr+12] := t2
```

Figure 14.1. Scheduling with alternating temporaries.

generator uses this technique in choosing which register to bind to a CPS variable. When a new variable is defined as the result of an operation, any unallocated register may be bound to it. The compiler chooses the least recently used register (or some approximation thereof), so the instruction scheduling phase will have more freedom in rearranging instructions to fill delay slots.

14.4   An example

To show the quality of target-machine code obtained by the Standard ML of New Jersey compiler, we can work an example. The program on page 83 counts the number of zeros in a list of integers. Pages 83 through 86 explain how it is in-line expanded and optimized. After closure-conversion with callee-save registers, it looks as shown in figure 14.2. In this example, f has no free variables, so closure analysis for f is pro forma; because f escapes, it requires a closure f'. Similarly, callee-save registers don't accomplish much here, but they don't do any harm either.

The continuation h has k as a free variable, so a "closure" must be made in which k_0 is saved. But this closure will be passed as the first callee-save argument of f, occupying the slot where k_1 has been. So k_1 must also go into h's closure.

In this example we use square brackets to indicate record-creation.

The spill phase leaves this program unaltered, since no subexpression has very many free variables.

Figure 14.3 illustrates final code generation into the assembly language of a RISC-like machine, but without delayed-branch or delayed-load instructions (for simplicity). The label f is the countzeros function. Like every function and continuation, it starts with an instruction to check for heap exhaustion; the preceding two words enable to garbage collector to understand the current context. The

```
let fun f(clos,l,k0,k1,k2,k3) =
       case l
         of _::_ => let val a = #0 l
                        val r = #1 l
                    in if ieql(0, a)
                       then let fun h0(n,h1,k2',k3') =
                                        let val k0' = #0 h1
                                            val k1' = #1 h1
                                            val n' = 1+n
                                        in k0'(n',k1',k2',k3')
                                        end
                                val h1 = [k0,k1]
                            in f(clos,r,h0,h1,k2,k3)
                            end
                       else f(clos,r,k0,k1,k2,k3)
                    end
          | nil => k0(0,k1,k2,k3)
       val f_clos = [f]
  in c0(f_clos,c1,c2,c3)
end
```

Figure 14.2. countzeros after closure-conversion.

```
        # dataptr=r12, datalimit=r13
        .word  0b1111110  # bit mask indicating live registers
        .word  f-L0       # offset to beginning of code string
f:      # clos=r1, l=r2, k0=r3, k1=r4, k2=r5, k3=r6
        r0 = r12+r13       # will overflow on heap exhaustion
        r7 = r2 & 1        # bitwise and to test boxity of l
        if r7<>0 goto L1   # branch away if nil
        r8 = M[r2+0]       # a=r8
        r2 = M[r2+4]       # r=r2   (targeting for variable r)
        if r8<>0 goto L2   # if ieql(0, a)
        M[r12] = 33        # store tag for a pair
        M[r12+4] = r3      # store first word of pair
        M[r12+8] = r4      # store second word of pair
        r4 = r12+4         # h1=r4
        r12 = r12+12       # adjust dataptr
        r3 = h0            # h0=r3
        goto f
L2:     goto f
L1:     r2 = 0             # first argument of k0
        jump r3            # invoke k0
        .word 0b1111000    # register mask for h0
        .word h0-L0        # offset to beginning of code string
h0:     # n=r2, h1=r4, k2'=r5, k3'=r6
        r0 = r12+r13       # will overflow on heap exhaustion
        r3 = M[r4+0]       # k0'=r3
        r4 = M[r4+4]       # k1'=r4
        r2 = r2+2          # n'=r2
        jump r3
```

Figure 14.3. Final code for countzeros.

comments at labels f and h_0 explain the standard register assignments for formal parameters of escaping user functions and continuations, respectively.

Since `nil` is not a pointer, it has a low-order 1 bit; this is used to test the boxity of the list l. If l is nil, control proceeds to label `L1`, otherwise it falls through. The variables a and r are fetched from l; targeting is used to select a register for r so that no **move** instruction is required when f is invoked just before `L2`. Anti-targeting is used for a, which is *not* a parameter to any function call, so that register 2 is not clogged up with a (which would prevent targeting from working on r).

To make the closure $h1$ requires three **store** instructions and two **add** instructions. Then it is time to call f; because of the success of register targeting, all the parameters except h_0 are already in the right place.

Label `L2` implements the `else` clause of the test $a = 0$; all arguments are in place, so only a jump is necessary. Here the compiler could use just a bit of peephole optimization to eliminate the jump to a jump.

Label `L1` implements the `nil` clause of the `case`. Again, all parameters but r_2 are in the right place.

The closure h_0 is quite straightforward: it fetches variables k_0' and k_1' from the closure h_1, increments n (remember that the representation of n is as $2n + 1$, so an increment must add 2), and invokes k_0'. The parameters k_2' and k_3' are already in the right place.

The only way to make this loop significantly faster is to make it tail-recursive. This could be done, in principle, by a transformation before the closure phase of the compiler. But it is difficult to make this transformation sufficiently general. For example, in this case we would have to rely on the associative law for addition in order to count the zeros left to right instead of right to left.

Since the function h_0 does not allocate any records, we could eliminate its heap-limit check and still be guaranteed that the heap would not overflow. However, this could make the asynchronous signal handler wait long periods between safe points (see Section 16.6).

CHAPTER FIFTEEN

PERFORMANCE EVALUATION

Clearly, some of the optimizations and representations described in this book must be more useful than others. To find out which ones are most important, we measured some real programs. We compiled each program with each of the optimizations disabled in turn, to see the effect of each optimization on the speed and size of the program. We measured the time taken (and instructions executed) by the compiled code, the amount of garbage collection, the code size, and other interesting statistics.

We used six benchmark programs. Each of these is a "real" program written for a "real" purpose (not just as a benchmark). The programs are described in figure 15.1 and some statistics about them are given in figure 15.2. For programs that used functions from the ML standard library (Lex, Yacc, Simple, and VLIW) the source code includes a copy of the commonly used library functions (244 non-blank lines) so the effect of the compiler on these functions could be measured.

Key	Name	Description
l	Life	The game of Life, written by Chris Reade and described in his book [68], running 50 generations of a glider gun.
x	Lex	A lexical-analyzer generator, implemented by James S. Mattson and David R. Tarditi [15], processing the lexical description of Standard ML.
y	Yacc	A LALR(1) parser generator, implemented by David R. Tarditi [87], processing the grammer of Standard ML.
k	Knuth–B	An implementation of the Knuth–Bendix completion algorithm, implemented by Gerard Huet, processing some axioms of geometry.
s	Simple	A spherical fluid-dynamics program, developed as a "realistic" FORTRAN benchmark [33], translated into ID [38], and then translated into Standard ML by Lal George.
v	VLIW	A Very-Long-Instruction-Word instruction scheduler written by John Danskin.

Figure 15.1. Description of the benchmark programs.

Key	Program	Source Lines	Compile Time	Code Size	Data Size	Non-GC Time	GC Time	System Time
l	Life	117	11.6s	16k	489k	21.1s	0.8s	0.38s
x	Lex	1223	71.5	84k	1033k	15.6	1.74	0.21
y	Yacc	5785	593.0	269k	1276k	4.41	2.04	0.47
k	Knu-B	439	29.1	35k	1619k	11.2	1.15	0.15
s	Simple	1002	87.1	75k	5391k	35.2	3.42	0.11
v	VLIW	3216	624.0	315k	3598k	28.2	2.19	0.28

Figure 15.2. "Standard" run of each program.

Some basic statistics about each benchmark program. **Source Lines** is the number of nonblank, noncomment lines in the source program. **Compile Time** is the real time to compile the program (this is higher than necessary, see page 198). **Code Size** is the number of bytes in the compiled program. **Data Size** is the maximum number of kilobytes ever observed by the garbage collector (and is therefore a lower bound for the largest amount of data simultaneously live). **Non-GC Time** is the amount of CPU time spent executing the program exclusive of garbage-collection or operating-system time. **GC Time** is the CPU time spent garbage collecting, and **System Time** is time spent in the operating system. Elapsed time was within 1.3 percent of the sum of the three times shown, except for Lex where it was 4.6 percent higher and Yacc where it was 18 percent higher.

Key	Program	Data size	Heap size	Cache Effectiveness
l	Life	.48 MB	2 MB	0.30
x	Lex	1.01	3	0.29
y	Yacc	1.25	4	0.62
k	Knuth–Bendix	1.58	8	0.69
s	Simple	5.26	16	0.72
v	VLIW	3.51	20	0.42

Figure 15.3. Cache effectiveness of the benchmark programs.

"Cache effectiveness" is number of instructions executed per second, divided by the clock rate of the machine. This definition is appropriate for the MIPS, which has few pipeline stalls unrelated to the memory hierarchy; on other machines a more complicated definition would be necessary. It is probable that cache misses cause the bulk of the effect noticed in this table.

15.1   Hardware

All the programs were run on a MIPS Magnum 3000 workstation with 128 mega-bytes of memory. However, for running the test programs substantially less memory was used to simulate a "realistic" environment; figure 15.3 shows the heap size used for each program. In general, the heap size we used for each program is about 3–5 times the amount of live data. When the Standard ML of New Jersey system is run normally, it resizes the heap after each garbage collection to keep the heap size at the same ratio (usually five) to the amount of live data. However, for benchmark purposes we kept a fixed size for each program, for the following reason: If an optimization we were measuring caused the program to use less live data, that would a very good thing because it can reduce the load on the garbage collector; and we didn't want this effect canceled by the automatic heap resizing.

For compiling the programs, we always used a fixed heap size of 70 megabytes, which is much more than sufficient for these programs; the larger heap size leads to faster compilation (because of less garbage collection), and we wanted to get the measurements done quickly.

The Magnum 3000 has a 32 kilobyte direct-mapped instruction cache and a 32 kilobyte direct-mapped write-through data cache "with an 8-deep write buffer and good DRAM page-mode smarts so that it writes at 1 word/2 cycles much of the time" [76]. The cache line size is eight words (32 bytes).

The MIPS is a Reduced Instruction Set Computer that "usually" executes one instruction per cycle; there are relatively few different kinds of pipeline interlocks that can stall the instruction issue (indeed, MIPS was originally an acronym for "Microprocessor without Interlocked Pipeline Stages"). However, we found that on our 25 megahertz workstation we often getting only 7 or 10 million instructions per second (see figure 15.3). Furthermore, recompiling and rerunning the same program would often change the execution time by 5–20 percent (see figure 15.13). There are several possible causes of these effects:

1. A fetch of an instruction not present in the instruction cache ("I-cache miss") can cause a several-cycle delay.

2. A fetch or store of a word not present in the data cache ("D-cache miss") can cause a several-cycle delay.

3. Several consecutive stores can fill up the write buffer, causing a stall.

4. The TLB (translation lookaside buffer) holds the virtual-memory translations of 56 user pages and eight kernel pages. If a virtual page not in the TLB is referenced (a "TLB miss"), then a 10-instruction trap handler is executed to reload it.

5. A page fault occurs if a virtual page is not in physical memory.

6. An integer multiply or divide, or a floating-point operation, can stall if the result is demanded before it's ready.

It is difficult to know what the causes of the stalls really are. However, all the benchmarks were run in very generous physical memory, so it's probably not page faults. And the programs don't do much multiplication or division, and only Simple does floating-point operations, so that's probably not the cause either. Therefore, the problem is likely to lie in the "memory subsystem" comprising I-cache, D-cache, write buffer, and TLB.

Without running a cache simulator, we can't tell exactly what is happening. Direct-mapped caches are especially susceptible to "interference" problems, where two frequently accessed addresses map to the same cache line and keep knocking each other out of the cache. This might explain the variation in recompiled programs, shown in figure 15.13; the ML system may choose to load the recompiled program at a different address relative to the data it manipulates, or relative to the ML runtime system, or the data records relative to each other, thus causing cache conflicts. But this is not a very well-founded explanation of the variability; it's just a guess.

ML programs are not alone in spending half their time waiting for cache misses; the same problem has been noticed in C programs that operate on large data, running on a Silicon Graphics workstation (also a MIPS processor, but with 64K primary data cache and 256K secondary cache): Szymanski noticed that CAD programs operating on data of about 2–3 megabytes spend 40–70 percent of their time waiting for cache misses [85].

In any case, we have chosen to present most of our results using instruction counts, rather than execution times, for two reasons:

1. The variability of cache hit rates, even for essentially similar programs, makes it much harder to compare optimizations that might only improve performance by a few percent.

2. Newer computers may have much larger caches, or may use set-associative caches, either of which will tend to make the cache-miss effects smaller; as the absolute cache-miss-wait time decreases, so will the relative impact of differing memory-reference patterns caused by compiler optimizations.

We measure instruction counts as follows: One register of the machine is dedicated to hold the instruction count. (As figure 15.8 shows, the loss of one register won't affect the quality of code generation.) At each branch (in the delay slot of the branch instruction), the register is incremented by the count of instructions since the last branch, *including all NOPs and the instruction-count increment itself.* The effect of the instruction-count-increment instructions on processing time is minimal; it's just like turning off branch-delay scheduling. (We still do load-delay scheduling.) Furthermore, this measurement technique has no effect whatsoever on memory reference patterns.

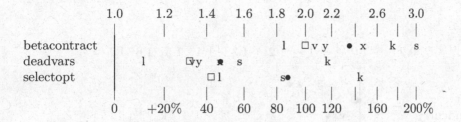

Figure 15.4. Crucial optimizations.

This graph shows the effect of disabling selected optimizations on the run time (instructions executed) of the compiled program. This is a log scale; the top labels indicate the ratio of performance, and the bottom labels indicate the percentage increase in instruction count. The letters indicate the individual programs (see figure 15.1 for the key). The dot • is the geometric mean of the increases for the individual programs. The square □ shows the average effect on *program size* of disabling the optimizations.

15.2   Measurements of individual optimizations

Figures 15.4 and 15.5 show the effect of disabling various individual optimizations. In most cases, the size and run time of the compiled code increases. It turns out that three optimizations are much more important than all the rest:

betacontract The in-line expansion of functions called only once (see page 68).

deadvars Eliminating the bindings of unused variables (page 70).

selectopt Constant folding of SELECTs from known records.

However, the amazing utility of these three optimizations may have less to do with the users' programs than with the method of translation into mini-ML and then into continuation-passing style. Danvy and Filinski have recently shown how to take more care converting into CPS, with the result that there are fewer "trivial" β-contraction redexes in the resulting expressions [35]. This would not affect the quality of code generated, but it might save the optimization phase some work; and it would reduce the size of the CPS expression when it's at its largest (i.e., before any contractions), which might save a large amount of memory. It seems, however, that our CPS-conversion algorithm already uses many of these techniques, so it's not clear how much room there is for improvement.

The optimizations listed in figure 15.5 are described in Chapters 6–14. We simply summarize them here.

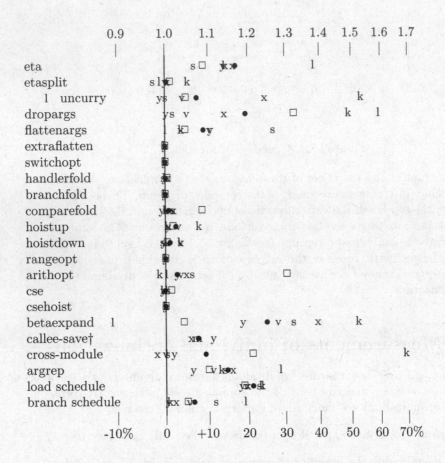

Figure 15.5. Effect of various optimizations.

This shows the effect on instructions executed of disabling various optimizations. A "good" optimization will appear farther to the right on this graph, indicating that the code runs slower when the optimization is disabled. The optimizations are described in the accompanying text. The letters v, l, x, y, s, k are the individual programs; the black dots are the averages; the squares show the effect on code size.

† Measurements for the **callee-save** optimization were done with a different set of benchmark programs; see the text.

eta Eta reduction (see page 76).

etasplit Inverse eta-reduction (see page 76).

uncurry Uncurrying of curried functions, at call sites where more than one argument is provided (page 76).

dropargs Eliminating unused arguments to functions (page 72).

flattenargs Replacing an n-tuple argument with n individual arguments (page 71).

extraflatten Replacing an n-tuple argument with n individual arguments, even if some of the call sites would then require extra SELECT operations (page 71).

switchopt Constant folding of SWITCH operators whose selector argument is an integer literal (page 73).

handlerfold Elimination of gethdlr operations in the scope of a sethdlr, and eliminating redundant sethdlrs (page 75).

branchfold Elimination of comparisons whose branch paths are the same (modulo α-conversion).

comparefold Constant folding of conditional branches (page 74).

hoistup Hoisting function definitions up to merge with other FIXes (see page 97).

hoistdown Pushing function definitions down to merge with other FIXes, and pushing function and other variable bindings inside conditionals and switches, if they are not used in more than one branch (page 96).

ifidiom Special recognition of an idiom involving if statements (page 75). Unfortunately, a bug prevented this idiom from being recognized in the test runs, so the transformation was never made, and there was no effect on run time.

rangeopt A very crude attempt at eliminating comparisons by range analysis on integer variables. As the graph shows, we didn't accomplish anything useful.

arithopt Constant folding of integer arithmetic expressions.

cse Common-subexpression elimination (page 99). Clearly a disappointing result.

csehoist An additional hoisting transformation useful for common-subexpression elimination (page 100). Also disappointing.

betaexpand In-line expansion of functions called more than once (Chapter 7).

callee-save Callee-save register allocation (Section 10.6). The measurements for this optimization were done on the programs **Lex**, **Yacc**, and the Standard ML of New Jersey **compiler** processing and optimizing its standard library; the change in *time* (not instruction count) is shown.

linked closures The "standard" closure representation used for these measurements is "flat" (Section 10.5), in which all free variables of a function appear directly in its closure (subject to modifications necessary for the callee-save technique). An alternate representation is "linked," so some variables do not appear directly in the closure; instead, a closure may point to the closure for a statically enclosing function, in which some of the free variables may be found. It turns out that switching between flat and linked closures makes no more than a 0.3 percent difference (in instruction count) in any of the benchmark programs.

cross-module Cross-module optimization. A word of explanation is necessary here. For the benchmark programs we put all the modules (typically, structure and functor definitions) into one file for each program, and compile them all at once. Normally, users would put each module of a program into a separate file (which is what we did for this line of the graph, to simulate "turning off cross-module optimization"). In the future, it would be nice to have the compiler automatically do cross-module optimizations across compilation units in different files.

argrep In the abstract-machine-code-generation phase, the first call to a known function can specialize the representation of arguments, so no register–register moves are necessary (page 159).

load schedule In the final target-machine-code-generation phase for the MIPS, one cannot use the result of a LOAD instruction in the immediately following instruction. The simplest solution is to put a NOP instruction (and waste a cycle); but a better solution is to reschedule so that some other useful instruction is put in the "delay slot" (page 170).

branch schedule On most RISC machines, one instruction after a branch gets executed even after a branch is taken. Branch scheduling can arrange to put a useful instruction (instead of a NOP) in that "delay slot" (page 170). This entry in the graph shows the effect of turning off branch scheduling. However, unlike all the other rows, here we measure *time* and not *instruction count*. This is because our instruction-counting code usually sits in the branch-delay slots, and we must remove that code to do branch scheduling. It should also be remarked that we do not do a state-of-the-art job of branch-scheduling; we move instructions into the delay slot from above the branch, but not from the destination of the branch [46].

It is natural to wonder whether all the improvements gained by the various optimizations of figures 15.4 and 15.5 are independent; that is, if optimization *A*

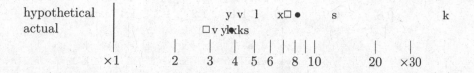

Figure 15.6. Many optimizations disabled at once.

This graph shows the effect of disabling all the optimizations of figure 15.4 and of figure 15.5 from **eta** through **csehoist**. The "hypothetical" row shows the product of all the individually measured effects of the individual optimizations; the "actual" row shows what actually happens. If the optimizations were all independent of each other, the two rows would be the same.

makes the program 1.1 times faster, and optimization B makes the program 1.3 times faster, then does the combination of A and B make it 1.43 times faster, or are they really doing the same thing redundantly? Figure 15.6 shows that, though it might seem that the first 19 optimizations listed provide eightfold speedup in combination, in fact they really provide only fourfold speedup. This isn't bad, however; it means (roughly) that an optimization that "claims" a 12 percent improvement (the 19th root of 8) may really be yielding an 8 percent improvement (the 19th root of 4). Thus, the individual "claims" are at least somewhat meaningful.

15.3 Tuning the parameters

The optimizer has several parameters that can be adjusted for better performance. The "uncurry" optimization requires a few passes of β-contraction to uncover redexes, but how many? The β-expansion phase has "fudge factors" C, D, and E; what should their values be? The entire cycle of contract–expand–hoist–CSE can stop when one round yields no optimizations, but perhaps it can almost as profitably stop when only n transformations are found. Finally, the runtime system has a tunable parameter: The ratio of heap-size to live data affects the efficiency of the garbage collector. Figures 15.7 through 15.12 illustrate the effects of tuning some of the compiler's and runtime system's parameters.

15.4 More about caches

All discussion so far of individual optimizations and parameter tuning has focused on instruction counts, for reasons explained in Section 15.1. Of course, the user of a compiler cares about execution time, not instruction count. And it may be

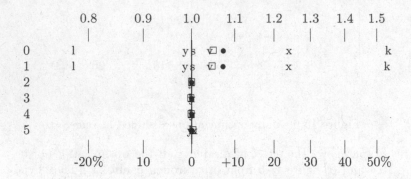

Figure 15.7. Rounds of contraction before η-reduction.

The "uncurrying" optimization is performed in the η-reduction phase (page 80). Some β-reduction is necessary to turn up instances of "uncurrying" that can be performed. This graph shows the effect of performing n iterations of the β-contraction/constant-folding phase before the η phase. Execution time for $n \leq 1$ is about 8 percent higher than for $n \geq 2$. Clearly, for these programs $n = 2$ suffices; $n = 2$ is used for all of the other benchmark runs described in this chapter.

that some individual optimization decreases the instruction count but increases the number of cache misses, for no net gain!

Figure 15.14 shows the effect that various optimizations and parameters have on cache effectiveness. It appears, for example, that load scheduling decreases cache effectiveness by about 10 percent; this is not surprising, since the effect of scheduling is to remove NOPs that were very kind to the cache. β-contraction decreases cache effectiveness by about 15 percent; though it actually increases the cache effectiveness in the Simple program by a large amount.

The change in cache effectiveness for any optimization can be multiplied by the change in instruction count (shown in figures 15.5, 15.8, 15.9, etc.) to get the effect on execution time *on this machine*. Note that the cache-effectiveness graph shows the *increase* in *effectiveness* caused by leaving an optimization *turned on*; figures 15.4 and 15.5 show the *increase* in *instruction count* caused by turning an optimization *off*.

The most remarkable thing about this graph is that the variance is so much larger than the average effects. It seems difficult to make useful generalizations or predictions from this data. Of course, as figure 15.13 shows, even a slight rearrangement of code and data can have large effects on the effectiveness of the cache.

Section 18.4 outlines a garbage-collection strategy that might significantly increase cache effectiveness.

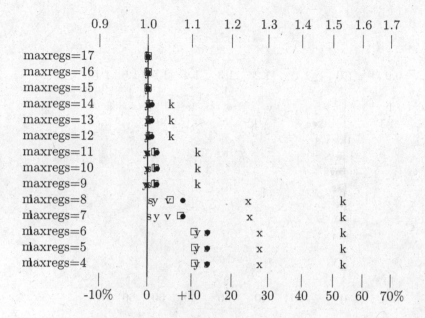

Figure 15.8. Registers on the target machine.

If we artificially limit the number of registers on the target machine for which code is generated, we expect to see the performance get worse as there are more spills, and as the arguments to known functions can less often fit in registers. This graph shows that the effect is not noticeable if there are 15 or more registers, and not severe with at least nine registers. Note that this does not include the "special-purpose" registers used by the code generator and runtime system, of which there are about six, or the register reserved for hardware or operating system, of which there are as many as six on some machines.

Curiously, the Life benchmark (1) runs *faster* with fewer than nine registers, as indicated by the datapoints at the extreme left.

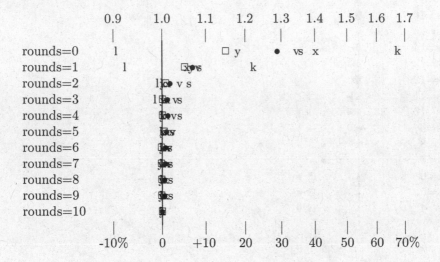

Figure 15.9. Effect of more rounds of in-line expansion.

This shows the effect of increasing the maximum number of rounds of β-expansion alternating with constant folding and contraction. Rounds=n indicates that contraction is iterated until convergence; then there are n rounds, each with one pass of β-expansion followed by contraction until convergence. Note that in most cases, this terminates naturally after a few rounds, which is why there is little difference between rounds=6 and rounds=9. For the other benchmarks in this chapter, rounds=10 was used.

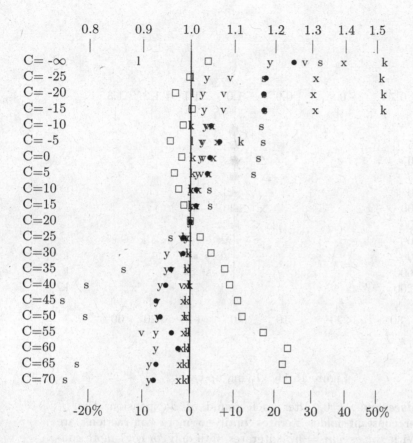

Figure 15.10. Optimism of the in-line expander.

The β-expansion phase has a parameter C that indicates the maximum amount of expected code growth it can tolerate in each individual in-line expansion (see page 91). The justification for C is that there may be further contractions in the expanded function body that the expander can't quite predict. This shows the effect of various degrees of optimism (large values of C) and pessimism (small values). The boxes $\square$ indicate the size of the resulting program; as expected, more eager in-line expansion leads to larger compiled code and faster execution.

For the other benchmarks in this chapter, $C = 20$ was used.

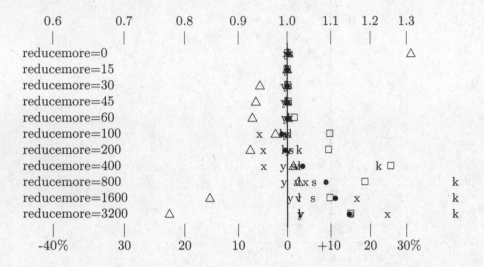

Figure 15.11. Giving up early.

With *reducemore* = 0, after each round of β-expansion, the β-contracter/constant folder iterates until no more contractions are found. With *reducemore* = n, it iterates until only "a few" more contractions are performed in one round; and if only n contractions and expansions are found in any round, no more rounds are done. This graph indicates the effect of varying n. The triangles $\triangle$ indicate compile time; the other points represent the change in run time and code size, as usual. Clearly on the medium-size programs used for these measurements, a value of 200 reduces compile time without affecting run time much. A value of 15 was used for all the other measurements in this chapter.

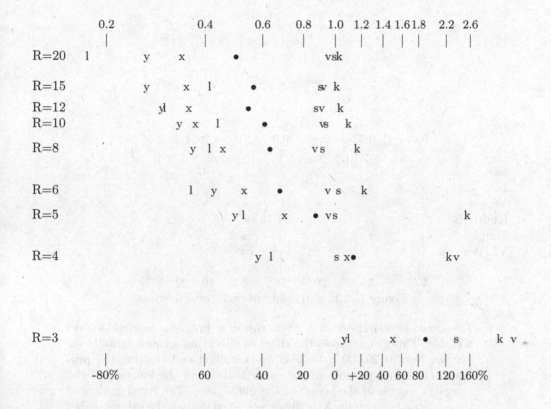

Figure 15.12. GC time vs. heap size.

As the ratio R of heap size to live data goes up, garbage-collection time should go down. In a nongeneration copying collector, GC time should be inversely proportional to $R - 2$, as described in Section 16.1. This is a log–log plot, where the spacing of the R-axis is according to $\log(R-2)$. We don't see a straight line because a generational collector is used, because it's impossible to keep R constant as the amount of live data varies, and probably for lots of other reasons. The data seem to indicate that $t \propto (R-2)^{-0.75}$ for $R < 6$ and $t \propto (R-2)^{-0.25}$ for $R > 6$, approximately

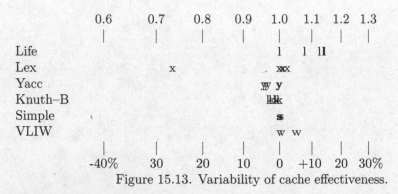

Figure 15.13. Variability of cache effectiveness.

The cache effectiveness of a given run of a program is quite unpredictable. This graph shows the effect of allocating a small array (sizes ranging from 0–20,000 bytes) before compiling and running the program. The only purpose of the array is to affect the location of the compiled code, and the layout of the data space. The running time of the program can vary by 5 to 20 percent, even though the same number of instructions is executed.

For each program, "1.0" (top axis) or "0" (bottom axis) represents the cache effectiveness of the "standard run" of the program, shown in figure 15.2.

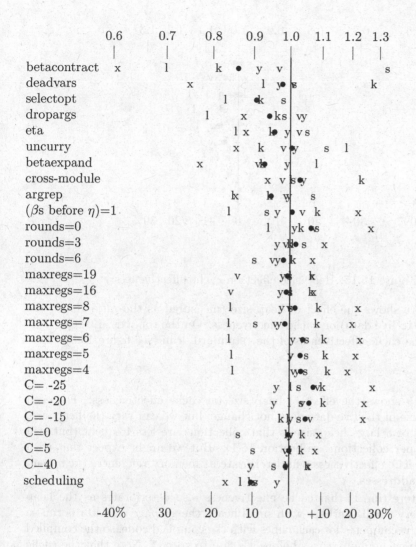

Figure 15.14. Cache effectiveness.

Some of the optimizations significantly alter the cache hit rate. This shows the gain or loss in instructions executed per second on a MIPS Magnum 3000 workstation. For example, using the *betacontract* optimization *decreases* cache effectiveness by 14 percent on the average. Setting $C = -25$ *increases* cache effectiveness by 8 percent on the average.

Only those optimizations that changed the instructions per second of at least one program by at least 10 percent are shown here. This graph should not be taken too seriously; figure 15.13 shows that much of the variation comes not from the properties of the optimizations but from accidents of program and data placement.

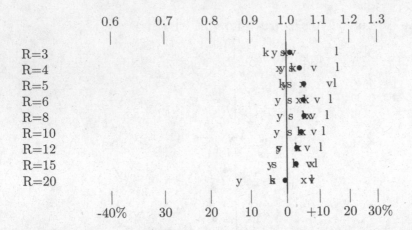

Figure 15.15. Heap size effect on cache effectiveness.

This figure shows the effect of heap size (measured as the ratio R of heap size to live data) on cache effectiveness. On the top axis, 1.0 represents the cache effectiveness of the "standard" run (see figure 15.3).

Figure 15.15 shows the effect of heap size on cache effectiveness. For each program, the size of the live data does not change, but we can vary the heap size. The advantage of a large heap size is that collections are less frequent (but still cost the same per collection, see Section 16.1). But we might expect that with a large heap, cache effectiveness will deteriorate as memory references are spread out over more addresses.

What is interesting is that cache effectiveness also deteriorates as the heap size becomes very small. Perhaps with small heaps the garbage collector is run so frequently that it competes for cache lines with the compiled code, so the compiled code misses the cache many times before it's "up to speed." Note that the cache effectiveness shown is for the compiled code only, not the garbage collector.

Unlike most compilers, Standard ML of New Jersey uses no runtime stack for activation records or closures. Instead, all closures are allocated on the garbage-collected heap. This means that programs allocate new records on the heap much more frequently than in most systems. Figure 15.16 shows that one word (four bytes) is allocated for every 3–7 instructions executed. Since assignments to already-existing reference variables are rare, almost all **store** instructions are for the initialization of words on the heap; thus, the "Allocation Rate" shown in the table can also be construed as the proportion of all instructions that are **store**s.

Initializing store instructions account for 20.7 percent of all instructions (the mean of the allocation rates given in the table). We can compare this with C

Key	Program	Allocation Rate	Data/Heap Ratio	GC Overhead
l	Life	.327	.24	.038
x	Lex	.234	.34	.11
y	Yacc	.140	.31	.46
k	Knuth–B	.191	.12	.10
s	Simple	.134	.33	.097
v	VLIW	.215	.18	.077

Figure 15.16. Allocation rates and GC overhead.

Standard ML of New Jersey programs do an enormous amount of allocation on the heap. The **Allocation Rate** shown in this table is the ratio of heap-words allocated to instructions executed. Since the vast majority of **store** instructions are to initialize words on the heap, the **Allocation Rate** is almost the same as the **proportion of store instructions**.

We also show the **Data/Heap Ratio** used in our measurements of the programs (the inverse of the parameter R shown in figure 15.12), and the overhead of garbage collection (GC time divided by non-GC time).

programs running on the MIPS, compiled by the MIPS C compiler, in which stores are 12 percent of all instructions.[1] This is quite a significant difference, and might mean any of the following:

1. ML and C are quite different programming models, and the programs being compared are doing quite different things.

2. The C compiler is optimizing stores nicely, but doesn't do as well as ML in eliminating nonstore instructions.

3. The ML compiler is poorly optimizing memory traffic, but doing well in eliminating other kinds of instructions.

In any case, it is hard to imagine a higher rate of heap allocation. Even so, garbage-collection overhead is a reasonable 14 percent (the average for the six programs); with better tuning of the collector (and by using more than two generations) this might be reduced by a factor of two.

An important lesson is that programmers should *not* strive to avoid "consing;" the system already allocates so much on the heap (especially continuation closures)

---

[1]Data taken from Appendix C.4 of Patterson and Hennessy [46], including SW (store-word) and SD (store-double-precision) instructions (counting the SD instructions twice, to simulate the two store instructions necessary to implement them on a MIPS R3000); and including only the GCC, Spice, and TeX benchmarks. The DLX machine used for Hennessy and Patterson's measurements is very similar to the MIPS.

that the impact of program transformations meant to avoid allocation is likely to be minimal.

15.5   Compile time

Standard ML of New Jersey takes a long time to compile. There are several culprits:

- The optimization phases (in many cases) are written "like prototypes," and too little attention is paid to how fast they run.

- A lot of work is done in nonproductive phases (such as hoisting, common-subexpression elimination, etc.).

- The translation into lambda-language, and then into CPS, generates a lot of unnecessary redexes; these redexes must then be reduced by the optimization phase. With a bit more sophistication, perhaps they could be generated "already-reduced" [35].

Some of these problems are easy to fix. For example, it is trivial to disable the hoisting and common-subexpression-elimination phases, to set the *reducemore* parameter to 400 (as described in figure 15.11), and so on. After making these adjustments, we measured the time to compile our six benchmark programs. The compile times and the breakdown by phases of the compiler, are shown in figure 15.17.

There's a real shocker here: The "assembly" phase—which includes the resolution of span-dependent instructions, instruction scheduling (which takes about a third of the time shown), and generation of the actual bit patterns of the instructions—takes more time than all the rest of the phases put together! Clearly, there is some problem with an algorithm or data structure; these simple tasks should not take nearly that long.

How much could the compile time be improved? We believe that the speed of the closure phase could be doubled without too much work; the speed of the assembly phase could be quintupled; and, by ripping out all the data gathering for optimizations that turned out to be useless (see figure 15.5) and implementing a smarter CPS converter, the speed of the optimization phase (β-contraction, in-line expansion, etc.) could be doubled. This would about double the speed of compilation overall.

Even so, the speed of compilation would then be about 25 lines per second on a twenty-MIPS machine. This is terrible; a good fast C compiler can compile about 400 lines of C per second [39] on a similar machine. There are two consolations, however:

1. With our compiler, you don't have to write your programs in C; and

2. Computers are getting faster at a faster rate than programs are getting bigger (we hope).

Compile time	Life 11s	Lex 88	Yacc 499	Knu-B 29	Simp 120	VLIW 328	Avg.
Parse	5.9%	4.7	3.4	5.9	3.8	3.6	4.6%
Semantics	8.1	7.3	4.0	6.4	7.7	4.7	6.4
Translate	0.7	0.5	0.3	0.7	0.4	0.4	0.5
Convert	1.1	0.8	0.6	1.2	0.7	0.7	0.8
Optimize	9.4	24.3	24.4	20.9	29.4	15.4	20.6
Closure	12.9	8.1	9.8	8.7	6.0	13.1	9.8
Spill	0.8	0.7	1.0	0.7	0.4	0.7	0.7
Generate	8.4	5.8	4.1	7.5	3.8	4.3	5.6
Assemble	52.6	48.0	52.4	48.0	47.9	57.1%	51.0

Figure 15.17. Time spent in different phases of the compiler.

This table shows the total compile time for each benchmark (when certain nonproductive optimizations are disabled), and the percentage of time spent in each phase. **Parse** includes lexical analysis and LALR(1) table interpretation. **Semantics** includes building the annotated abstract syntax tree and type checking. **Translate** is from abstract syntax to mini-ML (lambda language); **Convert** is from lambda language to CPS. **Optimize** includes the η, β-contract, and β-expand phases. **Generate** is the generation of abstract-machine instructions and the translation to "assembly" language for the MIPS. **Assemble** includes span-dependent jump resolution and instruction scheduling.

15.6   Comparison with other compilers

There are several Standard ML compilers available [21]:

- **Standard ML of New Jersey** as described in this book.

- **Poly/ML**, an implementation of ML in the Poly language [63], runs on Motorola 68020 and SPARC machines. Poly/ML is reported [21] to compile faster, and run slower than SML/NJ.

- **Poplog ML** is an implementation of ML in the Poplog system developed at the University of Sussex; it runs on VAX, MC68020, Intel 386, and SPARC machines. Poplog ML is reported [21] to compile faster, and run slower, than Poly/ML.

- **Edinburgh ML** is an implementation of the core language (without modules) that uses a byte-code interpreter written in C. It is portable to most machines with a C compiler but is quite slow.

- **The Kit Compiler**, a direct implementation by Nick Rothwell of *The Definition of Standard ML* [65]; this is intended for research and requires orders of magnitude more time and space (for compilation and for execution) than a "real" compiler.

- **ANU ML**, developed at the Australian National University, implements the core language of the *Definition* and an old version of modules. It compiles to native code on MC68020, VAX, and Pyramid.

- **MicroML**, developed at the University of Umea (Sweden), is an interpreter for an ML subset that runs on IBM PCs.

There are also two good compilers for CAML, a nonstandard ML developed at INRIA: the CAML compiler [25], which generates native code for several machines; and CAML Light [58], an amazingly fast byte-code interpreter that can compile in at least an order of magnitude less memory than SML/NJ. (See figure 15.19.)

We tested Poly/ML and SML/NJ on our six benchmark programs, running on a SparcStation 2 (the only modern platform on which they both run). Figure 15.18 shows the results. Poly/ML compiles about 2.7 times percent faster; but SML/NJ programs run 1.7 times faster than Poly/ML programs, on the average (geometric mean). SML/NJ reportedly uses about 1.5 times as much heap space for execution [21], and seems to use about 2–3 times as much for compilation. On a 68020-based platform (e.g., a Sun-3), SML/NJ probably generates only slightly better code than Poly/ML (since our translation from abstract to native code for that machine is not as good as it could be). So on obsolete architectures with tiny memories, Poly/ML may do better than SML/NJ.

Figure 15.19 compares implementations of several programming languages on the Knuth–Bendix benchmark. Standard ML of New Jersey does quite well, especially on the RISC machine (the DECstation 5000 has a MIPS processor).

| | Poly/ML 1.99 | | SML/NJ 0.73 | |
	Compile Time	Run Time	Compile Time	Run Time
Life	3	30.4	10	23.6
Lex	18	24.9	48	18.0
Yacc	91	11.0	180	7.9
Knuth–B	9	34.1	24	20.6
Simple	20	260.5	62	54.4
VLIW	55	50.3	157	39.3

Figure 15.18. Comparison of Poly/ML and SML/NJ.

This table shows compile time and run time in seconds (CPU time was within 1% of elapsed time) on a SparcStation 2 with 48 megabytes of memory. Both Poly/ML and SML/NJ were internal, not-yet-released versions of September, 1991. Poly/ML uses infinite-precision integers while SML/NJ uses finite precision; it's not clear how much of an advantage this gives SML/NJ. Commercially released versions of Poly/ML as of this date are significantly slower than 1.99.

15.7 Conclusions

What have we learned from all these measurements? There are some conclusions that can be drawn:

- If something could be done (hardware or software) about cache misses, programs would run about twice as fast. Perhaps the solution is to have a megabyte data cache that can hold the entire youngest generation.

- The three most important optimizations are β-contraction, dead-variable elimination, and constant folding of fetches from immutable records.

- In-line expansion, η-reduction, flattening of tuple arguments, and uncurrying save lots of time but not as much space.

- Elimination of unused procedure arguments, evaluation of arithmetic operators with constant arguments, and cross-module optimization save plenty of time but save even more space.

- Constant folding of comparisons doesn't save time but saves a significant amount of space.

	Sun 3/280 16 Mbytes		DECstation 5000/200 16 Mbytes	
	Execute	GC	Execute	GC
CAML V2-6.1	14.5	14.8	6.2	6.2
CAML Light 0.2	28.3		6.5	
SML/NJ 0.65	9.6	0.3	1.7	0.1
SML/NJ 0.65 x-mod	8.5	0.3	1.4	0.1
LeLisp 15.23	4.1		1.4	
SunOS 3.5, cc -O	4.35			
gcc 1.37.1, gcc -O	4.22			
Ultrix 4.0, cc -O2			0.90	

Figure 15.19. Comparison of several different compilers.

Xavier Leroy translated Gerard Huet's Knuth–Bendix completion program into several different languages, and ran it on two different machines [59]. (The program is the same as the Knuth–Bendix benchmark referred to elsewhere in this chapter, but with simpler input data.) This table shows non-GC run time and GC time for each version of the program. Since the program uses higher-order functions, Leroy had to do manual lambda lifting to write the program in Lisp and C, and in some places had to use explicit closures (structures containing function pointers).

CAML [25] is a different version of the ML language (i.e., not Standard ML) developed at INRIA; CAML V2-6.1 is a native-code compiler that shares the LeLisp runtime system, and CAML Light [58] is a compiler with a byte-code interpreter written in C. **SML/NJ x-mod** refers to Standard ML of New Jersey with all modules placed in one file to allow cross-module optimization.

- Choosing register assignments for formal parameters of known functions on the basis of the actual parameters of the first-encountered call (**argrep**) is quite useful.

- Several optimizations don't seem to accomplish anything at all: more aggressive flattening of tuple arguments; constant folding of SWITCH operators, analysis of exception handler variables, and arithmetic; range analysis of integers; common-subexpression elimination; and the recognition of comparisons whose **then** and **else** clauses are identical.

- After CPS conversion and callee-save register analysis, there is no appreciable difference between flat and linked closure representations.

- Hoisting of closures up and down to accomplish closure sharing does not accomplish much. Given the potential space-complexity danger of closure sharing (see Section 12.3), this optimization seems not to be worthwhile.

- About 17 general registers on the target machine (including five or six registers that ML uses for special purposes) seem to suffice, and 14 is almost as good. This does not include any registers reserved for special purposes by the hardware or operating system.

- Two rounds of in-line expansion will catch most useful β-reductions, except in unusual programs.

- The heuristics used by the β-expander seem to be robust.

- For the two-generation garbage collector currently used by Standard ML of New Jersey [6], increasing the heap size beyond six times the amount of live data gives diminishing returns.

- Standard ML of New Jersey "conses" furiously, but still manages to achieve good performance.

CHAPTER SIXTEEN

THE RUNTIME SYSTEM

The compilation technology described in this book uses heap allocation very heavily: for data constructors, n-tuples, closures, continuations, and references. The most important job of a runtime system—for compilers built this way—is to manage and garbage collect the heap, and do so as efficiently as possible. Therefore, this chapter concentrates on garbage collection; other aspects of the runtime system less relevant to optimization using continuations are described in our article on the runtime system [7].

16.1   Efficiency of garbage collection

We define the *amortized cost* of a garbage-collection algorithm as the time spent divided by the number of cells reclaimed. We assume that, in the long run, the number of cells allocated is approximately equal to the number of cells reclaimed. The "time spent" includes all time for *memory management*, including the execution of the collector itself, and the overhead for allocation of new records; but not the initialization of those records, which must occur no matter what the algorithm.

Consider two styles of collection algorithms: mark-and-sweep garbage collection and copying collection. Mark-and-sweep collection proceeds by first traversing the graph of all reachable records (starting at a specified set of "roots," see Sections 12.4 and 13.2), and marking anything it reaches. Then the collector sweeps through *all* records in order of address, putting any unmarked cells on a free list.

Copying collection works by traversing the graph of all reachable records starting at the roots, and *copying* any record it reaches to a *to-space*. As it copies a record, it leaves in the old copy a *forwarding pointer* that points to the new copy, so if another pointer to the old record is traversed, the same new copy is used. When the graph is completely traversed, the *from-space* containing old copies and garbage is now completely devoid of useful data, and is now usable as a large, contiguous free space for more allocation.

Now, either algorithm might work by a depth-first or a breadth-first traversal, or might traverse the live data in any other order. In any case, the time taken for the traversal is proportional to the amount of live data L. The sweep phase takes time proportional to M, the amount of memory swept. So the time taken by one mark and sweep is $c_1 L + c_2 M$, and the time taken by one copying collection is $c_3 L$.

The number of words reclaimed is just $M - L$, the size of the space collected minus the number of live words. Now the amortized cost of garbage collection is just

$$cost_{\text{mark\&sweep}} = \frac{c_1 L + c_2 M}{M - L} \qquad cost_{\text{copying}} = \frac{c_3 L}{M - L}$$

It is instructive to see how low these costs can become. If we just run the same program in a larger memory, L will not change but M can grow arbitrarily large. Larger M will decrease the cost; in the limit

$$\lim_{M \to \infty} cost_{\text{mark\&sweep}} = c_2 \qquad \lim_{M \to \infty} cost_{\text{copying}} = 0$$

Thus the cost per word of mark and sweep collection can never be less than c_2, whereas there is no inherent lower bound on the cost of copying collection.

But what if c_2 is quite small? This constant represents the size of the inner loop of the sweep phase, and c_2 might be as little as one or two instructions per word. Unfortunately, however, Standard ML of New Jersey allocates one new word on the heap for every five instructions executed (on the average); if there is an extra cost of one or two instructions to sweep this word, that's a 20–40 percent overhead just for the sweep phase of garbage collection. Clearly, then, to support code compiled to allocate at such a ferocious rate, copying collection is required.

M never quite reaches infinity, unfortunately, and we would like to get a realistic estimate of the cost per reclaimed word of garbage collection. A very useful—just about necessary—adjunct of the basic copying collection algorithm is *generational garbage collection*, described in Section 16.3. With generational collection, the copying collector can concentrate on a region of memory that has a very high proportion of garbage.

In fact, in the Standard ML of New Jersey collector, the copying collector finds an average of 98.7 percent garbage in its *from-space* when copying any given generation. This is an average taken from runs of the six benchmark programs described in Chapter 15, with a ratio of heap size to live data (summed over all generations) of six. With a simple two-space copying collector, of course, the percentage of garbage would be 66.6 in this amount of memory (each semispace would have a ratio M/L of 3). Clearly, generational garbage collection is very effective.

Thus the average proportion of live data in the from-space is only .013; let us suppose that c_3 is 20 instructions, more or less. Then for every word allocated, we'll have to pay $c_3 L/M$ or 0.26 instructions to collect it; if a word is allocated for every five instructions of execution, then the overhead for garbage collection is .052, or about 5 percent. This approximates (slightly optimistically) the overhead measured; see Chapter 15.

16.2   Breadth-first copying

Cheney's copying collection algorithm [28] is one of the simplest to implement. It is essentially a breadth-first search that copies live records from *from-space* to *to-space*. A breadth-first search requires a *queue* to keep track of nodes seen but not yet processed; Cheney's algorithm uses the to-space itself for the queue.

The basic operation of the algorithm is to *forward* a pointer. Given a p that points to a record in *from-space*, *forward*(p) points to the new copy in *to-space*. If the record has not yet been copied, it is first copied into *to-space* and a *forwarding pointer* is installed in the old copy. If a forwarding pointer is already there, then it is returned as the result of *forward*(p). In pseudo-code:

forward$(p) =$
    if $p[0]$ is a forwarding pointer
    then return $p[0]$
    else let L be the length of the object p points to
        for $i \leftarrow 0$ **to** $L - 1$
          do copy $p[i]$ to location $next + i$
        $p[0] \leftarrow next$
        $next \leftarrow next + L$
        return $p[0]$

How can we tell if $p[0]$ is a forwarding pointer? Well, the forwarding pointers are exactly those pointers in from-space that point to to-space; this is a simple address-range test.

Now, the "main loop" of the algorithm just tries to forward everything. First the root set is forwarded; then each field of every record in the to-space is forwarded. The pointer *scan* points at the first unforwarded object; the pointer *next* points at the first free word in to-space. When *scan* catches up with *next*, the collection is finished.

$scan \leftarrow next$
for $i \leftarrow 0$ **to** *number-of-roots*
  do $root_i \leftarrow forward(root_i)$
while $scan < next$
  do let L be the length of the object *scan* points to
      for $i \leftarrow 0$ **to** $L - 1$
        do $scan[i] \leftarrow forward(scan[i])$
      $scan \leftarrow scan + L$

16.3   Generational garbage collection

The technique of *generational garbage collection* [60] relies on two observations about Lisp and functional programs:

1. Newer cells tend to point to older cells.

2. Newer cells tend to be shorter lived than older cells.

When one writes `cons(a,b)` in a program, one constructs a newer cell that points to two older cells. The only way that an older cell can point to a newer cell is if it is modified after it is created, which is rare in Lisp and Scheme and impossible in ML (except for `ref` cells).

When a cell has been accessible for a long time, it's typically part of a global data structure that will continue to be necessary. New cells tend to be intermediate results of computations that will soon be useless. In this respect, dynamically allocated list cells are quite unlike radioactive atoms, whose future lifetimes are unrelated to their past lifetimes.

Now, we can take advantage of these two observations. Observation 2 implies that we should concentrate our garbage-collection efforts on the newer cells (which have a higher proportion of garbage), and observation 1 makes it possible to do so.

Allocated cells will be kept in several distinct areas G_i of memory, called *generations*. Cells in the same generation are of similar age, and all the records in generation G_i are older than the records in generation G_{i+1}. This implies (by observation 1) that for $i < j$, there are (almost) no pointers from G_i into G_j.

Consider the newest generation, G_n. The copying garbage collector may be applied to this generation, using the global variables and runtime stack as a root set. Because (almost) no pointers in the other generations can possibly point to records in G_n, the other generations (almost) need not be considered as roots. The garbage collector may copy the reachable objects of G_n into a new generation G_n' without touching the other generations. This is advantageous because G_n is expected (by observation 2) to have a higher proportion of garbage than any of the other generations.

In general, the garbage collector can work on generation G_i if it also works on all the newer generations; that is, it may work on any subset $G_i, G_{i+1}, ..., G_n$ of the generations. For greatest efficiency, the garbage collector should usually copy just G_n, but occasionally copy the older generations.

In practice, generational garbage collection performs extremely well; though it is typically implemented only for programming languages (such as Lisp, Scheme, ML, Smalltalk, etc.) where modification of older objects is relatively rare. In general, it is widely agreed that garbage collection need not take more than 5 percent of computation time.

The algorithm depends on the fact that cells contain pointers only to older cells. In the presence of assignments to older `ref` cells, this acyclic condition will not hold. Lieberman and Hewitt [60] handle this problem by making such fields point indirectly through an "assignment table." This requires either special hardware, or several instructions in software each time a reference variable is accessed.

A simpler scheme devised by Ungar [89] keeps a set of addresses of cells that point to newer cells; this set must be maintained with the help of the allocating program—whenever it assigns a pointer into an existing cell, it must add the address of that cell to the modified set. Then, when collecting generations $G_k, ..., G_n$, the modified sets of generations $G_0, ..., G_{k-1}$ must be treated as root pointers.

This scheme makes fetching the contents of a `ref` very cheap—since the data structure for the modified set need not be consulted—but assigning a ref requires a few instructions (or special hardware). An update that stores a nonpointer value cannot create a root of garbage collection, though; if these updates can be identified at compile time, it is not necessary to generate code to augment the modified set for them. Therefore, to support Ungar's scheme, it is helpful to have two different operators for assignment (called `:=` and `unboxedassign`) for storing pointers and nonpointers, respectively. Then nonpointer assignment can go at full speed. The choice of pointer or nonpointer assignment operator should be made early in compilation; see Section 4.4. Of course, when it is not known at compile time whether a particular value is a pointer, the `:=` operator must be used.

Shaw [79] uses the virtual memory of the machine. All the pages in the older generations are initially made read-only. An attempt to update a `ref` cell will cause a page fault; the fault handler can put the page in a set of modified older-generation pages, and make the page writable. Subsequent updates to that page will go at full speed, and the entire contents of each page in the modified set must be scanned at garbage-collection time.

With this virtual-memory method, it is helpful to separate the older generations into at least three parts:

1. Immutable records, list cells, closures, and other pointer-containing objects. These will never be updated.

2. Mutable, pointer-containing, references and arrays. These must be marked read-only, and handled as described in the previous paragraph.

3. Mutable byte arrays, immutable strings; references and arrays that contain only unboxed values. These never contain pointers, so even though they may be updated they cannot cause problems for generational garbage collectors; they are marked as writable in the virtual-memory system.

The static type system of ML makes it easy to achieve this separation; for other languages, where all objects are potentially mutable even though few updates may be performed, it is not possible to separate mutable from immutable objects.

This separation might not help enormously; good measurements have not yet been done. In any case, to separate objects of different kinds it is helpful to have different operators for making immutable records, possibly pointer-containing `ref`s, nonpointer-containing `ref`s, and immutable strings (of bytes) and mutable byte arrays. Thus, for example, we have `makeref` and `makerefunboxed` to make possibly pointer-containing and nonpointer-containing references, respectively.

Note that an implementation is unlikely to need *both* the distinction between `:=` and `unboxedassign` and between `makeref` and `unboxedmakeref`, since it is unlikely that Ungar's technique and Shaw's will *both* be used in the same runtime system. We provide both in the CPS language to maintain some implementation independence.

16.4   Runtime data formats

One way to streamline the garbage collector is to make the formats of runtime data as simple as possible. For Standard ML, we divide all objects into two categories:

1. Pointer containing: Each word is either a pointer or a tagged integer. These objects include n-tuples, records, closures, data constructors, arrays, and references.

2. Nonpointer containing: There are no pointers anywhere in the object, so each word or byte can have an arbitrary bit pattern. These objects include strings, byte arrays, floating-point numbers, floating-point arrays, machine instructions.

An object starts with one descriptor word, which indicates the *kind* of the object (not the source-language *type*) and its length. There are just two different kinds of pointer-containing objects: immutable records (including closures, data constructors, etc.) and mutable arrays. Similarly, there are two kinds of nonpointer-containing objects: immutable strings (including real numbers, float vectors, machine-code segments, etc.) and mutable byte arrays (including float arrays). In a Lisp or Smalltalk system, where there is runtime type checking, descriptors would need to include much more information to distinguish types of objects.

Usually, a pointer contains the address of the first (nondescriptor) word of an object, and the descriptor may be found by looking at the previous word. But it is often convenient to allow pointers to point to the middle of objects:

- When several functions share a closure (see page 107), some function pointers must point into the middle of the closure record.

- When accessing elements of an array sequentially, the compiler may use a strength-reduction optimization that allows pointers into the middle of the array (we have not implemented this).

- One compilation unit usually has many entry points in the same machine-code string, each of which may be pointed to from closures.

- When accessing characters of a string or float array sequentially, strength reduction may allow pointers into the middle of the array (we have not implemented this, and cannot; see below).

We solve this problem in one way for pointer-containing objects and another way for string objects. For pointer-containing objects, we observe that all integers (and other unboxed values) have a low-order 1 bit; all pointers (to word-aligned data) have low-order 00 bits. Therefore, we make descriptors (at the beginnings of objects) have low-order 10 bits. Given a pointer to the middle of an object, one simply searches backward sequentially to find a word whose low-order bits are 10.

If we have a large object with many pointers to the middle of it, this backward sequential search would have to be done for each pointer. We can solve this problem, if necessary, by filling the from-space version of the object with special forwarding pointers that point to the appropriate places in the middle of the to-space copy; then the full backward search will only be done once.

For machine-code objects, we require that the entry points be specially marked. For any location l in the object that can be pointed at directly, the previous bytes $(l-4)\ldots(l-1)$ must contain a *back-pointer* descriptor that indicates the distance backward to the beginning of the object.

This solution works well for the entry points to a machine-code string. However, it is not useful for strength reduction in traversing arbitrary strings and byte arrays, because there is no room for the back pointers when any element of the array may be addressed by the program. Thus, we can't point into the middle of arbitrary byte data.

Because nonpointer-containing objects don't need to be scanned by the collector, it is helpful for the *forward* procedure to copy them to a different region of the to-space, so the region between *scan* and *next* contains only pointer-containing objects. Then the nested loop of the garbage-collection function (above) can be unnested to process each word individually: Integers and descriptors are left unchanged, and pointers are forwarded. The ability to scan objects word-by-word becomes even more valuable for virtual-memory-based concurrent or generational collectors [7, 8].

16.5 Big bags of pages

It's a bit wasteful to use a full word for the descriptor of each object. The solution is to group many objects together on the same page, and let one descriptor cover the whole page [45]; this is known as a BIBOP (BIg Bag Of Pages) scheme. For example, if we have a large number of two-word records (as is the case), we can reserve one or more regions of memory for them, and store them without descriptors. Testing the size of an object now requires looking up the high-order bits of its address in a "BIBOP table." John Reppy is experimenting with 64-kbyte "BIBOP pages" in the Standard ML of New Jersey compiler, so a single 64-kbyte array can hold eight-bit descriptors for all the BIBOP pages in a 32-bit address space.

To keep things simple for the compiled code, we don't have to use the BIBOP table for the youngest generation of data. That is, compiled code will allocate everything, with descriptors, on the heap as it did before. But the garbage collector will strip the descriptors off some objects and put them in BIBOP pages. The separation of pointer-containing and nonpointer-containing objects for a generational collector, described earlier in the chapter, may also be done by the garbage collector when moving objects out of the youngest generation.

Of course, this complicates the procedure for determining the kind of an object (its size, and whether it contains pointers) at runtime. But ML has a static type system, so the program never needs to perform this procedure. Only the garbage collector and the polymorphic equality function need to determine the kind of an object at runtime.

Using the BIBOP scheme might save 33 percent of memory, except in the youngest generation, assuming that most objects that survive the first garbage collection are two-word records (which is very likely true!). It turns out that closures are the majority of objects allocated (and they are usually larger than two words), but closures tend to become garbage before the first collection, and the longer-lived objects have a narrow distribution of object sizes.

The garbage collector (scanner) may now be slowed down by a constant factor as it looks up descriptors in BIBOP tables. But Section 16.1 shows that an increase in the constant factor c_3 can be compensated for by increasing the amount of memory M; and the savings in memory from the BIBOP scheme could provide this extra M. On the whole, then, the BIBOP trick might save time and space, or it might not.

16.6   Asynchronous interrupts

Often it is desired to interrupt the program asynchronously (e.g., when a timer interrupt occurs). Suppose we take a naive approach to this, and just write all the registers (including the program counter) to a record. When it is desired to resume the interrupted program, we can load the registers from this record and continue.

But what if a garbage collection occurs while this special saved-register record exists? Some of the fields of this record are pointers, some are nonpointers, some are unboxed integers that masquerade as pointers, and so on. The garbage collector does not have enough information to decode this record.

Furthermore, there may be dozens, or thousands, of such records. In a multithreaded system in which timer interrupts are used to switch between threads (see Chapter 17), each suspended thread will be a special continuation made by interrupting a running process.

A simple solution is to interrupt the program only at safe points (see page 148). We can get the program to stop at the very next safe point just by setting the limit register to *maxint*; at the next safe point an overflow interrupt will occur. Thus, the action taken on an asynchronous interrupt should be to modify the limit register.

In a typical Unix operating system, the sequence of events upon reception of a signal would be [72]:

1. Event occurs; operating system notifies client program by "calling" client's signal-handler procedure according to standard C-language calling convention. Registers are pushed on stack.

2. C-language signal handler sets saved copy of limit register (on the stack) to *maxint*, then returns.

3. Operating system pops saved registers (including modified limit register) from stack, "resumes" client.

4. At the next safe point, the limit check overflows, causing a trap.

5. Operating system notifies client program by calling client's signal-handler procedure. Now, registers can be saved safely. All the registers including the saved PC are written into a special continuation closure. The function pointer of this closure is just a special code fragment that loads all the registers from the closure and jumps to the saved PC (also extracted from the special closure).

6. The ML signal handler is invoked, with the specially constructed continuation closure as an argument. If and when the ML signal handler wants to resume the program that was running at the time of the signal, it just throws to this continuation.

In reality, things are more complicated. First, in most versions of Unix the order that the operating system pushes registers on the stack is not documented or repeatable; this problem can be solved by appropriate trickery [7] that costs about two extra memory references per register (plus a few more instructions). Second, it is necessary to tell the operating system to reenable the signal that occurred; this is usually done by "returning" from the C-language signal handler, so this return must be made to happen [72]. Third, those registers indicated by the register mask to hold nonpointers must be held in a separate, nonpointer-containing object that the closure points to.

Suppose the boon of changing the operating-system interface were granted to us. Then we could have a much more efficient response to a signal: The operating system could notify the client process that a signal had arrived *by setting its limit register*.[1] This would replace steps 1–3 above, saving *two* context switches: from the operating system into the client and back to the operating system.

Since fantastic wishes usually come in threes, we could also desire to change the hardware. Let us wish for an overflow exception (a compare-and-trap instruction would be just as good) that traps *in user mode, without entering the hardware's privileged mode.* Then another context switch or so could be avoided.

We still have one wish left over, which we could expend on a larger, write-back cache (see Section 18.4).

Although our method of handling asynchronous signals on conventional hardware and operating systems is cumbersome, it is not prohibitively expensive: Total signal-handling time (into the ML signal handler and back) is about 0.3 milliseconds on a SparcStation 2, for example [73].

---

[1] Eric Cooper [30] is now experimenting with this technique in a special-purpose machine on which ML is used for writing device drivers.

CHAPTER SEVENTEEN

PARALLEL PROGRAMMING

The *call-with-current-continuation* primitive allows Standard ML of New Jersey to support several different models of shared-memory parallel and concurrent programming. Examples of such models are:

- A generalization of Hoare's *Communicating Sequential Processes* [49, 50] known as *Concurrent ML*, in which different threads communicate synchronously through unidirectional channels [70, 71, 73].

- *ML-Threads* [31], inspired by Modula-2+ threads (lightweight processes with shared variables and locks) [22, 23], which was based on Mesa processes [56], a generalization of Hoare's *Monitors* [48].

- A version of *Futures* similar to those in Multilisp [44] that allows a graph-reduction style of synchronization even in a strict functional language.

In any of these models, we take a standard sequential programming language (e.g., Standard ML, C, or Modula-2) and add primitives for starting new threads (lightweight processes, threads of execution that share memory) and communicating and synchronizing between threads.

In implementing any of these parallel-programming languages on a multiprocessor, there are two problems to be solved:

1. **Scheduling** threads of execution; managing queues of threads that are ready to run, that are waiting for events generated by other threads; encapsulating the state of a thread so control may be transferred to the scheduler, and then back to resume the encapsulated state of another thread.

2. **Multiprocessing:** arranging for several processors to be running simultaneously in the same address space; communication between processors; concurrent garbage collection of a program running on several processors.

In addressing these problems it is necessary to have cooperation among the compiler, the runtime system and garbage collector, the scheduler, and the operating system. For example, the compiler must generate reentrant code, so two different threads can be executing the same function at the same time without

215

trashing each others' variables. The runtime system must allow for individual local storage for each thread. The operating system should allow for nonblocking input/output operations, so one thread's attempt to do input will not prevent the other threads from running.

The *call-with-current-continuation* primitive provides a way to encapsulate the state of a thread (as a continuation) so neatly that almost the entire **scheduling** problem can be solved at the level of the source langauge (in this case ML) without involving the compiler or the runtime system [93].

To illustrate this, we will describe the (uniprocessor) implementation of a very simple concurrency package. In a later section we will address issues related to multiprocessing.

17.1   Coroutines and semaphores

To show how threads may be implemented without modification of the compiler or runtime system, we will invent a very crude model of concurrent computation using coroutines and semaphores. We are not advocating the use of this model as a programming language, since it relies on the programmer to avoid race conditions and is expressed at a low level. But it makes a good short illustration of the use of first-class continuations to implement schedulers.

The signature of our concurrency package includes a function fork to start a new thread, a type semaphore with operations P and V:

```
signature COROUTINES =
  sig   val fork:  (unit->unit) -> unit
        val yield: unit -> unit
        type semaphore
        val semaphore: unit -> semaphore
        val P: semaphore -> unit
        val V: semaphore -> unit
  end
```

Given a function f, fork(f) starts f running in parallel; in essence, the call to $f()$ returns immediately so f is running at the same time as the caller. This package does not have preemptive scheduling, however, so each thread should periodically call yield to let some other thread(s) run for a while.

A semaphore is a special variable with two states, *free* and *busy*. When a thread performs P on a free semaphore, it becomes busy; but P on a busy semaphore blocks the thread until some other thread performs a V. When V is performed on a busy semaphore, either the semaphore becomes free (if there was no thread blocked by P on that semaphore), or one thread waiting (by P) is resumed. V on a free semaphore is undefined.

We can write a simple program with coroutines and semaphores to illustrate. There are two arrays A and B of integers. One thread takes numbers out of A, doubles them, and puts them into B; the other thread takes numbers from B,

```
fun back_and_forth(initial) =
let open Coroutines
   fun busy() = let val s = semaphore()
                in P s; s
                end
   val free = semaphore
   type slot = {value: int ref, put: semaphore, get: semaphore}
   fun nlist 0 f = nil | nlist i f = f i :: nlist (i-1) f
   val A = arrayoflist(
             map(fn i => {value=ref i, put=busy(), get=free()})
               initial)
   val B = arrayoflist(nlist 10
             (fn j => {value=ref 0, put=free(), get=busy()}))
   val Alen = Array.length A and Blen = Array.length B
   fun thread1 (i,j) =
             let val {value=Av,put=Ap,get=Ag} = A sub i
                 val {value=Bv,put=Bp,get=Bg} = B sub j
                 val x = (P Ag; !Av)
              in V Ap; P Bp; Bv := 2*x; V Bg;
                 yield();
                 thread1((i+1) mod Alen, (j+1) mod Blen)
             end
   fun thread2 (i,j) =
             let val {value=Av,put=Ap,get=Ag} = A sub i
                 val {value=Bv,put=Bp,get=Bg} = B sub j
                 val x = (P Bg; !Bv)
              in V Bp; P Ap; Av := x div 2; V Ag;
                 yield();
                 thread2((i+1) mod Alen, (j+1) mod Blen)
             end
 in fork(fn()=>thread1(0,0)); thread2(0,0)
end
```

Figure 17.1. A program using coroutines and semaphores.

```
structure Coroutines : COROUTINES =
struct
    val queue : unit cont list ref = ref nil
    fun enqueue k = queue := !queue @ [k]
    fun dispatch() = let val head::rest = !queue
                     in queue := rest; throw head ()
                     end
    fun fork f = callcc(fn k => (enqueue k; f(); dispatch()))
    fun yield() = if random() then ()
                  else callcc(fn k => (enqueue k; dispatch()))
    datatype sem = FREE | BUSY of unit cont list
    type semaphore = sem ref
    fun semaphore () = ref FREE
    fun P sem = case !sem
                  of FREE => sem := BUSY nil
                   | BUSY waiters =>
                         callcc(fn k =>
                              (sem := BUSY(waiters@[k]);
                               dispatch()))
    fun V sem = case !sem
                  of BUSY nil => (sem := FREE)
                   | BUSY(w::rest) => (sem := BUSY rest;
                                       enqueue w)
end
```

Figure 17.2. The implementation of coroutines with semaphores.

Note that @ is list concatenation in ML.

halves them, and puts them back into A. But a thread may not remove a value from an array until it has been put there by the other thread, that is, it can't grab the same value twice. And a thread may not overwrite a value in its output array until the previous element in that slot has been read by the other thread. This style of interaction is reminiscent of "I-structures" [16].

Each "slot" is implemented by an *int ref* and two semaphores. When the slot is "full," then the **put** semaphore for that slot is busy and the **get** semaphore is free; when it is "empty," **put** is busy and **get** is free. Before putting something into a slot, a thread must P the **put** semaphore; afterward, it should V the **get** semaphore to signal the availability of the data. To extract data from a slot, it's the other way around.

The complete program is shown in figure 17.1. The initial contents of the A array are specified by the list *initial*; the B array starts out with 10 empty slots.

The implementation of this coroutine package is even simpler than its client. We need a *run queue* of ready-to-execute threads. Each suspended thread is represented by a *unit cont*, a continuation to which we throw a place-holder "unit" value. The queue itself is a reference to a list of suspended threads; we add to the queue by appending to the end of the list, and remove items from the queue at the head of the list (there are, of course, more efficient ways of implementing queues). *Enqueue* adds a thread to the tail of the queue; *dispatch* removes a thread from the queue and resumes it.

The *fork(f)* function is implemented by first using `callcc` to make a continuation k that will resume the caller of *fork*. Then k is enqueued, and the function f is executed. Thus, the "child" is executing and the "parent" is put on the run queue. Presumably, the child will *yield* from time to time, and then eventually be resumed each time. Finally, the function f will return; we *dispatch* another thread and the child thread terminates (*dispatch* never "returns"); the number of threads on the run queue (plus the number of threads on semaphore queues) goes down by one).

To *yield* is even simpler: We use `callcc` to encapsulate the state of the current thread, enqueue that state, and dispatch the head of the run queue. However, we don't have to yield every time; just for fun, we can flip a *random* coin and yield only if tails comes up.

A semaphore is represented as a *ref* to a datatype with two constructors, BUSY and FREE. A busy semaphore also has a list of threads that are blocked trying to do a P operation on that semaphore. Semaphores are created initially free.

To P a free semaphore, one just makes it busy (with no waiters) and returns. To P a busy semaphore, one adds oneself to the list of waiters and dispatches a ready thread from the run queue.

To V a busy semaphore with no waiters, one just makes it free. If there are waiters, any one of the waiters is removed from the list and enqueued on the run queue.

Because this is a coroutine package, in which there are never two threads running at exactly the same time, it is unnecessary to worry about simultaneous execution of P and V (or P and P, etc.). In a true multiprocessor version, or in a uniprocessor version with preemptive scheduling, the usual techniques for mutual exclusion (interlocked test-and-set instructions, etc.) would be used.

17.2 Better programming models

Concurrent threads using P and V are quite low level. For the convenience of the programmer, and for the robustness of the application, one might wish to program using monitors, synchronous channels, futures, directed logic variables [53], or I-structures. Any of these models can be implemented with P and V. However, it may be better to think of `callcc` and *interlocked test-and-set* instructions as the primitives, since semaphores already introduce a notion of queuing, and the implementation of any concurrency package may have its own preferred arrangement of queues.

As shown in the previous section, `callcc` is a clean and expressive tool for managing threads and resumption points. However, one would like it to be efficient. Since a parallel program might be expected to use its concurrency primitives (P, V, *fork*, and *yield* in our example) quite frequently, they should not be expensive.

In a language implementation with a runtime stack, *call with current continuation* must copy the stack and *throw* must restore it. Since the stack can grow arbitrarily high, `callcc` can get quite expensive. The problem can be partially avoided by keeping the stack small, and dumping the stack into the garbage-collected heap when it grows too big; but this adds many complications of its own [47].

Since Standard ML of New Jersey has no runtime stack, there is nothing to copy. Call with current continuation (and throw) costs no more than an ordinary procedure call, plus the cost of installing an exception handler: perhaps a dozen instructions, depending on the number of free variables in the continuation. This makes a very attractive system for implementing concurrency packages. At least two such packages are under serious development [73, 31].

17.3 Multiple processors

Call with current continuation solves the problem of multiple *threads* very nicely. When it is desired to run those threads on more than one *processor*, more work is needed [31].

We first consider the case where there is a fixed number of processors, all dedicated to the same parallel program. There are several resources to manage: registers, stack, heap, input/output, and so on.

In principle, SML/NJ uses no runtime stack. But ML functions can call C functions that do use the stack. In our runtime system, a thread is never preempted while executing a C function (since there are no "safe points" in C code; see Section 16.6). Therefore, it suffices to have one stack segment *per processor*; we don't need a stack for each thread.

What about the heap? If several processors are simultaneously allocating on the same heap, some sort of locking is required to avoid overwriting the same new record. But since allocation is so frequent, locking on each allocation would be prohibitively expensive. A better solution is to have each processor allocate in its own area of the heap. That is, we give each processor a large chunk of contiguous free space in which to allocate, and we guarantee that no two processors are allocating in the same place. If one processor allocates faster than the others, it will exhaust its chunk first; we can just give it another chunk. When we run out of chunks, a garbage collection must be initiated.

Again, we don't need one chunk *per thread*, just *per processor*. Different threads on the same processor are never allocating simultaneously (since they are never running simultaneously, and are never preempted in the middle of an allocation).

Any thread may attempt to perform input or output that might block. In this case, the processor should somehow proceed with the execution of another ready thread. Finally, on a real multicomputer the number of processors available to a client process may not be fixed, as the operating system reallocates processors among clients. Both of these problems can be solved by an appropriate operating system interface [3].

17.4 Multiprocessor garbage collection

When a garbage collection is required, it seems like a good idea to take advantage of the multiprocessor. There are two basic approaches: indexgarbage collection!multiprocessor

1. Make the garbage collector run in parallel on all the processors [44].

2. Make the garbage collector run at the same time as some of the allocating threads [36, 10].

Both of these problems are reasonably well studied; and there is undoubtedly further work to be done on each. We should remark our preference for the latter scheme, based on the following observation: If the overhead of garbage collection is about 5 percent, then one garbage-collector processor should be able to keep up with about 20 allocating processors; furthermore, the overhead of collection can be adjusted as desired by adding more memory to the system. Of course, in a system with many more than 20 processors, some combination of the two approaches may be necessary.

CHAPTER EIGHTEEN

FUTURE DIRECTIONS

A piece of software is never finished. We have several ideas for improvements to optimizer and code generator of the SML/NJ compiler.

One big problem is the slowness, and the vast amount of memory required, for compilation; Section 15.5 shows the time taken by each phase of the compiler. It appears that the front end is much faster than the back end; much of the credit goes to David MacQueen's designs for the fast pattern-match compiler [19], the fast module system [61], and the fast type checker; these have proved to be bottlenecks in some other Standard ML compilers. The problem lies in the optimizer, code generator, and instruction scheduler; Section 15.5 discusses how we plan to speed up the back end by a large factor.

18.1   Control dependencies

There are some new kinds of information we could exploit in the CPS optimizer and instruction scheduler. The idea is to make a more precise model of control dependencies. Consider the following CPS fragment:

```
if        PRIMOP( > , [VAR i, 0], [], [
then                 SELECT(2, VAR a, w, ...),
else                 ...])
```

If $i > 0$, the second field of record a will be fetched and execution will continue from there; if $i \leq 0$, the fetch won't be done.

Now, suppose we would like to hoist the SELECT above the comparison. There are several reasons we might like to do this: to remove loop-invariant code from a loop, to perform common-subexpression elimination, to do instruction scheduling on a superscalar computer, or to "flatten" an n-tuple function parameter. Since the SELECT is not a "side effect," we should be able to execute it even if it's not called for. If $i \leq 0$ then w will turn out not to be useful, but the program should not be incorrect.

The problem is that if $i \leq 0$ there is no guarantee that a is a valid address. Suppose i is the tag of a data constructor and a is the carried value. Depending on the value of i, a could be a record-pointer, an integer, a real number, or a string.

Fetching a might cause a page fault immediately (if a is an integer), or load a "bad pointer" into registers (if a is a string or real value, whose second field is an arbitrary bit pattern).

This problem occurs in all compilers. To hoist a fetch above a conditional jump, it's necessary to prove that the address fetched is a valid address even when the "else" path is taken. (If the address is invalid in the "then" case, that's the programmer's responsibility; or, in safe languages such as ML, an impossibility.) This proof can be quite difficult using dataflow analysis.

We can exploit the properties of the ML language, however. The CPS-language SELECT is from a lambda-language SELECT, which in turn is from a pattern match of a record or data constructor. The CPS-language *greater-than* comparison is either from a lambda-language primop or from a lambda-language SWITCH operator. If from the former, then the type of a cannot possibly depend on the value of i— integer comparisons in ML programs can't affect the types of variables. If from the latter, however, there can be a dependence: The comparison may be checking which data constructor has been applied to a value.

Unfortunately, during the conversion from lambda language to CPS, information about the source of the comparison is lost. To hold on to this information, we need to augment the CPS language with some extra control-dependence information. For each branching operator, we can "bind" an artificial variable; at any of the operators after the branch, we can "use" this variable. As an example, consider this ML program fragment:

```
case (z,i)
 of (x::r,0) => x+2
  | (y::r,_) => y+i
  | _ => i
```

After translation to CPS, it might look like this:

```
1        PRIMOP(boxed, [VAR z], [], [
2           PRIMOP( ieql, [VAR i, INT 0], [], [
3              SELECT(0, VAR z, x,
4                 PRIMOP( + , [VAR x, INT 2], [w], [
5                   APP(VAR k, [VAR w])])),
6              SELECT(0, VAR z, y,
7                 PRIMOP( + , [VAR x, VAR i], [u], [
8                   APP(VAR k, [VAR w])])))]),
9           APP(VAR k, [VAR i])])
```

The SELECTs of lines 3 and 6 can be hoisted above the comparison of line 2, but not above the boxity test of line 1. This information could be generated trivially by the pattern-match compiler. We might augment the CPS to bind an artificial variable v in line 1, and note the dependence on v of lines 3 and 6. Then lines 3 and 6 could both be hoisted above line 2 to eliminate the common subexpression; but they could not be hoisted above line 1 without violating a scope rule for v.

There are several kinds of operations that we might like to hoist above comparisons, and that could benefit from this kind of control-dependency information:

- Fetches from records (SELECT), as described above.

- Fetches from and updates to arrays; these are dependent on the pattern-match comparisons just like SELECT, and also on array-bounds checks and comparisons.

- Unboxing of floating-point values; since floats are represented as pointers to double-precision numbers, unboxing them requires a fetch. This fetch can fail—just as a SELECT can—if hoisted above a pattern-matching comparison. However, such hoisting becomes very desirable if we want to be able to pass *unboxed* floating-point values to known functions, especially in loops.

To make use of this technique in the instruction scheduler, it would be necessary to propagate the dependency information all the way into assembly language, which would be tedious but not difficult in principle.

18.2 Type information

A different solution to the problem described in the previous section is to carry information about static types from the source language through the λ-language into the CPS. Then we could know that the type of variable x is *real*, so it can definitely be unboxed without harm; that a is *int×int*, so it can be fetched from without harm; and so on.

However, having a typed CPS language would require the manipulation and reduction of types whenever β-reductions (and other transformations) are performed. Although this is certainly possible to do, it is painful enough that we have decided to avoid this approach.

18.3 Loop optimizations

Many compilers have special optimizations for loops: hoisting of loop-invariant computations, induction-variable analysis, strength reduction, and loop unrolling. As explained in Chapter 9, hoisting of loop-invariant computations can be done by common-subexpression elimination and β-reduction without knowing what a loop is; and loop unrolling is just a special case of in-line expansion.

But loop unrolling can be made more profitable with special attention to loop-exit tests. Consider a typical case:

```
fun dotprod(A,B) =
   let val N = length(A)
       fun f(s,i) = if i>=N then s
                    else f(s+(a sub i)*(b sub i), i+1)
   in f(0.0, 0)
   end
```

In continuation-passing style the program looks substantially the same:

```
fun dotprod(A,B,k) =
  let val N = length(A)
      fun f(s,i) =
        if i>=N then k(s)
                else let val x = A sub i
                         val y = B sub i
                         val z = x*y
                         val s' = s+z
                         val i' = i+1
                      in f(s',i')
                     end
   in f(0.0, 0)
  end
```

Now, for efficiency we might unroll the loop by substituting for f(s',i'):

```
fun dotprod(A,B,k) =
  let val N = length(A)
      fun f(s,i) =
          if i>=N then k(s)
          else let val x = A sub i
                   val y = B sub i
                   val z = x*y
                   val s' = s+z
                   val i' = i+1
                in if i'>=N then k(s')
                   else let val x' = A sub i'
                            val y' = B sub i'
                            val z' = x'*y'
                            val s'' = s'+z'
                            val i'' = i'+1
                         in f(s'',i'')
                        end
               end
   in f(0.0, 0)
  end
```

Our compiler can get this far already, without knowing about loops. But we haven't really accomplished much, because the loop-exit tests are still sprinkled through the unrolled loop.

A useful optimization here would be to eliminate the test $i' \geq N$ by modifying the test at the top of the loop to compare $i + 1 \geq N$; if this modified test failed, then a special loop-exit sequence would test whether $i \geq N$. Thus:

```
fun dotprod(A,B,k) =
  let val N = length(A)
      fun f(s,i) =  ... (as before)
      fun f'(s,i) =
          let val i' = i+1
              val i'' = i'+1
          in if i'>=N then f(s,i)
             else let val x = A sub i
                      val y = B sub i
                      val z = x*y
                      val s' = s+z
                      val x' = A sub i'
                      val y' = B sub i'
                      val z' = x'*y'
                      val s'' = s'+z'
                  in f'(s'',i'')
                  end
          end
  in f'(0.0, 0)
  end
end
```

This already runs significantly faster because there are fewer branches. But now the problem (especially on a pipelined, VLIW, or superscalar machine) is that there is a long chain of data dependencies in the computation of i'' and s''. To solve the problem for i'', we can calculate $i'' = i + 2$. The result is a loop on which software pipelining [2] would get very good performance on a typical superscalar machine.

So far in the discussion of this program, we have ignored the array-bounds check on the subscripting of A and B. We might like to continue to write programs in a "safe" language, in which case we can't "turn off" the array-bounds checking. But *induction-variable* analysis can be used in this case (and others) to determine that i is always safely within the bounds of the array A. With a little extra work, the bounds check for B might also be hoisted outside the loop. (A is treated differently from B in that N is defined to be the length of A.)

Shivers [80] has implemented (and proven correct) several kinds of loop optimizations in a continuation-passing-style Scheme compiler.

18.4 Garbage collection

According to the data shown in Chapter 15, half of the execution time of a typical program is spent waiting for cache misses. It may be possible to use the garbage collector as a tool for *improving* the locality of reference of the program.

With a generational garbage collector, performance might be greatly improved by putting the youngest generation entirely in the cache. Heap allocations touch the entire youngest generation cyclically, so "locality of reference" is only achieved by caching it all. Furthermore, only a few percent of the youngest generation are copied to older generations; a write-back cache would avoid any main-memory traffic for most data, which become garbage before the first collection.

Collections should not be too frequent, however, for two reasons: Starting the collector incurs nontrivial overhead (7600 cycles in Standard ML of New Jersey on the MIPS); and the longer one waits before a collection, the more records have turned into garbage. Therefore, the strategy of fitting the youngest generation in cache will probably perform well only with half-megabyte caches, or larger.

Zorn [98] has detailed measurements of the interaction of garbage collection and cache performance (in Common Lisp), as well as some recommendations for collector and cache design that can significantly improve cache performance.

18.5   Static single-assignment form

The CPS language shares an important property with static single-assignment form [34]: Each variable is assigned (bound) only once. However, what in SSA is just an edge in the flow graph is—in CPS—a call to a known function. Calls to known functions have an implicit assignment of actual parameters to formal parameters; in SSA these are represented by "ϕ-functions," which maintain the fiction of single assignment. By gathering information in our CPS optimizer about all the different actual parameters passed into a given formal parameter of a known function, we can get the effect of the ϕ-functions in CPS. Doing this would allow us to implement some of the efficient optimization algorithms (constant propagation [94], etc.) that work on static single-assignment form.

18.6   State threading

It might be a good idea to make the creation and use of the updateable store more explicit, by having state variables produced as the result of assignment (:= and `update`) operations and consumed as arguments of fetch (! and `subscript`) operations. Then CPS would truly be a "functional" language. Many constraints on CPS transformations (i.e, that an `update` should not be hoisted above another `update`) that are implictly present in various phases of the compiler would now be direct consequences of variable-scope rules.

Introducing store-valued variables allows the possibility that the program would no longer have a *single-threaded store*; that is, to evaluate a program it might be necessary to have more than one copy of the memory. While this might be very useful (in a replay debugger, for example [88]), it doesn't fit naturally on a von Neumann machine. Thus, it would be necessary to restrict programs (or CPS-conversion algorithms) to be single-threaded.

INTRODUCTION TO ML

This appendix describes enough of the ML language to understand the examples in the rest of the book. We cover only the core language (without the module system) here, though a summary of the module system is given in Section 4.8. For more thorough coverage, see Reade [68], Paulson [67], or Sokolowski [81].

One of the distinguishing features of Standard ML is its facility for data structuring. As in other languages, there are atomic types (such as *integer*), cartesian product types (*records*), and disjoint sum types (which are like *variants* in Pascal or *unions* in C); but everything seems to fit together more safely and elegantly in ML.

The atomic types include *int* (integers), *real* (floating point numbers), and *string* (sequences of zero or more characters).

Given types $t_1, t_2, ..., t_n$ with $n \geq 2$, one can make the cartesian product type $t_1 \times t_2 \times \cdots \times t_n$. (In ML syntax, the $\times$ is written using a star *.) This is called an n-tuple; for example, `int*int*string` is a 3-tuple type containing values like `(3,6,"abc")`.

A *record* type is a syntactic sugaring of an n-tuple (for $n \geq 0$) in which each "field" is given a name. For example, the type

```
{wheels: int, passengers: int, owner: string}
```

contains values like

```
{wheels=4, passengers=6, owner="Fred"}
```

and is much like—though not interchangeable with—the type `int*int*string`.

A *union* type can have values of several different forms; for example, a *list* value can be either a *pair* or *nil*. Unlike the union of C (or the variant record of Pascal), ML requires a tag on each value to distinguish which of the kinds it belongs to. It is impossible to extract information from the value without first checking the tag, so unions in ML are much safer to use. (The tag is called a *constructor* in ML.)

The `datatype` keyword is used to declare union types. In a datatype declaration, there is a list of constructor names, each of which specifies the *type* of value associated with it. For example,

```
datatype vehicle =
          CAR of {wheels: int, passengers: int, owner: string}
        | TRUCK of real
        | MOTORCYCLE
```

each value of type *vehicle* can be a car, a truck, or a motorcycle. If a car, it carries a record value (two integers and a string). If a truck, it carries a real value indicating its gross weight. And motorcycles all look the same: MOTORCYCLE is called a *constant constructor* because it carries no value.

Types can be *polymorphic*: a function or constructor can operate on objects of different—though similar—types. For example, the *list* datatype can be used to make lists of integers, lists of reals, lists of integer-lists, etc.

```
datatype 'a list = nil | :: of 'a * 'a list
```

The symbol :: is just an identifier like TRUCK or nil. The *type variable* 'a before list indicates that *list* is not a type, it's a type constructor: that is, it must be applied to a type argument like *int* or *string* before it is meaningful as a type. Type constructors are written *after* the types they are applied to, so int list is the type of lists of integers.

The :: (pronounced "cons") constructor carries a value of type 'a * 'a list; that is, a pair whose first element is type 'a and whose second element is a list of 'a. If we have a list of strings, the first element is a string and the second is another list of strings (the "tail" of the list).

Though 'a can stand for any type—one could make an int list list—the elements of any one list must all be the same type. If it is necessary to have a list containing different types of objects, one can use a datatype as the argument of the list type constructor: a vehicle list can contain both cars and trucks.

Most data structures are *immutable*: they can't be modified by assignment statements. For example, if the variable *a* holds the record value describing Fred's 6-passenger car (shown above), then it is not possible to alter the *passengers* field to be 7, nor is it possible to alter *a* to point to a different record. What you might do instead is make an entirely new record equal to

```
{wheels=4, passengers=7, owner="Fred"}
```

and bind it to the variable *b*.

However, there is an exception to this rule. There is a special datatype *ref* of *mutable references*:

```
datatype 'a ref = ref of 'a
```

This built-in datatype has "special" properties, unlike the *list* datatype which—though predefined in Standard ML—could just as easily be part of a user's program. In particular, if *r* is a reference variable (say an int ref), then *r* may be assigned (using an assignment operator :=) to hold a different value. And if a field of a record or tuple is a reference:

```
{wheels=4, passengers=ref 6, owner="Fred"}
```

then that field can be assigned a different value. But note that this record has type

```
{wheels: int, passengers: int ref, owner: string}
```

which is not the same as the type of Fred's original car.

A.1 Expressions

Expressions in ML take several forms:

exp → id

An expression can be a single identifer. ML has two kinds of identifiers: *Alphanumeric* identifiers are composed of letters and digits starting with a letter (just like in Pascal; except that underscore and apostrophe are also allowed in alphanumeric identifiers). *Symbolic* identifiers are made up of the characters !%&$+-/:<=>?@\~\^|#*' in any combination. Some alphanumeric combinations are *reserved words* (like **let** and **end**); so are some symbolic combinations (like | and =>).

exp → exp id exp

An infix operator can be put between two expressions, like a+b or (a+b)*c or a*b+c. Different operators have different precedences, as in Pascal or C. In ML, however, any identifier can be made infix with a specified precedence; and operators like + and * are just ordinary identifiers that are infix by default.

exp → (exp)

An expression may be enclosed in parentheses without changing its meaning; this is useful to override the usual precedence of operators, just as in Pascal.

exp → exp exp

Function application is expressed in ML by writing the function followed by its argument. Thus f x is *f* applied to *x*. If you write f(x) it looks a bit more like Pascal, but the parentheses are not necessary—you could just as well write (f)x. An expression can evaluate to a function; if g y returns a function as a result, then that function can be applied to x by writing (g y) x. But in fact, function application associates to the left, so g y x parses the same as (g y) x. On the other hand, the argument to a function call might also be a function call, as in f(g y) or even (g y)(h x). Every function in ML takes exactly one parameter.

$exp \rightarrow id$
$exp \rightarrow id\ exp$
$exp \rightarrow exp\ id\ exp$

Datatype values are constructed either with a constant data constructor (the first of these three rules), or with a value-carrying constructor applied to an argument (the second rule). A value-carrying constructor may be declared *infix* as long as the value it carries is a 2-tuple; in this case the constructor is written *between* its two arguments, as in the third grammar rule above. The list constructor `::` is an example of this: `3::nil` is a singleton list in which `::` is applied to the pair `(3,nil)`. And `::` is declared right-associative, so `1::2::3::4::nil` is a list of four integers.

$exp \rightarrow (exp,\ exp)$
$exp \rightarrow (exp,\ exp,\ exp)$

One can construct n-tuples in ML by writing two or more expressions separated by commas, surrounded by parentheses. When the tuple expression is evaluated, a record is built in memory. This is a bit like *cons* in Lisp or *new* (with initializing assignments) in Pascal. The record `(3,"a",7)` is a 3-tuple that contains an integer, a string, and an integer; it's not the same as `((3,"a"),7)` which is a 2-tuple containing a 2-tuple and an integer.

The restriction that functions take only one argument may seem rather harsh; in fact, one commonly passes an n-tuple to a function, as in `f(x,y,z)`. This looks comfortably like an n-argument function.

$exp \rightarrow \{\,exprow\,\}$
$exprow \rightarrow id\ =\ \texttt{exp}$
$exprow \rightarrow exprow\ ,\ id\ =\ \texttt{exp}$

A record expression is a series of field expressions, enclosed in braces, with associated field names. The field names need not be declared in advance.

$exp \rightarrow \texttt{let}\ dec\ \texttt{in}\ exp\ \texttt{end}$

A `let` expression introduces a local declaration *dec*. The names defined by this declaration are visible only between the `let` and the `end`. The forms of declaration are given in section A.3.

$exp \rightarrow \texttt{fn}\ pat\ \texttt{=>}\ exp$

The keyword `fn` is pronounced *lambda*, and defines anonymous functions. The grammar-symbol *pat* stands for *pattern*; an example of a simple pattern is just an identifier (but see below). Thus `fn x => x+3` is a function that adds three to its argument, so `(fn x=>x+3)7` is 10.

Lambda-expressions can be nested, as in `fn x=> fn y=>x+y` which is a function that returns a function. ML has lexical (static) scope, so `(fn x=> fn y=>x+y)3` is identical in meaning to `fn y=>3+y` in all contexts. Nested lambdas provide an alternate way of making multiple-argument functions, so if f is `fn x=>fn y=>fn z=>x+y+z` then one could apply f to three arguments by writing `f a b c`; in this case f is called a "curried" function.

Actually, the syntax for fn-expressions is richer than implied by the grammar rule above. More precisely:

$exp \rightarrow$ **fn** $match$
where a $match$ is a list of rules separated by bars:

$match \rightarrow rule$
$match \rightarrow match \mid rule$
$rule \rightarrow pat \Rightarrow exp$

When a function defined with several rules is applied to an argument, the patterns are examined in order to find the first one that matches. Then the expression corresponding to that pattern is evaluated.

$exp \rightarrow$ **case** exp **of** $match$

A **case** expression evaluates its exp argument, and tests the patterns in the $match$ to find the first one that matches; then the variables (if any) of the matching pattern are bound, and the right-hand-side expression is evaluated.

A.2   Patterns

The simplest $pattern$ is just a variable (which always matches), but there are other kinds:

$pat \rightarrow constant$

When the pattern is an integer, real, or string constant c, it matches only the value c. If the argument is not equal to c, it fails to match the pattern. Note that the compile-time type checking ensures the type of the constant (e.g. int) will always be the same as the type of the argument.

$pat \rightarrow id$

When the pattern is a constant constructor (defined by a previous **datatype** declaration), it matches only that constant. Compile-time type checking ensures that the argument will be a member of the right datatype. If the identifier has not been declared a constructor by a **datatype** declaration, then it stands for a variable in the $match$—with quite a different behavior (see below). This is often a source of great confusion (and bugs). The problem can be ameliorated by the convention that constructors (except, unfortunately, **nil**) start with capital letters and variables do not.

$pat \rightarrow id\ pat$

When the pattern is a constructor applied to a pattern p, then the pattern matches if the argument was built using the same constructor *and* if p matches the value carried by that constructor in the argument. Thus the pattern TRUCK 3.5 matches a value built by the expression TRUCK(2.5+1.0) but not the values MOTORCYCLE or TRUCK(3.0).

pat → (*pat*)

 A pattern may be parenthesized to disambiguate syntax, without changing its meaning.

pat → (*pat, pat*)
pat → (*pat, pat, pat*)

 An *n*-tuple pattern (for any $n \geq 2$) matches an *n*-tuple argument if and only if each of the elements of the tuple pattern matches the corresponding element of the argument. Static type checking ensures that the argument is an *n*-tuple (for the right *n*).

pat → {*patrow*}
patrow → *id* = *pat* , *patrow*
patrow →
patrow → . . .

 A record pattern is a sequence of *id=pat*, where the *id*s are the record labels. Like a tuple pattern, the record pattern matches if all of the fields match the fields of the argument. A record pattern may end with an ellipsis (. . .), in which case the remaining fields of the argument automatically match; but the names of the remaining fields must be determinable at compile time.

pat → _

 The underscore _ is a wild-card pattern that matches any argument.

pat → *id*

 When the pattern is an identifier not declared as a constructor, then a new variable is bound to the argument, which always matches. Thus the function `fn x=>x+3` has a pattern `x` which is a variable. When the function is applied to an argument, a new instantiation of `x` takes on the value of the argument. The scope of x is the entire right-hand-side of the function (i.e., `x+3`); so this function adds three to its argument. Static type checking will ensure that the argument is always an integer.

 The function `fn(a,b)=>a+b*2` has a pair (2-tuple) pattern as its formal parameter; the first element of the pair will be bound to the variable a, and the second to the variable b. So even though ML requires all functions to have exactly one argument, multiple-argument functions can be simulated in a very conventional style.

 Now consider a function that treats empty and singleton lists differently from longer lists:

```
fn nil => 0
 | x::nil => 1
 | z => 2
```

The first rule matches only the empty list. the second rule matches a *cons* cell if the head and the tail match; but the head always matches (since `x` is a variable) and the tail matches only the empty list (`nil`); so the second rule matches lists of length one. The final rule catches anything that didn't match the first two rules.

A.3 Declarations

Several kinds of things can be declared in ML, each with a different keyword to introduce the declaration:

dec → `val` *pat* = *exp*

A `val` declaration can be used to define a new variable, as in `val x=5` which binds x to 5. In this case, the pattern is a simple variable pattern which always matches.

Another use of the `val` declaration is to extract fields of records:

```
val (a,(b,c),d) = g(x)
```

In this case, the type returned by $g(x)$ must be a 3-tuple whose second element is a pair. The first and last components of the 3-tuple are bound to a and d, and the elements of the pair are bound to b and c.

Finally, it is possible to make `val` declarations that are not guaranteed to match, as in

```
val TRUCK gross_weight = v
```

If the vehicle v is indeed a truck, then the variable *gross_weight* will be bound to the value carried by the `TRUCK` constructor. Otherwise, the `val` declaration fails by raising the `Bind` exception.

dec → `val rec` *pat* = *exp*

Normally, the scope of the identifiers bound by a `val` declaration *does not include* the expression *exp* in the declaration. However, the keyword `rec` indicates a recursive declaration; in this case the *exp* must start with the keyword `fn`. Thus, a function to compute the length of a list:

```
val rec length = fn nil => 0 | fn a::r => 1+length(r)
```

dec → `fun` *clauses*

It is convenient to have syntactic sugar for `val rec` declarations. Some examples (and their meanings without using `fun`) are shown here:

```
fun length nil = 0              val rec length = fn nil => 0
  | length (a::r) =                            | (a::r) =>
        1+length(r)                                1+length(r)


fun f a b c = a+b+c            val rec f = fn a=>fn b=>fn c=>a+b+c
```

Note that even though f is not recursive, the `rec` keyword does no harm.

$dec \rightarrow$ `datatype` *datbind*

  Datatypes are declared using the syntax described at the beginning of this appendix.

$dec \rightarrow$ `type` *type-binding*

  Type abbreviations declare a new type equivalent to some existing (perhaps unnamed) one. For example,

```
type intpair = int*int
type comparison = int*int -> bool
```

  The type *intpair* will now be the same as $int \times int$, and *comparison* is an abbreviation for "function from pair of integers to Boolean." Type abbreviations can be parametrized, as in

```
type 'a pair = 'a * 'a
type 'b predicate = 'b -> bool
```

$dec \rightarrow$ *dec dec*

  Several declarations in a row may be used wherever one is permitted. The identifiers bound by the earlier declarations may be used by the later ones.

$dec \rightarrow$ **etc.**

  There are several other kinds of declarations, which we lack the space to explain here.

A.4   Some examples

To illustrate the use of ML, we will explain some of the examples used elsewhere in the book. First, the `countzeros` program from page 83:

```
fun count p = let fun f (a::r) = if p a then 1+f(r) else f r
                    | f nil = 0
              in f
              end

fun curry f x y = f(x,y)

val countzeros = count (curry (fn (w,z)=> w=z) 0)
```

  The function `count` takes an argument `p` and returns as a result another function that takes a list argument. That function returns an integer. A simpler way to understand this is that `count` is a *curried* function of two arguments. In any case, its type is

```
count:  ('a -> bool) -> (('a list) -> int)
count:  ('a -> bool) -> 'a list -> int
```

The type is written twice, the second time with the minimal number of parentheses (note that -> associates to the right).

The compiler can automatically infer the type of count (and, in fact, of all functions). In this case, since p is applied to an argument, it must be a function; and since the result of this application is used in an if expression, p must return a bool as a result. The fact that the second argument is written variously as a::r and nil implies that it must be a list; furthermore (because of the repetition of a) the elements of the list must match the type of p's argument. Finally, the expression 1+count(r) returned by the then clause implies that count returns an integer.

So what does count do? The argument p is a predicate that is applied to each element of the list. If the list is empty (count p nil), then 0 is returned. Otherwise, if p yields true on the first element of the list, we return 1 plus count p of the tail of the list; if p yields false, we don't add 1. Thus, count tells us how many elements of the list match the predicate.

The curry function takes a function f as an argument. f is a function that takes a 2-tuple as an argument. The result of curry f is a function fn x=>fn y=>... that takes a single argument x and returns a function fn y=> that takes a single argument y. The result of this function is just f(x,y). So curry f returns the "curried" version of f.

The countzeros function counts the number of zeros in a list of integers. It does this by applying count to the apropriate predicate. Before count actually executes, of course, it must be applied to another argument (a list); so countzeros won't do much until applied to a list of integers.

Now consider the eq function from page 27. Here we have omitted some cases for conciseness:

```
fun eq(RECORD(a,i),RECORD(b,j)) =
                arbitrarily(i=j andalso eqlist(a,b), false)
  | eq(INT i, INT j) = i=j
  | eq(STRING a, STRING b) = arbitrarily(a=b, false)
  | eq(ARRAY nil, ARRAY nil) = true
  | eq(ARRAY(a::_), ARRAY(b::_)) = a=b
  | eq(FUNC a, FUNC b) = raise Undefined
  | eq(_,_) = false
and eqlist(a::al, b::bl) = eq(a,b) andalso eqlist(al,bl)
  | eqlist(nil, nil) = true
```

The fun...and syntax allows the definition of mutually recursive functions eq and eqlist. The function eq gives the semantics of pointer equality on a pair of dvalue arguments (see page 24), and eqlist simulates pointer equality on a pair of dvalue lists.

Call eq's two arguments x and y. If they are both RECORDs, then the field-list of x will be bound to a and the field-list of y will be bound to b; their offsets will be bound to i and j respectively. Then the function arbitrarily will be evaluated with two arguments. The first argument uses the `andalso` keyword, which does short-circuit Boolean evaluation; equivalently,

```
if i=j then eqlist(a,b) else false
```

The second argument is just `false`; `arbitrarily` just returns one of its arguments (see page 3).

Thus, testing the equality of records will result (if `i=j`) in a call to the `eqlist` function, which may recursively call `eq`.

If one argument is a `RECORD` and the other is not, then the first pattern to match is `(_,_)`; the corresponding expression returns `false`.

If both arguments are `STRING`s, then the third pattern matches.

If both arguments are `ARRAY`s, then either the fourth or the fifth pattern matches depending on whether the element-lists are both `nil`.

If both arguments are `FUNC`s, then the sixth pattern matches. Then the expression `raise Undefined` is evaluated, which raises an exception. In this case, `eq` returns no result at all, and control passes to the nearest enclosing exception handler.

The function `eqlist` has two clauses; one that matches nonempty lists and one that matches empty lists. The nonempty case tests equality of the first elements, and recurs on the rest of the lists. But what if the lists are of different lengths, in which case the recursion will eventually lead to a case where one list is `nil` and the other is not? Then neither of the patterns matches; the runtime exception `Match` will be raised.

SEMANTICS OF THE CPS

This semantics is explained in Chapter 3.

```
functor CPSsemantics(
        structure CPS: CPS
        val minint: int    val maxint: int
        val minreal: real  val maxreal: real
        val string2real: string -> real
        eqtype loc
        val nextloc: loc -> loc
        val arbitrarily: 'a * 'a -> 'a
        type answer
        datatype dvalue = RECORD of dvalue list * int
                        | INT of int
                        | REAL of real
                        | FUNC of dvalue list ->
                            (loc*(loc->dvalue)*(loc->int))->
                            answer
                        | STRING of string
                        | BYTEARRAY of loc list
                        | ARRAY of loc list
                        | UARRAY of loc list
        val handler_ref : loc
        val overflow_exn : dvalue
        val div_exn : dvalue
                ) :
           sig val eval: CPS.var list * CPS.cexp ->
                        dvalue list ->
                        (loc*(loc->dvalue)*(loc->int)) ->
                        answer
               end =
struct
type store = loc * (loc -> dvalue) * (loc -> int)
fun fetch ((_,f,_): store) (l: loc) = f l
fun upd ((n,f,g):store, l: loc, v: dvalue) =
```

```
                         (n, fn i => if i=1 then v else f i, g)
fun fetchi ((_,_,g): store) (l: loc) = g l
fun updi ((n,f,g):store, l: loc, v: int) =
                         (n, f, fn i => if i=1 then v else g i)
exception Undefined

fun eq(RECORD(a,i),RECORD(b,j)) =
                arbitrarily(i=j andalso eqlist(a,b), false)
  | eq(INT i, INT j) = i=j
  | eq(REAL a, REAL b) = arbitrarily(a=b, false)
  | eq(STRING a, STRING b) = arbitrarily(a=b, false)
  | eq(BYTEARRAY nil, BYTEARRAY nil) = true
  | eq(BYTEARRAY(a::_), BYTEARRAY(b::_)) = a=b
  | eq(ARRAY nil, ARRAY nil) = true
  | eq(ARRAY(a::_), ARRAY(b::_)) = a=b
  | eq(UARRAY nil, UARRAY nil) = true
  | eq(UARRAY(a::_), UARRAY(b::_)) = a=b
  | eq(FUNC a, FUNC b) = raise Undefined
  | eq(_,_) = false
and eqlist(a::al, b::bl) = eq(a,b) andalso eqlist(al,bl)
  | eqlist(nil, nil) = true

fun do_raise exn s = let val FUNC f = fetch s handler_ref
                     in f [exn] s
                     end

fun overflow(n: unit->int,
             c: dvalue list -> store -> answer) =
      if (n() >= minint andalso n() <= maxint)
            handle Overflow=> false
        then c [INT(n())]
        else do_raise overflow_exn

fun overflowr(n,c) =
     if (n() >= minreal andalso n() <= maxreal)
             handle Overflow => false
        then c [REAL(n())]
        else do_raise overflow_exn

fun evalprim (CPS.+ : CPS.primop,
              [INT i, INT j]: dvalue list,
              [c]: (dvalue list -> store -> answer) list) =
                              overflow(fn()=>i+j, c)
  | evalprim (CPS.-,[INT i, INT j],[c]) =
                              overflow(fn()=>i-j, c)
```

```
| evalprim (CPS.*,[INT i, INT j],[c]) =
                        overflow(fn()=>i*j, c)
| evalprim (CPS.div,[INT i, INT 0],[c]) = do_raise div_exn
| evalprim (CPS.div,[INT i, INT j],[c]) =
                        overflow(fn()=>i div j, c)
| evalprim (CPS.~,[INT i],[c]) = overflow(fn()=>0-i, c)
| evalprim (CPS.<,[INT i,INT j],[t,f]) =
                        if i<j then t[] else f[]
| evalprim (CPS.<=,[INT i,INT j],[t,f]) =
                        if j<i then f[] else t[]
| evalprim (CPS.>,[INT i,INT j],[t,f]) =
                        if j<i then t[] else f[]
| evalprim (CPS.>=,[INT i,INT j],[t,f]) =
                        if i<j then f[] else t[]
| evalprim (CPS.ieql,[a,b],[t,f]) =
                        if eq(a,b) then t[] else f[]
| evalprim (CPS.ineq,[a,b],[t,f]) =
                        if eq(a,b) then f[] else t[]
| evalprim (CPS.rangechk, [INT i, INT j],[t,f]) =
                  if j<0
                  then if i<0
                       then if i<j then t[] else f[]
                       else t[]
                  else if i<0
                       then f[] else if i<j then t[]
                       else f[]
| evalprim (CPS.boxed, [INT _],[t,f]) = f[]
| evalprim (CPS.boxed, [RECORD _],[t,f]) = t[]
| evalprim (CPS.boxed, [STRING _],[t,f]) = t[]
| evalprim (CPS.boxed, [ARRAY _],[t,f]) = t[]
| evalprim (CPS.boxed, [UARRAY _],[t,f]) = t[]
| evalprim (CPS.boxed, [BYTEARRAY _],[t,f]) =t[]
| evalprim (CPS.boxed, [FUNC _],[t,f]) = t[]
| evalprim (CPS.!, [a],[c]) =
                  evalprim(CPS.subscript, [a, INT 0],[c])
| evalprim (CPS.subscript, [ARRAY a, INT n],[c]) =
                  (fn s => c [fetch s (nth(a,n))] s)
| evalprim (CPS.subscript, [UARRAY a, INT n],[c]) =
                  (fn s => c [INT(fetchi s (nth(a,n)))] s)
| evalprim (CPS.subscript, [RECORD(a,i), INT j],[c]) =
                  c [nth(a,i+j)]
| evalprim (CPS.ordof, [STRING a, INT i],[c]) =
                  c [INT(String.ordof(a,i))]
| evalprim (CPS.ordof, [BYTEARRAY a, INT i],[c]) =
                  (fn s => c [INT(fetchi s(nth(a,i)))] s)
```

```
| evalprim (CPS.:=, [a, v],[c]) =
                evalprim(CPS.update, [a, INT 0, v], [c])
| evalprim (CPS.update, [ARRAY a, INT n, v],[c]) =
              (fn s => c [] (upd(s,nth(a,n),v)))
| evalprim (CPS.update, [UARRAY a, INT n, INT v],[c]) =
              (fn s => c [] (updi(s,nth(a,n),v)))
| evalprim (CPS.unboxedassign, [a, v], [c]) =
            evalprim(CPS.unboxedupdate, [a, INT 0, v], [c])
| evalprim (CPS.unboxedupdate,
          [ARRAY a, INT n, INT v],[c]) =
                (fn s => c [] (upd(s,nth(a,n), INT v)))
| evalprim (CPS.unboxedupdate,
          [UARRAY a, INT n, INT v],[c]) =
                (fn s => c [] (updi(s,nth(a,n),v)))
| evalprim (CPS.store,
          [BYTEARRAY a, INT i, INT v],[c]) =
       if v < 0 orelse v >= 256
          then raise Undefined
          else (fn s => c [] (updi(s,nth(a,i),v)))
| evalprim (CPS.makeref, [v],[c]) = (fn (l,f,g) =>
            c [ARRAY[l]] (upd((nextloc l, f,g),l,v)))
| evalprim (CPS.makerefunboxed, [INT v],[c]) = (fn (l,f,g) =>
            c [UARRAY[l]] (updi((nextloc l, f,g),l,v)))
| evalprim (CPS.alength, [ARRAY a], [c]) =
                                   c [INT(List.length a)]
| evalprim (CPS.alength, [UARRAY a], [c]) =
                                   c [INT(List.length a)]
| evalprim (CPS.slength, [BYTEARRAY a], [c]) =
                                   c [INT(List.length a)]
| evalprim (CPS.slength, [STRING a], [c]) =
                                   c [INT(String.size a)]
| evalprim (CPS.gethdlr, [], [c]) =
                (fn s => c [fetch s handler_ref] s)
| evalprim (CPS.sethdlr, [h], [c]) =
                (fn s => c [] (upd(s,handler_ref,h)))
| evalprim (CPS.fadd, [REAL a, REAL b],[c]) =
                         overflowr(fn()=>a+b, c)
| evalprim (CPS.fsub, [REAL a, REAL b],[c]) =
                         overflowr(fn()=>a-b, c)
| evalprim (CPS.fmul, [REAL a, REAL b],[c]) =
                         overflowr(fn()=>a*b, c)
| evalprim (CPS.fdiv, [REAL a, REAL 0.0],[c]) =
                         do_raise div_exn
| evalprim (CPS.fdiv, [REAL a, REAL b],[c]) =
                         overflowr(fn()=>a/b, c)
```

```
| evalprim (CPS.feql, [REAL a, REAL b],[t,f]) =
                            if a=b then t[] else f[]
| evalprim (CPS.fneq, [REAL a, REAL b],[t,f]) =
                            if a=b then f[] else t[]
| evalprim (CPS.flt,[REAL i,REAL j],[t,f]) =
                            if i<j then t[] else f[]
| evalprim (CPS.fle,[REAL i,REAL j],[t,f]) =
                            if j<i then f[] else t[]
| evalprim (CPS.fgt,[REAL i,REAL j],[t,f]) =
                            if j<i then t[] else f[]
| evalprim (CPS.fge,[REAL i,REAL j],[t,f]) =
                            if i<j then f[] else t[]


type env = CPS.var -> dvalue

fun V env (CPS.INT i) = INT i
  | V env (CPS.REAL r) = REAL(string2real r)
  | V env (CPS.STRING s) = STRING s
  | V env (CPS.VAR v) = env v
  | V env (CPS.LABEL v) = env v

fun bind(env:env, v:CPS.var, d) =
                fn w => if v=w then d else env w

fun bindn(env, v::vl, d::dl) =
                bindn(bind(env,v,d),vl,dl)
  | bindn(env, nil, nil) = env

fun F (x, CPS.OFFp 0) = x
  | F (RECORD(l,i), CPS.OFFp j) = RECORD(l,i+j)
  | F (RECORD(l,i), CPS.SELp(j,p)) = F(nth(l,i+j), p)
```

```
fun E (CPS.SELECT(i,v,w,e)) env =
                let val RECORD(l,j) = V env v
                 in E e (bind(env,w,nth(l,i+j)))
                end
  | E (CPS.OFFSET(i,v,w,e)) env =
                let val RECORD(l,j) = V env v
                 in E e (bind(env,w,RECORD(l,i+j)))
                end
  | E (CPS.APP(f,vl)) env =
                let val FUNC g = V env f
                 in g (map (V env) vl)
                end
  | E (CPS.RECORD(vl,w,e)) env =
                E e (bind(env,w,
                       RECORD(map (fn (x,p) =>
                                      F(V env x, p)) vl, 0)))
  | E (CPS.SWITCH(v,el)) env =
                let val INT i = V env v
                 in E (nth(el,i)) env
                end
  | E (CPS.PRIMOP(p,vl,wl,el)) env =
                evalprim(p,
                       map (V env) vl,
                       map (fn e => fn al =>
                             E e (bindn(env,wl,al)))
                         el)
  | E (CPS.FIX(fl,e)) env =
          let fun h r1 (f,vl,b) =
                 FUNC(fn al => E b (bindn(g r1,vl,al)))
               and g r = bindn(r, map #1 fl, map (h r) fl)
           in E e (g env)
          end

val env0 = fn x => raise Undefined

fun eval (vl,e) dl = E e (bindn(env0,vl,dl))

end
```

APPENDIX C

OBTAINING
STANDARD ML OF NEW JERSEY

Standard ML of New Jersey is the work of many people (see page ix). The system was developed jointly at Princeton University and AT&T Bell Laboratories, with contributions from other places.

Standard ML of New Jersey can be obtained from http://smlnj.org

READINGS

This book covers the optimizer and code generator of the Standard ML of New Jersey compiler. The following works describe other aspects of the system:

Appel and MacQueen [13] A Standard ML Compiler. Describes the state of the work at a very early stage.

Appel and MacQueen [14] Standard ML of New Jersey. Summarizes the work done to date.

Baudinet and MacQueen [19] Tree Pattern Matching for ML. Describes an efficient algorithm for generating good decision trees from pattern matches.

MacQueen [61] The Implementation of Standard ML Modules. An efficient algorithm that avoids much copying of static semantic information when functors are applied.

MacQueen [62] A Higher-Order Type System for Functional Programming. A rationale for the Standard ML module language design.

Appel, Duba, and MacQueen [9] Profiling in the Presence of Optimization and Garbage Collection. A simple, mostly conventional approach to execution profiling with call counts and timer interrupts.

Appel and Jim [11] Continuation-Passing, Closure-Passing Style. A short paper summarizing some of the representations and algorithms described in this book.

Appel [6] Simple Generational Garbage Collection and Fast Allocation. Covers the two-generation garbage collector (vintage 1988–91) and the (no longer used) page-fault-trap method of heap-overflow detection.

Appel [7] A Runtime System. Describes in some detail the runtime system (vintage 1990) of Standard ML of New Jersey, with the exception of the two-generation garbage collector.

Duba, Harper, and MacQueen [37] Typing First-Class Continuations in ML. Formalizes the polymorphic type checking of *call-with-current-continuation*.

Tolmach and Appel [88] Debugging Standard ML Without Reverse Engineering. A novel and efficient replay debugger for SML/NJ, which takes advantage of first-class continuations and is independent of the code generator and the runtime system.

Tarditi, Acharya, and Lee [86] No Assembly Required: Compiling Standard ML to C. The translation to abstract-machine instructions (after the spill phase of the SML/NJ compiler) is replaced by a translation to unreadable but quite portable C code.

Reppy [72] Asynchronous Signals in Standard ML. Describes the design, implementation, and use of a mechanism for handling asynchronous signals, such as user interrupts.

Reppy [73] Concurrent Programming with Events—The Concurrent ML Manual. Concurrent ML (CML) is a system for concurrent programming in Standard ML. A CML program consists of a set of *threads* (or lightweight processes). Communication with other threads is done by synchronous message passing on channels.

Reppy and Gansner [74] The eXene Library Manual. A Concurrent-ML interface to X windows that allows a much cleaner style of programming than the usual kind of X interface.

Cooper and Morrisett [31] Adding Threads to Standard ML. Multiple threads of control added to Standard ML of New Jersey, using shared variables, mutex locks, conditions, and signals.

BIBLIOGRAPHY

[1] Alfred V. Aho, Ravi Sethi, and Jeffrey D. Ullman. *Compilers: Principles, Techniques, and Tools*. Addison-Wesley, Reading, MA, 1985.

[2] Alexander Aiken and Alexandru Nicolau. Optimal loop parallelization. *SIGPLAN Notices (Proc. SIGPLAN '88 Conf. on Prog. Lang. Design and Implementation)*, 23(7):308–17, 1988.

[3] Thomas E. Anderson, Brian N. Bershad, Edward D. Lazowska, and Henry M. Levy. Scheduler activations: Effective kernel support for the user-level management of parallelism. In *Proc. 13th Symp. on Operating System Principles*, October 1991. ACM Press, New York. (in press).

[4] Andrew W. Appel. Allocation without locking. *Software—Practice and Experience*, 19(7):703–5, 1989.

[5] Andrew W. Appel. Runtime tags aren't necessary. *Lisp and Symbolic Computation*, 2:153–62, 1989.

[6] Andrew W. Appel. Simple generational garbage collection and fast allocation. *Software—Practice and Experience*, 19(2):171–83, 1989.

[7] Andrew W. Appel. A runtime system. *Lisp and Symbolic Computation*, 3(343-80), 1990.

[8] Andrew W. Appel. Garbage collection. In *Topics in Advanced Language Implementation Techniques*, Peter Lee, editor. MIT Press, Cambridge, MA, 1991.

[9] Andrew W. Appel, Bruce F. Duba, and David B. MacQueen. Profiling in the presence of optimization and garbage collection. Technical Report CS-TR-197-88, Princeton University, Dept. Comp. Sci., Princeton, NJ, 1987.

[10] Andrew W. Appel, John R. Ellis, and Kai Li. Real-time concurrent collection on stock multiprocessors. *SIGPLAN Notices (Proc. SIGPLAN '88 Conf. on Prog. Lang. Design and Implementation)*, 23(7):11–20, 1988.

[11] Andrew W. Appel and Trevor Jim. Continuation-passing, closure-passing style. In *Sixteenth ACM Symp. on Principles of Programming Languages*, pages 293–302, 1989. ACM Press, New York.

[12] Andrew W. Appel and Trevor T. Y. Jim. Optimizing closure environment representations. Technical Report 168, Dept. of Computer Science, Princeton University, Princeton, NJ, 1988.

[13] Andrew W. Appel and David B. MacQueen. A Standard ML compiler. In *Functional Programming Languages and Computer Architecture (LNCS 274)*, Gilles Kahn, editor, pages 301–24, 1987. Springer-Verlag, New York.

[14] Andrew W. Appel and David B. MacQueen. Standard ML of New Jersey. In *Third Int'l Symp. on Prog. Lang. Implementation and Logic Programming*, Martin Wirsing, editor, August 1991. Springer-Verlag, New York. (in press).

[15] Andrew W. Appel, James S. Mattson, and David R. Tarditi. A lexical analyzer generator for Standard ML. Distributed with Standard ML of New Jersey, December 1989.

[16] Arvind, Riyashur S. Nikhil, and Keshav K. Pingali. I-structures: Data structures for parallel computing. In *Proc. PARLE Conference, LNCS 259*, September 1986. Springer-Verlag, New York.

[17] Lennart Augustsson. Garbage collection in the $< \nu, g >$-machine. Technical Report PMG memo 73, Dept. of Computer Sciences, Chalmers University of Technology, Goteborg, Sweden, December 1989.

[18] Joel F. Bartlett. Compacting garbage collection with ambiguous roots. Technical Report 88/2, DEC Western Research Laboratory, Palo Alto, CA, 1988.

[19] Marianne Baudinet and David MacQueen. Tree pattern matching for ML. Available from David MacQueen, AT&T Bell Laboratories, 600 Mountain Avenue, Murray, Hill, NJ 07974, 1986.

[20] Robert L. Bernstein. Producing good code for the case statement. *Software — Practice and Experience*, 15(10):1021–24, October 1985.

[21] David Berry. SML resources. Sent to the SML mailing list by db@lfcs.ed.ac.uk, May 1991.

[22] A. D. Birrell, J. V. Guttag, J. J. Horning, and R. Levin. Synchronization primitives for a multiprocessor: A formal specificati on. In *Proceedings of the 11th ACM Symposium on Operating Systems Princi ples*, pages 94–102, November 1987. ACM Press, New York. Published as *Operating Systems Review*, 21(5).

[23] Andrew D. Birrell. An introduction to programming with threads. Research Report 35, DEC Systems Research Center, Palo Alto, CA, January 1989.

[24] Hans-Juergen Boehm and Mark Weiser. Garbage collection in an uncooperative environment. *Software—Practice and Experience*, 18(9):807–20, 1988.

[25] CAML: The reference manual (version 2.3). Projet Formel, INRIA-ENS, June 1987.

[26] Luca Cardelli. Compiling a functional language. In *1984 Symp. on LISP and Functional Programming*, pages 208–17, 1984. ACM Press, New York.

[27] Luca Cardelli, James Donahue, Lucille Glassman, Mick Jordan, Bill Kalsow, and Greg Nelson. Modula-3 report. Technical Report Research Report 31, DEC Systems Research Center, Palo Alto, CA, 1988.

[28] C. J. Cheney. A nonrecursive list compacting algorithm. *Communications of the ACM*, 13(11):677–78, 1970.

[29] Douglas W. Clark. Pipelining and performance in the VAX 8800 processor. In *Proc. 2nd Intl. Conf. Architectural Support for Prog. Lang. and Operating Systems*, pages 173–79, 1987. ACM Press, New York.

[30] Eric C. Cooper. Carnegie Mellon Univ., Pittsburgh, PA, personal communication, 1991.

[31] Eric C. Cooper and J. Gregory Morrisett. Adding threads to Standard ML. Technical Report CMU-CS-90-186, School of Computer Science, Carnegie Mellon University, Pittsburgh, PA, December 1990.

[32] G. Cousineau, P. L. Curien, and M. Mauny. The categorical abstract machine. In *Functional Programming Languages and Computer Architecture, LNCS Vol 201*, J. P. Jouannaud, editor, pages 50–64, 1985. Springer-Verlag, New York.

[33] W. P. Crowley, C. P. Hendrickson, and T. E. Rudy. The SIMPLE code. Technical Report UCID 17715, Lawrence Livermore Laboratory, Livermore, CA, February 1978.

[34] Ron Cytron, Jeanne Ferrante, Barry K. Rosen, Mark N. Wegman, and F. Kenneth Zadeck. An efficient method of computing static single assignment form. In *Proc. 16th ACM Symp. on Principles of Programming Languages*, pages 25–35, January 1989. ACM Press, New York.

[35] Olivier Danvy and Andrzej Filinski. Representing control. Technical Report TR-CS-91-2, Kansas State University, Manhattan, KS, February 1991.

[36] Edsger W. Dijkstra and Leslie Lamport. On-the-fly garbage collection: An exercise in cooperation. *Communications of the ACM*, 21(11):966–75, 1978.

[37] Bruce Duba, Robert Harper, and David MacQueen. Typing first-class continuations in ML. In *Eighteenth Annual ACM Symp. on Principles of Prog. Languages*, pages 163–73, Jan 1991. ACM Press, New York.

[38] K. Ekanadham and Arvind. SIMPLE: An exercise in future scientific programming. Technical Report Computation Structures Group Memo 273, MIT, Cambridge, MA, July 1987. Simultaneously published as IBM/T.J. Watson Research Center Research Report 12686, Yorktown Heights, NY.

[39] Christopher W. Fraser and David R. Hanson. A retargetable compiler for ANSI C. *SIGPLAN Notices*, 26(8), August 1991. to appear.

[40] Christopher W. Fraser and David R. Hanson. Simple register spilling in a retargetable compiler. *submitted for publication*, 1991.

[41] Michael R. Garey and David S. Johnson. *Computers and Intractability: A Guide to the Theory of NP-completeness*. W. H. Freeman and Co., New York, 1979.

[42] M. J. C. Gordon, A. J. R. G. Milner, L. Morris, M. C. Newey, and C. P. Wadsworth. A metalanguage for interactive proof in LCF. In *Fifth ACM Symp. on Principles of Programming Languages*, 1978. ACM Press, New York.

[43] Michael J. C. Gordon. *The Denotational Description of Programming Languages*. Springer-Verlag, New York, 1979.

[44] Robert H. Halstead Jr. Multilisp: A language for concurrent symbolic computation. *ACM Transactions on Programming Languages and Systems*, 7(4):501–38, October 1985.

[45] David R. Hanson. A portable storage management system for the Icon programming language. *Software—Practice and Experience*, 10:489–500, 1980.

[46] John L. Hennessy and David A. Patterson. *Computer Architecture: A Quantitative Approach*. Morgan Kaufmann, San Mateo, CA, 1990.

[47] Robert Hieb, R. Kent Dybvig, and Carl Bruggeman. Representing control in the presence of first-class continuations. In *Proc. ACM SIGPLAN '90 Conf. on Prog. Lang. Design and Implementation*, pages 66–77, 1990. ACM Press, New York.

[48] C A. R. Hoare. Monitors: An operating system structuring concept. *Comm. ACM*, 17(10):549–57, October 1974.

[49] C. A. R. Hoare. Communicating sequential processes. *Comm. ACM*, 17(8):666–77, August 1978.

[50] C. A. R. Hoare. *Communicating Sequential Processes*. Prentice-Hall, Englewood Cliffs, NJ, 1985.

[51] Gerry Kane. *MIPS Risc Architecture*. Prentice-Hall, Englewood Cliffs, NJ, 1988.

[52] Richard Kelsey and Paul Hudak. Realistic compilation by program transformation. In *Sixteenth ACM Symp. on Principles of Programming Languages*, pages 281–92, 1989. ACM Press, New York.

[53] Alon Kleinman, Yael Moscowitz, Amir Pnueli, and Ehud Shapiro. Communication with directed logic variables. In *Proc. 18th ACM Symp. on Principles of Programming Languages*, pages 221–32, January 1991. ACM Press, New York.

[54] D. Kranz, R. Kelsey, J. Rees, P. Hudak, J. Philbin, and N. Adams. ORBIT: An optimizing compiler for Scheme. *SIGPLAN Notices (Proc. Sigplan '86 Symp. on Compiler Construction)*, 21(7):219–33, July 1986.

[55] David Kranz. *ORBIT: An optimizing compiler for Scheme*. PhD thesis, Yale University, New Haven, CT, 1987.

[56] Butler W. Lampson and David D. Redell. Experience with processes and monitors in Mesa. *Communications of the ACM*, 23(2):105–17, February 1980.

[57] P. J. Landin. The mechanical evaluation of expressions. *Computer J.*, 6(4):308–20, 1964.

[58] Xavier Leroy. The ZINC experiment: an economical implementation of the ML language. Technical Report No. 117, INRIA, February 1990.

[59] Xavier Leroy. INRIA, personal communication, 1991.

[60] Henry Lieberman and Carl Hewitt. A real-time garbage collector based on the lifetimes of objects. *Communications of the ACM*, 23(6):419–29, 1983.

[61] David B. MacQueen. The implementation of Standard ML modules. In *ACM Conf. on Lisp and Functional Programming*, pages 212–23, 1988. ACM Press, New York.

[62] David B. MacQueen. A higher-order type system for functional programming. In *Research Topics in Functional Programming*, pages 353–68, 1990. Addison-Wesley, Reading, MA.

[63] David C. J. Matthews. Papers on Poly/ML. Technical Report T.R. No. 161, Computer Laboratory, University of Cambridge, February 1989.

[64] Robin Milner. A proposal for Standard ML. In *ACM Symposium on LISP and Functional Programming*, pages 184–97, 1984. ACM Press, New York.

[65] Robin Milner, Mads Tofte, and Robert Harper. *The Definition of Standard ML*. MIT Press, Cambridge, MA, 1989.

[66] Motorola, Inc. *MC68020 32-Bit Microprocessor User's Manual*. Prentice-Hall, Englewood Cliffs, NJ, 1985.

[67] Laurence C. Paulson. *ML for the Working Programmer*. Cambridge University Press, Cambridge, 1992.

[68] Chris Reade. *Elements of Functional Programming*. Addison-Wesley, Reading, MA, 1989.

[69] J. Rees and W. Clinger (eds.). Revised report on the algorithmic language Scheme. *SIGPLAN Notices*, 21(12):37–79, 1986.

[70] John H. Reppy. Synchronous operations as first-class values. *SIGPLAN Notices (Proc. SIGPLAN '88 Conf. on Prog. Lang. Design and Implementation)*, 23(7):250–59, 1988.

[71] John H. Reppy. First-class synchronous operations in Standard ML. Technical Report TR 89-1068, Cornell University, Dept. of Computer Science, Ithaca, NY, 1989.

[72] John H. Reppy. Asynchronous signals in Standard ML. Technical Report TR 90-1144, Cornell University, Dept. of Computer Science, Ithaca, NY, 1990.

[73] John H. Reppy. Concurrent programming with events. Technical report, Cornell University, Dept. of Computer Science, Ithaca, NY, 1990.

[74] John H. Reppy and Emden R. Gansner. The eXene library manual. Cornell Univ. Dept. of Computer Science, March 1991.

[75] J. C. Reynolds. Types, abstraction, and parametric polymorphism. In *IFIP Conference*, R. E. A. Mason, editor, pages 513–24, 1983.

[76] Chris Rowen. Mips Corporation, personal communication, 1991.

[77] David A. Schmidt. *Denotational Semantics: A Methodology for Language Development*. Allyn and Bacon, Boston, 1986.

[78] Ravi Sethi. Complete register allocation problems. *SIAM J. Computing*, 4(3):226–48, 1975.

[79] Robert A. Shaw. Improving garbage collector performance in virtual memory. Technical Report CSL-TR-87-323, Stanford University, Palo Alto, CA, 1987.

[80] Olin Shivers. *Control-Flow Analysis of Higher-Order Languages*. PhD thesis, Carnegie-Mellon University, Pittsburgh, PA, May 1991. CMU-CS-91-145.

[81] Stefan Sokolowski. *Applicative High Order Programming: the Standard ML perspective*. Chapman & Hall Computing, London, 1991.

[82] *The SPARC Architecture Manual*. Sun Microsystems, Inc., Mountain View, CA, 1987.

[83] Guy L. Steele. Rabbit: a compiler for Scheme. Technical Report AI-TR-474, MIT, Cambridge, MA, 1978.

[84] Joseph E. Stoy. *Denotational Semantics: The Scott-Strachey Approach to Programming Language Theory*. MIT Press, Cambridge, MA, 1977.

[85] Thomas Szymanski. AT&T Bell Labs, personal communication, 1991.

[86] David R. Tarditi, Anurag Acharya, and Peter Lee. No assembly required: Compiling Standard ML to C. Technical Report CMU-CS-90-187, Carnegie-Mellon Univ., Pittsburgh, PA, November 1990.

[87] David R. Tarditi and Andrew W. Appel. ML-Yacc, version 2.0. Distributed with Standard ML of New Jersey, April 1990.

[88] Andrew P. Tolmach and Andrew W. Appel. Debugging Standard ML without reverse engineering. In *Proc. 1990 ACM Conf. on Lisp and Functional Programming*, pages 1–12, June 1990. ACM Press, New York.

[89] David M. Ungar. *The Design and Evaluation of a High Performance Smalltalk System.* MIT Press, Cambridge, MA, 1986.

[90] *VAX Architecture Handbook.* Digital Equipment Corp., Maynard, MA, 1979.

[91] Philip Wadler. Strictness analysis aids time analysis. In *Fifteenth Annual ACM Symp. on Principles of Prog. Languages*, pages 119–32, Jan 1988. ACM Press, New York.

[92] Philip Wadler and Stephen Blott. How to make *ad-hoc* polymorphism less *ad hoc*. In *Sixteenth Annual ACM Symp. on Principles of Prog. Languages*, pages 60–76, January 1989. ACM Press, New York.

[93] Mitchell Wand. Continuation-based multiprocessing. In *Conf. Record of the 1980 Lisp Conf.*, pages 19–28, August 1980. ACM Press, New York.

[94] Mark N. Wegman and F. Kenneth Zadeck. Constant propagation with conditional branches. *ACM Trans. on Prog. Lang. and Systems*, 13(2):181–210, April 1991.

[95] J. Welsh, W. J. Sneeringer, and C. A. R. Hoare. Ambiguities and insecurities in Pascal. *Software—Practice and Experience*, 7(6):685–96, 1977.

[96] N. Wirth. The programming language Oberon. *Software—Practice and Experience*, 18(7), July 1988.

[97] W. Wulf, R. K. Johnsson, C. B. Weinstock, C. B. Hobbs, and C. M. Geschke. *Design of an Optimizing Compiler.* Elsevier North-Holland, New York, 1975.

[98] Benjamin Zorn. The effect of garbage collection on cache performance. Technical Report CU-CS-528-91, University of Colorado, Boulder, CO, May 1991.

INDEX